THE WALL STREET JOURNAL.

NATIONAL BUSINESS EMPLOYMENT WEEKLY

Premier Guides

RESUMES

P. 45 - Getting information
interviews
P. 58 - Resume headings
P. 74 - Action verbs
P. 116 - Functional resume
categories

THE NATIONAL BUSINESS EMPLOYMENT WEEKLY
PREMIER GUIDES SERIES

Published:

Resumes, Third Edition,	ISBN# 0-471-32259-8 paper
Interviewing, Third Edition,	ISBN# 0-471-32257-1 paper
Cover Letters, Third Edition,	ISBN# 0-471-32261-X paper
Jobs Rated Almanac,	ISBN# 0-471-05495-X paper
Love Your Work,	ISBN# 0-471-11956-3 paper
Self-Employment,	ISBN# 0-471-10918-5 paper
Personal Best: 1001 Great Ideas for Achieving Success in Your Career,	ISBN# 0-471-14888-1 paper

THE WALL STREET JOURNAL.

NATIONAL
BUSINESS
EMPLOYMENT
WEEKLY

Premier Guides

RESUMES

Third Edition

Taunee S. Besson

John Wiley & Sons, Inc.

New York • Chichester • Weinheim • Brisbane • Singapore • Toronto

Copyright © 1999 by National Business Employment Weekly. All rights reserved.

Published by John Wiley & Sons, Inc.
Published simultaneously in Canada.

This publication is designed to provide accurate and authoritative information in regard to the subject matter covered. It is sold with the understanding that the publisher is not engaged in rendering professional services. If professional advice or other expert assistance is required, the services of a competent professional person should be sought.

Library of Congress Cataloging-in-Publication Data:

Besson, Taunee S.
    National business employment weekly guide to resumes / Taunee S.
  Besson, National business employment weekly. — 3rd ed.
        p.   cm. — (The national business employment weekly premier
  guides series)
    Rev. ed. of: Resumes. 2nd ed. c1996.
    Includes index.
    ISBN 0-471-32259-8 (pbk. : alk. paper)
    1. Resumes (Employment)   I. Besson, Taunee S.   Resumes.   II. Title.
  III. Title: Guide to resumes.   IV. Series.
  HF5383.B435   1999
  808'.06665—dc21   98-53411

Printed in the United States of America.

10 9 8 7 6 5 4 3 2 1

This book is dedicated to Larry, Amber and Teal Besson.

Foreword

With all the free advice about resume-writing available on the Internet, why would job seekers need to buy a book on the topic? All you need to do to create a resume is point, click, and fill in the blanks of a template on your computer screen. A few minutes later, you can download and print out a new document. Or, if you prefer not to consult one of the thousands of career sites in cyberspace, you can visit a computer store and purchase job-hunting software that includes resume-writing instructions.

The drawback to either of these approaches is that the resume you ultimately produce will be prepared in a format designed for the average candidate. Yet anyone who's conducted a job search lately knows that to land the right job, average isn't good enough. Even in the blistering job market of recent years, employers aren't so desperate that they'll hire the first person to walk through their doors. They're looking for candidates who demonstrate they have the combination of skills, abilities, and experience necessary to solve an immediate problem.

Cyberspace advice is comprehensive and generic, but to prepare a great resume, a step-by-step, research-intensive approach is still the best way to produce a document that answers an employer's question, "Is this someone I should interview right away?" with a resounding "Yes!" While this approach may take more effort and angst, you owe it to yourself to try.

In creating a document that's uniquely your own, where do you start? Certainly not by adding your most recent position to the bottom of your old resume says career counselor Taunee Besson. In every edition of her book, she has maintained that candidates must tailor their resumes to each individual employer or die a quiet death in the job market. She strongly promotes the concept that when it comes to resumes, one size doesn't fit all. Whether you're a seasoned professional, first-time job hunter, career changer or returning to the workforce after an extended absence, her book shows you how to construct a resume that reflects your circumstances and supports your objectives.

Not only does Taunee explain how to write a resume, but she clearly illustrates the difference between a merely adequate and an excellent document with "before" and "after" examples of actual job hunters' resumes. And, since nearly every large company now uses resume scanners and computerized databases to track candidates, she shows how to prepare a scannable version of your document.

For this third edition of *Resumes,* Taunee wanted her examples to be as relevant now as when the book was first published. For each chapter, she collected fresh resumes from job hunters who recently sought—and found—new positions. By following her suggestions, you'll be equally prepared for job hunting as you approach and enter the millennium.

PERRI CAPELL
Managing Editor,
National Business Employment Weekly

Acknowledgments

Many people have been very helpful as I put this book together. While I cannot name them all, I'd like to thank Tony Lee and Perri Capell for choosing me to write this book, and for their help in editing it and soliciting sample resumes from readers. Many newspapers nationwide also published our request for great resumes, and these fellow journalists have my gratitude and a promise to return the favor should they ever need a little help from a friend.

I also want to recognize Jim Henry, Tom Arterburn, the staffs of Options Resource and Career Center in Houston and the Career Action Center in Cupertino, California, as well as their clients, for contributing an excellent selection of sample resumes. They are responsible for many of the specialized examples in this book. Special thanks also to cartoonist Tom Cheney and Robert Half, the creator of Resumania, for their wonderful, humorous contributions to this book.

My thanks also go to Wendy Enelow of Enelow Enterprises International, Holly Tullis and Jim Caraway at EDS, Max Davis at Raytheon Systems, and John Kuzma from Motorola for their invaluable advice in developing the chapter on resume scanning.

My own clients and newsletter readers deserve a tremendous thank you for allowing me to use their resumes, and for showing uncommon understanding when I needed to concentrate on the book instead of them. Richard Bolles has my gratitude for cultivating my healthy disrespect for run-of-the-mill resumes, and for inspiring my adaptation of his transferable skills exercise. Delores Smith, my office manager, deserves my heartfelt appreciation for spending days checking quotes, updating resource information, editing and typing revisions, and generally keeping me on track. Her exceptional phone presence, eagle-eye attention to detail, perseverance and nurturing personality paved the way for this third edition getting to press on time and error free.

I also want to acknowledge the support of my family and friends who saw a lot less of me as this book came together. While they've always been sympathetic to my need to spend lots of time with clients and the community, this past year has demanded a level of forbearance verging on saintliness.

T.S.B.

About the Author

Taunee S. Besson is president of Career Dimensions, a Dallas consulting firm that helps individuals and companies with issues such as career change, networking, executive coaching, Internet job search and recruiting techniques, small-business strategies, spouse relocation/employment and outplacement. She also collaborates with corporations that want to enhance their recruitment, retention, promotion and marketing to women by establishing corporate advisory boards composed of prominent female nonprofit and business executives and entrepreneurs. Ms. Besson is an award-winning columnist for the *National Business Employment Weekly*, a frequent speaker and guest author, and a Certified Career Management Fellow. Ms. Besson has taught courses at numerous Dallas-area colleges and universities and is an active community volunteer.

Contents

Introduction   1

☆ Resume Angst . . .   1
☆ . . . And Its Cure   3
☆ Reasons for Writing Resumes   3
☆ A Note from the Author   5

1 What a Resume Can and Can't Do for You   9

☆ To Whom It May Concern   10
☆ I'm Available   11
☆ I'm OK   13
☆ A Resume Doesn't a Job Search Make   13
☆ A Resume Quiz   13

2 Getting Organized   19

☆ Laying Your Resume Foundation   21
☆ Your Functional and Transferable Skills Inventory   24
☆ Gathering Information to Tailor Your Resume   24

☆   Resume Information from Information Interviews   41
☆   Resume Information from Executive Search Firms   49

3 Resume Guidelines 51

☆   Tailor Your Resume to Employer Needs   51
☆   Use Humor Sparingly   55
☆   Be Brief and Concise   55
☆   Write Your Own Resume   56
☆   Be Neat and Error Free   57
☆   Prioritize Everything   57
☆   Make Your Resume Easy to Read   58
☆   Omit Negative Information   60
☆   Curb Your Anger   61
☆   Don't Make Demands of the Employer   61

4 The Parts of Your Resume 65

☆   Your Name, Address and Phone Number   65
☆   Your Resume Objective   66
☆   The Professional Qualifications Brief (Summary of Qualifications)   70
☆   Experience   72
☆   Education   77
☆   Organizations   78
☆   Awards   79
☆   Personal Data   79
☆   Salary History   80
☆   Reason for Leaving   81
☆   References   83
☆   How to Find Resume Help   84

5 The Chronological Format 87

☆   The Good News   87
☆   The Bad News   88

☆ Before-and-After Examples   89
☆ Success Stories   103
☆ Other Good Chronological Resumes   107

6 Functional Resumes   113

☆ Experience by Functional Area   113
☆ Experience by Job Objective   114
☆ The Pros   115
☆ The Cons   115
☆ Example of a Personal Profile   116
☆ Success Stories   118
☆ Other Good Functional Resumes   118

7 Hybrid Resumes   131

☆ The Pros   131
☆ The Cons   132
☆ Using the Same Experience in Chronological and
  Hybrid Formats   132
☆ Matching Functions to Objectives   141
☆ Success Stories   145
☆ Other Good Hybrid Resumes   151

8 Resumes for Consulting, Freelancing, Volunteer and Internal Company Use   161

☆ Internal Resumes   162
☆ Consultant Resumes   165
☆ Freelance Resumes   173
☆ Resumes for Board or Committee Positions   177

9 Resumes for First-Time Job Seekers and Recent College Graduates   181

☆ Volunteer Work   181
☆ A Variety of Useful Experience, Not Necessarily Paid   182

☆ Education   184
☆ Honors and Awards   185
☆ Personal or Other Facts   185
☆ References   185
☆ Before-and-After Resume   186
☆ A Success Story   187
☆ Other Good Resumes   196

10 Resumes for Women Returning to the Paid Workforce   203

☆ Volunteer Experience   205
☆ Hobbies   206
☆ Previous Paid Experience   207
☆ Success Stories   208
☆ Other Good Resumes   208

11 Resumes for Career Changers   217

☆ Points to Ponder   218
☆ Example Resumes   221
☆ Military Resumes   226

12 Resumes for Seasoned Professionals   235

☆ Points to Ponder   235
☆ Success Stories   237

13 Scannable Resumes   249

☆ What Is Resume Scanning?   250
☆ Who Uses Resume Scanning and Why   250
☆ The Good News about Resume Scanning   252
☆ And the Bad News . . .   253

☆ And Yet, There's Hope!   254
☆ Dos and Don'ts for Writing Scannable Resumes   254
☆ Scannable Resumes That Work   264
☆ Other Resume Examples   269

14 Resume Follow-Up   277

☆ The Components of a Tracking System   278
☆ Do You Want a Computerized or a Manual System?   281
☆ Follow-Up Calls and Letters   282

Index   287

Introduction

Resume Angst . . .

"I would rather have a root canal than write another resume."

"I've been working on this resume day and night for the last two weeks and I'm not going to stop until I get it perfect."

"Frankly, I think that resumes are totally pointless. Why people bother to write them is completely beyond me."

"You and I both know a job search is strictly a numbers game. To get 5 interviews, I'll have to send out 500 resumes. To get 10 interviews, I'll have to mail 1,000."

"A resume should always have an objective . . . a resume should never have an objective. I read two different books and they give diametrically opposing advice. If the experts can't agree on something as simple as this, how am I supposed to get my act together?"

Why are people so intense about resumes? Bringing up the subject is almost as likely to heat up a discussion as mentioning religion or politics, yet resumes don't have nearly the significance of the other two subjects. Or do they?

Have you noticed that job seekers seem to fall into two camps: those who have absolute convictions about their resume strategy and those who

1

constantly second-guess themselves? Why do reasonable people with good self-esteem tend to turn into overbearing control freaks or indecisive wimps when confronted with writing a resume? What is behind this Dr. Jekyll becomes Mr. Hyde/Mr. Milquetoast syndrome? Consider the following:

☆   Finding the ideal job can become a crusade instead of a research project if job seekers believe a career is crucial to personal identity. When a resume serves as an initial introduction to a potential employer, its author may endow it with far more importance than it really deserves. In this kind of self-imposed pressure-cooker situation, job seekers may protect themselves by locking on to one approach and denying all others, or trap themselves in a web of indecision to avoid making a wrong choice.

☆   Therapists say the American culture has generated a "stroke-deprived economy" by teaching us not to give, receive or ask for positive feedback. Unfortunately, resumes require us to break the rules and brag about ourselves. Faced with the distasteful prospect of committing a social taboo, we often respond with classic avoidance behavior.

☆   Because we don't learn about resumes as part of our formal or informal education, we feel a little lost when forced to write one. Consider how you would react to someone asking you to parallel park an 18-wheeler. You know it can be done, because you've seen other people pull it off who are no more intelligent than you. Yet because you have had no exposure to the technique, the process takes on an unnerving mystique. With a few lessons and a little practice, you could whip that sucker into a loading dock as well as the next guy, but for the moment, you can't trust yourself to do it without causing major damage. From this perspective, resumes and really big trucks have a lot in common.

☆   Going to the library or bookstore and looking through the resume section can be a baffling experience. Every expert seems to have a different opinion of what employers want. Chances are that the more information you gather, the more confused you'll become. It's easy to get frustrated and angry when answers aren't black and white when you desperately want them to be. Unfortunately, resumes are both an art and a science. Every expert gives good advice based on personal opinion and experience. Yet only you can determine which suggestions fit your specific situation. If you're a novice at selling yourself to potential employers, figuring out which recommendations make the most sense can be very difficult.

. . . And Its Cure

You can rise above the resume fray and confidently make your own decisions by keeping a few key facts in mind:

☆ Should you find yourself looking upon a resume as your only lifeline to employment, lighten up. It's just one tool in your job search arsenal.

☆ Remind yourself that bragging is a healthy and admirable activity when you're selling yourself to a new employer. She wants to know what you can do for her and she needs to be certain that her number one candidate is an outstanding performer. Telling her about your accomplishments helps her to justify the decision to hire you.

☆ Target each resume for a particular job. If you determine what a specific employer wants, then select past achievements that correlate with the requirements of his opening, you can be confident your resume will capture his attention and get you an interview.

☆ Ask for advice if you need it. Read resume books, talk to friends and fellow job seekers or visit a career counselor. Just don't allow any of these resources to usurp your power to choose what should be in your resume. People can determine what's right for them by trusting their instincts. There's nothing magic about writing a good resume. As long as you address both your needs and the needs of your potential employer, you'll be fine.

Reasons for Writing Resumes

Now that we have dealt with the emotion surrounding resumes, let's take a look at the reasons for writing them. As everyone knows, a resume is the usual vehicle for responding to an ad. Employers who advertise for candidates to fill a position want to screen potential employees before they OK them for interviews. Reviewing applicants' resumes is an excellent way to sort out the real contenders from those whose qualifications match poorly. To survive the winnowing process, your resume must speak concisely and directly to the needs of the recruiter. It must entice him to get to know you better.

Resumes serve a similar purpose at executive search firms. Sending a resume to a headhunter notifies her of your interest in being considered for search assignments on which she's working. To capture her attention, you must discuss your most important accomplishments in a format she will appreciate. Search firms don't work for you, so to be considered as a viable candidate, you must meet their strongest expectations.

You can also use a resume for a limited direct mail campaign to employers who particularly interest you. After identifying each company's likely requirements for potential employees, tailor your resume to highlight relevant achievements. By addressing specific needs, you should pique a recruiter's curiosity sufficiently for him to grant you an interview.

Resumes can also remind a potential employer of ways that your background might be useful. Talking to company representatives informally can help you to learn valuable facts about what the firm wants in an ideal associate. Then, if your experience seems to be a good match, you can send a resume targeting its needs. This may lead to your filling a current opening or creating a new position for yourself.

When used properly, this approach puts you miles ahead of competitors who rely on paper versus personal communication, and assumptions instead of facts about the employer's preferences.

Writing a resume is also great mental exercise before an interview. When meeting hiring managers, you should have two main goals:

1. Convincing your interviewer that you are the best candidate for the job.
2. Ascertaining if the position and the company are right for you.

Because a resume distills the achievements most relevant to the job you seek, organizing and writing this sales document requires you to consider carefully what you have to offer a particular employer. As your brain processes and refines this information, it wears comfortable little paths to its data storage centers. Then, when you need to cite your accomplishments in an interview, the information will come to you in a flash because your brain has been programmed to retrieve it easily.

What's another name for an unemployed person? A consultant. But if you're genuinely operating a consulting business, you'll probably need a resume to reinforce your credibility. Potential customers are just as concerned about your background and expertise as potential employers. They want to know you deserve to be called an expert and aren't using the title "Consultant" because you have delusions of grandeur.

Having a resume also is helpful if you work for a company that provides products or service to clients. Even if you represent one of the Big Five or a prestigious department in your corporation, you should be prepared to explain on paper why your credentials are more suited to an assignment than a competitor's. Institutions don't have the clout and credibility they once had. As the power and influence of the individual gains importance, potential users of your talents and expertise will demand to know more about you—regardless of the organization you represent.

Finally, you need a resume if you're contemplating a job change within your organization.

While resumes are valuable tools in your job search, they'll never substitute for person-to-person contact. Use them effectively to get your foot in the door, remind an employer why you should be hired, prepare for an interview or reinforce your credibility, but never assume a resume can take the place of building mutual rapport. Since the dawn of history (and probably even before that), people have done business together because they like and trust each other. This is an irrevocable trait of human nature. Use it to your advantage.

A Note from the Author

When the *National Business Employment Weekly* asked me to author a book on resumes, I struggled with many conflicting questions: How could I put together a resource that would be different from the others already on the market? What kinds of information should I include? How should I explain the resume's role in the overall job-search process? What were the best methods for illustrating how to write good resumes? What did job seekers want to know about this subject that other books weren't telling them?

To answer these questions, I read many resume books available from the library and local bookstores, then asked clients and colleagues what they expected to find in the ultimate resume guide. Here's what I discovered.

People have a number of misconceptions about resumes, especially concerning their role in a typical job search. Without discounting the importance of resumes, I wanted to dispel the myth that they're the "Open Sesame" to a new career. I chose to make my point by telling the saga of Larry and Joe and giving the resume quiz in Chapter 1.

As with any worthwhile project, preparing to put together a resume may take as long or longer than actually writing it. So often, job seekers become frustrated because they lack key items of information. Unless they first determine their marketable expertise and who's interested in buying it, they'll miss the mark in developing a truly effective written sales tool. Chapter 2 outlines how to identify your most relevant skills and accomplishments and learn from an employer how you can specifically benefit his organization.

As I looked through the books currently available on resumes, I noticed that they generally seemed to follow a prescribed format that leaves little room for individuality. Because an outstanding resume must be a personal expression of who you are, I didn't want this book to take a cookie-cutter or fill-in-the-blank approach. I especially didn't want, say, a financial planner to be able to turn to a financial planning resume, delete the name and address, put in her own and think her resume work was complete. So I used two techniques to encourage independent thinking:

1. The resumes in this book belong to real people from throughout the United States. While these examples represent and reinforce the principles I've suggested, they depict a variety of approaches for putting together an attention-getting document.

2. To help you create a unique product that gets results, I have provided lots of ideas and examples to guide you through the process. The old cliche, "If you give a person a fish, he will eat today, but if you teach him how to fish, he will never go hungry," represents the philosophy behind this book. If you use the system I recommend instead of just cloning an example, you'll never have to grapple with the uncertainty of writing a resume, no matter what career you're in.

One client gave me some particularly valuable advice when she suggested that I include some "before" and "after" examples that were actually quite good in the "before" stage but even better in the "after" version. She said, "Don't insult your readers' intelligence by offering truly terrible 'befores.' Make people think about why seemingly subtle improvements spell the difference between a resume that gets an interview and one that doesn't." You will find before-and-after examples in most of the chapters.

A veteran career planner who had also been a successful engineer, minister and trainer, admonished me to tell the stories behind the resumes. He said, "Wouldn't it be wonderful for your readers to hear how people in similar circumstances have changed their lives and moved on to positions and organizations that use their best skills and appreciate their contributions?" I hope you'll enjoy the true stories in this book as much as I have.

If you've read many resume guides, you've probably noticed that resume examples are usually categorized by type of career or industry. Yet I've found that accountants, engineers and other pros who want to remain in their fields have less trouble putting together resumes than those making major career or lifestyle changes. The professionals most in need of a map are the ones who are charting new territory. Consequently, I've targeted four groups of adventurers for my specialized resume categories: first-time job seekers, homemakers returning to the workforce, career changers and seasoned professionals who've been with one company for a long time. If you aren't in one of these groups, however, don't feel neglected. The other examples purposely encompass a broad spectrum of careers. It's likely your vocation is among them.

Finally, I received much feedback about the need for a system to keep track of the voluminous amounts of information and paperwork generated during a typical job search. Chapter 14 deals with this issue. If you're the kind of person who despises organizing things, take some of my suggestions. However, if you love devising the most efficient method for creating order out of chaos, have at it and send me your ideas. I'm not too proud to use them (and give you the credit) in our next edition.

So that's how this book evolved. It came together much like a typical job search. It had its ups and downs, quick inspirations and frustrating obstacles, but I had an unyielding goal throughout. It took about six months of continuing effort supported by my editors, colleagues, friends, clients and family. Now that the book is done, you and other job seekers will be its final judge. Let me know what you think.

"I'm going to level with you, Stan . . . your resume is a lemon."

1

What a Resume Can and Can't Do for You

Larry woke up full of anticipation. Today, he was to begin his career as Chief Financial Officer for Acme Software Systems, a position ideally suited to his background and skills. In the past four months, Larry had pursued his job search full time, networking with at least 50 people, collaborating with headhunters, answering ads in the *National Business Employment Weekly* and his local newspaper, mounting a targeted direct mail campaign and following up on potential leads. To stay balanced, he also scheduled time to relax, play ball with his daughter, and work off that extra 10 pounds he'd been wanting to shed for the past two years.

He's both enthusiastic and a little nervous about moving into a challenging position where he will be working with a team that fits him like a glove. While the past few months have had their ups and downs, Larry knows his job search approach produces results. Should he ever need to use it again, he's confident his winning formula will find him a great match.

Meanwhile, across town, Joe looks at the clock and notices it's already 9:30 A.M. He sighs, stares at the ceiling, and tries to convince himself to get out of bed and face another day unemployed. After six months of effort, Joe doesn't feel any closer to finding work than he did when he began looking for a job. In fact, when he was laid off, he was a lot more confident about moving easily into another midmanagement position than he is today. With his seemingly marketable experience, excellent reviews, sterling references, and dynamite resume that took days to perfect, he can't help wondering, "Where did I go wrong?"

Joe's problems stem from a combination of erroneous assumptions and macho attitudes. He's made a series of mistakes that have sabotaged his opportunities and heightened his depression. Unless he changes his approach, he'll spend many more mornings under the covers pondering his fate.

Let's take a look at Joe's job search versus Larry's. The differences should speak for themselves.

To Whom It May Concern

After he was laid off, Joe worked to perfect his resume like a man possessed. He carefully constructed a chronological listing of his job responsibilities to impress even the fussiest employer. He consulted his thesaurus, fine-tuning every phrase for maximum impact. After days of exhaustive labor, he pronounced his masterpiece complete and ready to catapult him into any position a contact, executive search firm, ad or direct mail campaign might offer. He honestly believed this resume was one of his life's proudest achievements.

Having produced the perfect resume and an equally perfect cover letter, Joe spent several hundred dollars on typesetting and laser printing to make hundreds of perfect copies at a local graphics firm.

While Joe put a lot of effort into his resume, he confined his networking effort to just a few friends and relatives. He was embarrassed about being laid off, so he didn't want to broadcast his unfortunate situation to people who respected him, or put his friends in an awkward position by asking for their help.

Instead he decided to make extensive use of executive search firms. In fact, he was really enthusiastic about other people's marketing him to potential corporations. To get names of qualified headhunters, he looked up Employment Recruiters and Executive Search Consultants in the yellow pages and sent all but the specialized ones his all-purpose resume and cover letter addressed: To Whom It May Concern. Then he waited for them to call.

Like many job seekers, Joe spent most of his job search pouring over want ads in his local newspaper, *National Business Employment Weekly,* and major dailies in other cities where he was willing to relocate. He responded to every ad remotely similar to his experience, assuming that at least a few would bear fruit.

Joe targeted companies in his industry as well. He went to the library and found a list of the top 250 software firms in the United States, and sent the human resources department at each company an identical resume and cover letter with a note asking them to call him if they wanted more information.

Joe, confident in the knowledge he had "papered the world" with his resume, decreased his job search efforts and eagerly anticipated an avalanche of calls and letters from prospective employers. Much to his surprise and frustration, 400 resumes generated six responses and one job offer he didn't want.

Joe started his job search believing his experience would be marketable in any number of places. In a burst of frenzied activity, he sent hundreds of unsolicited resumes to search firms and companies, answered many want ads, and did a little networking with friends. By the second month, when he began receiving rejection letters, he experienced the sinking feeling his job search would be more difficult than expected. In fact, the task began to loom larger and larger until Joe felt crushed by its weight and scope. Was he really as good as he thought? Would he ever find another job? Negative expectations overwhelmed him, crowding out all the positive feelings he had about himself, and usurping the time and effort he should have been spending looking for a job.

Every time he picked up the want ads and saw nothing worthwhile; every time he read about another layoff; and every time receipt of his resume went unacknowledged, he sank deeper into despair. Yet he did nothing to seek support from his family, friends and community because he was embarrassed and afraid.

Why didn't Joe talk to his minister, a career counselor or a therapist? Pride. Strong men don't need help. They solve their own problems.

I'm Available

When he started his job search, the first thing Larry did was list contacts who might be able to help him find a new position. Then he systematically met with each of them to explore a new career.

Recognizing that 80 to 90 percent of jobs are filled through networking, he talked extensively with potential employers. When he uncovered an opportunity, he constructed a resume to parallel the position's requirements and sent it along with a "Thank you for the appointment" note. As you might imagine, Larry eventually developed quite a stack of resume variations. But the thought and effort he put into them paid major dividends by showing potential employers how his background uniquely fit their particular needs.

While Larry knew the highest percentage of job seekers found positions through networking, he recognized that executive search firms, ads, and targeted resume campaigns sometimes yield results as well. Consequently, he researched headhunters and selected several who specialized in his field. Before he left his position at Snyder Systems, he talked to each of them to find out what they prefer in a resume and how they match candidates to search assignments. Then, focusing on his most relevant experience, he followed each firm's favored format and sent a copy of his revised resume.

Perusing his local paper and *National Business Employment Weekly* ads, he selected a few that required his particular combination of skills and experience. He carefully tailored his resume to parallel what each ad requested by rearranging the priority of his accomplishments, altering jargonal phrases, highlighting key personality traits, and even changing his objective to match the position, title and company name. He became a dedicated stickler for detail. Friends in human resources positions had forewarned him, "Resumes are screening tools. Even one 'off the mark' element can be the kiss of death."

Instead of beginning his cover letter with the usual, "I am sending my resume in response to your ad for a CFO," he did some library research that enabled him to focus his first paragraph on why the company interested him. Having attracted the attention of the human resources department with this unique approach, Larry summarized his most relevant experiences in his second paragraph. At the end of the letter, he promised a follow-up call to answer any immediate questions and discuss the mutual benefit of scheduling an initial interview. He addressed the letter to a specific person, even if it required a little sleuthing to discover the name, while also sending a copy to the CEO when possible.

To launch his very selective direct mail campaign, Larry spent several days at the library researching companies to determine his best corporate candidates. He looked for those whose philosophy, growth, organization, and products or services intrigued him. As he read annual reports and trade journal articles, he searched for specific needs or niches he might uniquely fill. After having tailored his cover letters and resumes, he sent them to the targeted CEOs most likely to hire him, then followed up on the phone to find out if a get-acquainted interview would be worthwhile.

By carefully pursuing chosen markets through networking, search firms, ads and direct mail, Larry maximized his chances for generating serious responses. By the time his job search ended, he had produced 20 inquiries, 10 initial interviews, 6 second interviews and 4 job offers, all of which were good matches for his background and interests.

I'm OK

Larry knew his job search would be a roller coaster of "king of the hill" highs and "crawl under a snake with a high hat on" lows. Consequently, he built a variety of activities into his days to keep himself on an even keel.

While he pursued a new job five days a week, he didn't obsess about it. As a recovering workaholic, he didn't want to backslide by concentrating on his job search every waking hour. He knew actively seeking a balance of work, fun and learning was a healthy approach whether he was employed or not. And he was hoping if he practiced his new lifestyle during his job search, he would be more likely to maintain it when he returned to work.

A Resume Doesn't a Job Search Make

Larry's and Joe's stories illustrate that a perfect resume doesn't produce a satisfying career. Unless your job search strategy combines a savvy resume with lots of networking, targeted marketing, persistent follow-up and psychological support, you, too, may find yourself depressed, unemployed and wondering what went wrong.

A Resume Quiz

The saga of Larry and Joe has alluded to a number of activities and attitudes involving resumes. Now that you have read it, here's a quiz to test your resume acumen. Don't worry if you don't answer all the questions correctly. If you were an expert, you would be writing this book, not reading it (the correct answers follow the quiz):

_F_ 1. Any well-planned job search begins with a great resume. (True or False?)

_A_ 2. When putting together a cover letter and resume for an ad, you:

    A. Tailor both the letter and the resume.

    B. Send a generic letter and resume.

    C. Tailor the cover letter, not the resume.

_F_ 3. Armed with a good resume, a headhunter has all he needs to market you to a variety of potential employers. (True or False?)

___F___ 4. A resume is your most important job search tool. (True or False?)

___F___ 5. Potential employers would rather hire an employed person than someone without a job. (True or False?)

___T___ 6. The research you conduct to formulate your resume is also an important key to preparing for an employment interview. (True or False?)

___F___ 7. Employers consider your resume follow-up a waste of their time. (True or False?)

___F___ 8. You can expect to get a reply from everyone to whom you send a resume. (True or False?)

___F___ 9. There is one resume format most employers prefer. (True or False?)

___B___ 10. The most effective job search activity is:

    A. Answering ads.

    B. Networking with follow-up.

    C. Using a search firm.

    D. Mounting a direct mail campaign.

___T___ 11. The best way to begin a cover letter is with a unique reason for your interest in the company and available position. (True or False?)

___F___ 12. Looking for a job is much harder than filling an opening, because the employer is always in the driver's seat. (True or False?)

___T___ 13. In real estate, the three keys to success are location, location, and location. In writing resumes, it's tailoring, tailoring, tailoring. (True or False?)

___T___ 14. Use the name of the person and company to whom you are sending your resume in cover letters, even if it takes some sleuthing to discover it. (True or False?)

_____ 15. Resumes that will be scanned into a computer should be written differently from those that will be reviewed by human eyes only. (True or False?)

___F___ 16. With the perfect resume, you will be able to leap tall buildings in a single bound, catch bullets in your teeth, and land a position that pays $500K, plus stock options. (True or False?)

Answers

False   1. Despite conventional wisdom, you do not want to start your job search with a major resume effort. To do this puts the cart before the horse. A resume is really a kind of ad or brochure. Before developing an ad campaign, an advertising agency carefully targets its market and defines its customers' needs and priorities. Only after identifying these factors, does the copywriter describe features and benefits most useful to the targeted market. In your case, you are the product. You bear the responsibility of selling your most important experiences and attributes to potential employers on a person-to-person basis. If you write your resume before you have found out what they need, you are missing an opportunity to present your best case.

A. _____ **2.** Tailor both the resume and cover letter. How many times have you heard people say they customize their cover letter, but send the same resume to everyone? Usually they are very proud of themselves for doing this, as many job seekers send one form letter and resume to everyone. Unfortunately, when a resume is competing with 200 to 400 others, it has to stand out from the crowd. Recruiters don't have time to separate the "diamonds from the dirt" in the 10 to 60 seconds they spend skimming for relevant experience. It is the candidate's responsibility to sort the valuable stuff from the extraneous, using only 20-carat material to land an interview.

False _____ **3.** Executive search firms need a good resume from you, but they also must have a search assignment that matches your background before they can be of service. Headhunters do not market you. They find the best candidates for client job openings. Their clients are companies that pay their fee or retainer. Don't expect a headhunter to make you her number one marketing project. Conducting your search campaign isn't her job, it's yours.

False _____ **4.** A resume is an important tool, but it can't get you a job. Only people can do that. If you want your job search to be successful, concentrate on people and prepare your resume to suit their needs.

False _____ **5.** It used to be true that firms preferred to hire employed people because only the deadwood were let go from a company. However, in the past 10 years, corporate mergers and acquisitions, hostile takeovers, and right-sizings have put many highly qualified professionals on the street through no fault of their own. Prospective employers are aware of this trend. If you maintain your self-confidence and tell a potential employer what you can do for him, he will consider another firm's loss his gain.

True _____ **6.** Resume search is important for the job interview, too. Most of us are more comfortable moving into unfamiliar territory if we have a map of the terrain. When you have researched an individual company to tailor your resume, you know a great deal about its products—services, mission, philosophy, revenues, and so forth. This information can be very valuable in preparing good questions and answers for initial and subsequent interviews. Employers like candidates who are savvy enough to do some homework before their first meeting.

In customizing your resume, you are pursuing two objectives simultaneously: You are creating a powerful written sales tool, and you are developing a verbal testament about why a specific employer should hire you. If you think of your resume-writing process as the best preparation for a rigorous interview session, you will be more likely to give it the time it deserves.

False   **7.** Employers don't consider your resume follow-up a waste of their time. While there will always be potential employers who are firm believers in the "don't call us, we'll call you" approach, most recruiters admire candidates who make an effort to follow up on their resumes. Follow-up shows both initiative and persistence, traits good managers love, especially in individuals who are applying for positions with major responsibilities. Don't worry about seeming too enthusiastic. Company representatives enjoy being pursued. It massages their egos and reminds them their company is worth courting.

False   **8.** Replying to all resumes would be the polite thing to do, but often it simply isn't practical. If a company receives 200 responses for an ad, or experiences a continual deluge of unsolicited resumes, it would spend an inordinate amount of time sending acknowledgments. If you really want a receipt for your resume, send a stamped, self-addressed postcard asking for one. If you make it easy, the human resources department will comply.

False   **9.** There is no universally preferred format. Many job seekers spend days perfecting their resumes, agonizing over whether to use a chronological format or a functional one. This question may be akin to figuring how many angels will fit on the head of a pin. There is no one perfect resume to suit every employer's needs. But there is a perfect resume for a specific opportunity. If you are going to focus on perfection, do it on an individual, rather than a global basis.

B.   **10.** Networking with follow-up is the most effective. The key to a successful job search is contacts. Most people can sell themselves better in person than on paper. While the tailored resumes you send to search firms, ads and direct mail targets are important and deserve your attention, they will never possess the power of a good relationship.

True ___ **11.** Just about every cover letter sent in response to an ad begins in the following style, "To Whom It May Concern: This letter is in response to your ad in the *National Business Employment Weekly* for . . ." Rather uninspiring, isn't it? Is it any wonder the few individuals who research a company, then use the information to formulate their cover letter's first paragraph, have a tremendous advantage over their complacent competitors? In the resume derby, everything you do to distinguish yourself moves you another length ahead of the pack.

False ___ **12.** Have you ever tried to hire a new employee? While looking for a job is tough, finding a good employee is no picnic either. Picture yourself as the CEO of a small to midsize company looking for a new CFO. After carefully constructing your ad, you wade through scores of resumes, schedule and conduct several rounds of interviews, screen the princes from the frogs, and hope when you choose the best candidate, he will say yes. For a busy executive, this can be a long, expensive, and nerve-racking process with no guarantee of a positive result.

True ___ **13.** Tailor, tailor, tailor.

True ___ **14.** People and companies like to see their names in print, especially if it took some effort to find them. Chapters 2 and 5 include tips to help you find the real addressee even when the person is trying to be incognito.

Both ___ **15.** **Both true and false.** If your resume will be read by a resume scanning program for key words, it's absolutely imperative that those key words be included in your text. Consequently, tailoring your resume to an ad, networking recommendation or job description is probably even more important than if a person were doing the initial screening. In this respect people-scanned and computer-scanned resumes are very similar.

However, because some computer scanners have difficulty reading vertical lines, italics and unusual type fonts, techniques you might use to grab the attention of recruiters can be misinterpreted by a computer. If your resume is likely to be scanned, keep the format simple and use only boldface type and bullets to highlight major points.

False ___ **16.** **Unfortunately, false, superexec.** However, a great resume can get you invited to the penthouse, where your masterful interviewing techniques will lead to a great opportunity complete with a substantial raise and a covered parking spot with your name on it.

2

Getting Organized

Before you make your first networking call or circle any ads in the newspaper, prepare an office at home or at an outplacement facility to maximize your productivity and keep frustration to a minimum.

If you haven't already acquainted yourself with the power and ease of desktop publishing, do it now. With a current word-processing package and a PC, you can produce a variety of professional looking, tailored resumes and cover letters without having to retype each version or pay an expensive resume service. And while the computer is saving you time, money and aggravation on your resumes, it can also store your contact and company data, keep your weekly calendar, monitor your cash flow, remind you to follow up on resumes and appointments and even play a game with you if you need a little diversion.

If you don't have a computer or can't gain easy access to one through a friend, college lab, or outplacement center, copy businesses such as Kinko's rent them by the hour. You might also check the cost of having your resumes and cover letters typed by personnel at an executive office service, especially if you are contracting with them to receive your mail and answer your calls during the day.

Aside from a computer, you'll need a few other important resources to create professional resumes. A laser or ink jet printer is one of them. While a dot matrix printer may be perfectly presentable for your son's sixth-grade science project, its product will not serve you well in a competitive job market. If you don't have a good printer or the funds to buy one, take your resume disk to a local print shop where it will be translated into a hard copy for you.

If you have read any older resume books, you have probably noticed how outdated the typefaces look. With the advent of desktop publishing, your little computer can produce beautiful documents from software that contain a variety of type sizes, italics, bold lettering and other techniques previously seen only in expensive documents. Before you type your resume, be sure you have at least one modern font available which reflects your personality. When your resume is competing with 200 others, you don't want it to be eliminated because it looks as if you wrote it wearing a leisure suit.

You should order some fine-quality stationery for your cover letters and resumes. Quality paper has a high rag content and a watermark you can see if you hold it up to the light. There isn't any one color preferred over others. So you can assert your independence and select something in the white, cream, light blue, or gray color family without concern about being incorrect.

You may want to have your name, address, phone number and e-mail address printed on your letterhead, and your name and address on the envelopes. While it isn't necessary to do this, it can save you some time, and it has a finished quality that lends an added touch of distinction.

Aside from a computer, printer, diskholder and stationery, you will want to stock your work space with the following important tools:

☆ *Stamps*—both first and third class varieties—in case you need to send some heavier packages.

☆ A *Rolodex*—manual or computerized—for quick reference to contact and company names, addresses and phone numbers.

☆ A *wall* or *desk calendar* for scheduling blocks of time for research, phone calls, resumes and cover letters, thank-you notes, brainstorming, reading ads, articles and books, interviews, notes on appointments, and appropriate follow-up strategies.

☆ A *manual* or *computerized system* for keeping track of your job search activities and the follow-up needed for each.

☆ A *dictionary* or *thesaurus* for checking spelling and finding just the right word whenever you need it.

Laying Your Resume Foundation

Writing a great resume is a lot like painting a house. Before you apply the paint, you have to buy the right materials, assemble them, and prepare your surface. If you neglect these initial steps, your final product will probably fall short of your standards. Taking a systematic approach may seem to require more time at the outset, but sticking to it will save you a lot of frustrated effort and produce superior results.

Accomplishments History

Before writing one word of your resume, put together an accomplishments history, including your most significant achievements from work, hobbies, volunteer projects, school, extracurricular activities, travel, and other life experiences you feel are worth noting. Doing this is essential to preparing a good resume, and it's a wonderful boost for the bruised ego commonly found in job seekers.

For each of your chosen accomplishments, create a list of chronological activities, transferable and specialized skills, and results. Mention names of clients, companies, participants, states, clubs, institutions, and individuals that would impress a potential employer. Quantify where applicable. Some examples of relevant statistics might include sales volume, percentage increase in revenue, inventory turns, money saved, percentage of shrinkage decrease or worker hours saved. You can also give a better idea of the scope of your job or project by quantifying the number of people you supervise, coordinate, collaborate with or serve as customers.

Be creative and inclusive in describing what you've done. This is not the appropriate time for modesty. You might want to involve your spouse or a friend in this process. Often they remember your accomplishments better than you do, and they can encourage you to give yourself credit for efforts you might dismiss as trivial. The following are some examples of achievements to help get your brainstorming started:

☆ Designing a brochure, poster or newsletter.

☆ Mediating a dispute between two parties.

☆ Determining the political realities in choosing a course of action.

☆ Selling a product, service or decision to senior executives or clients.

☆ Developing, promoting and teaching in-house training programs.

☆ Putting together a yearly project or budget.

☆ Investigating the options for installing a new system.

☆   Supervising and mentoring professional or blue-collar workers.

☆   Inventing a new product or service.

☆   Speaking to large or small groups or chairing committee meetings.

☆   Writing and editing an employee or product documentation manual.

☆   Spearheading organizational change.

☆   Working on a team to design a mission statement and policies.

☆   Fixing a product design problem.

☆   Establishing rapport with people whose perspectives are different from yours.

☆   Opening a new facility.

☆   Recruiting and interviewing potential employees.

☆   Planning an advertising or public relations campaign.

☆   Using your imagination to solve a pressing or recurring problem.

☆   Testing a hypothesis to determine if your hunch is correct.

☆   Implementing a total quality program.

☆   Acting quickly and decisively to avert a crisis or take advantage of an opportunity.

☆   Prioritizing, juggling a variety of tasks.

☆   Inspiring people to do difficult things.

☆   Coaching a soccer team.

☆   Planning and hosting a 25th-anniversary party.

☆   Traveling to a new and exotic place.

☆   Building and flying a model airplane.

☆   Renovating and managing rental houses.

☆   Doing your own income tax return.

☆   Serving as an officer for a nonprofit agency.

☆   Managing your own portfolio.

☆   Losing 25 pounds and maintaining your new weight.

☆   Adding a gameroom to the house.

Once you've made a list of your accomplishments, give each of them its own sheet of paper and write about the step-by-step process you used to make it successful. The following is an example of a typical achievement:

Larry's Number One Accomplishment

My most significant accomplishment as chief financial and administrative officer was starting an Investor Relations program from scratch after my company went public in 1995. For the first year, I handled IR personally, but then recognized we needed a much more proactive program than I was able to provide using 25 percent of my available time. Basically, I was just responding to securities analysts' questions and was not able to court new analysts or visit existing shareholders.

In 1997, I hired a top-notch IR VP from a giant competitor. He spent about 75 percent of his first year traveling. He had phone conversations with 100 analysts and face-to-face meetings with another 115 of the most important analysts or potential investors. Our CEO, the IR VP and I made formal slide presentations to 10 industry analyst meetings. Our shareholder list improved from 5 percent retail (individual stockholders as opposed to institutions who owned stock) to 25 percent, and we increased the number of analysts who wrote reports on our company from 2 to 10.

The experience utilized several of my skills/attributes that are important to me:

1. My ability to find and motivate good people—everyone thought very highly of our IR VP, and he worked tirelessly during the time he was with us.

2. My credibility—we were honest and forthright with analysts and they thanked us for it.

3. My presentation skills—I was able to bring to the process all the key ingredients in effective presentations:

   • Understanding the important aspects of the business.

   • Understanding what the audience wants to know about the company.

   • Good charts and written materials.

   • Good verbal skills.

Once you have written your accomplishments, put them on a skills summary sheet. Doing this will help you select action verbs and phrases to describe your most marketable activities to potential employers. The functional and transferable skills inventory starting on page 25 shows how Larry has identified the functional skills he used to achieve his IR department goal.

While most people think they know the skills they use on a regular basis, they often neglect to identify some of their most important competencies, especially those that are inborn and come naturally. Yet these functional skills are primary keys to an individual's effectiveness and are usually essential ingredients to a satisfying position.

Your Functional and Transferable Skills Inventory

Creating a resume without having a solid grasp of the skills you use best (and enjoy most) is an impossible task. To gain a better understanding of your key abilities and how they might transfer to new functional areas, complete a skills inventory worksheet like the sample on pages 25–36, which documents Larry's IR experience.

Gathering Information to Tailor Your Resume

With your accomplishments history complete, you are almost ready to begin working on your resume. So far, you have laid a foundation for describing the most important things you can offer an employer. Now you need to determine exactly what the employer wants from you. There are a variety of ways to do this by using ads, information interviews and library research.

Resume Information from Ads

Let's take a look at a typical ad in the *National Business Employment Weekly* to determine what is particularly important to the company that placed it, and how you might best respond.

Crandall Corporation, a medium-sized, fast-growing plastics manufacturer is looking for a VP of Sales and Marketing. If you have experience with a medium-sized company on a high growth curve, be sure to include this information in your resume, and provide increasing sales figures to back it up. Since your background is similar, it will pique the recruiter's interest and entice him to continue reading for other parallels.

Crandall has multiple product lines and serves a global market. Most of its lines have been around for a while, but it also has a fast-growing new one at the forefront of its market niche. If you have experience in a worldwide market, focus on it. If you have worked with any fast-moving, cutting-edge products, this will be a key selling point for you.

The next part of the ad makes your job of interpreting what the company wants very simple. They've listed their major requirements for you. Consequently,

FUNCTIONAL AND TRANSFERABLE SKILLS INVENTORY

DIRECTIONS:

☆ Choose seven experiences from any time (current, childhood, teen years, college, etc., 5-10-20 years ago, etc.) and any area (work, family, school, volunteer work, hobbies, special projects, relationships, etc.) of your life using two criteria:

1. They were satisfying.

2. You enjoyed their *process* as well as their result.

☆ Write a paragraph or outline giving a step-by-step account of each one.

☆ Think about why you chose these seven experiences and what you particularly enjoyed about them.

☆ On this skills exercise, put the title of your first experience at the top of Column 1. Then—keeping in mind its step-by-step process—look at each box of transferable skills. If you used one or more of the skills in a box, put a check in Column 1. If you enjoyed using the skill(s), make a second check (in the same box).

☆ As you work through Column 1, you will find that some skills have no checks because you didn't use them in your experience. Some will have one check: You used them but they weren't enjoyable. Others will have two checks: You had fun applying them.

☆ After completing Column 1, use the same procedure for your other six experiences.

☆ Your completed exercise will give an excellent picture of your transferable skills, where they cluster, and which ones are most satisfying.

Experiences	IR. Program 1	2	3	4	5	6	7
I. THE SOCIAL THEME (People and Idea Skills)							
A. Written Communication Skills							
Love of reading voraciously or rapidly. Love of printed things.							
Comparing. Editing effectively.	✓✓		✓				
Publishing imaginatively.			✓				
Explicit, concise writing. Keeping superior minutes of meetings.	✓✓		✓				
Uncommonly warm letter composition.	✓✓						
Flair for writing reports. Skilled in speechwriting.							
B. Verbal Communication Skills							
Effective verbal communication. Expressing self very well. Making a point and cogently expressing a position.	✓✓						
Encouraging communication and participation.	✓✓						
Thinking quickly on one's feet.	✓						
Translating. Verbal skills in foreign languages. Teaching languages. Adept at translating jargon into relevant and meaningful terms to diverse audiences or readers.	✓✓						

Proof reader
Print shop
Research notes
records

	IR. Program						
	1	2	3	4	5	6	7
Summarizing. Reporting on conversations or meetings accurately.							
Informing, enlightening, explaining, instructing, defining.	✓✓						
Developing rapport and trust.	✓✓		✓				
Adept at two-way dialogue. Ability to hear and answer questions perceptively. Accepting differing opinions. Helping others express their views.	✓✓						
Listening intently and accurately. Good at listening and conveying awareness.	✓✓						
Dealing with many different kinds of people. Talks easily with all kinds of people.							
C. Instructing, Guiding, Mentoring Skills							
Fostering stimulating learning environment. Creating an atmosphere of acceptance. Patient teaching. Instills love of the subject. Conveys tremendous enthusiasm.			✓				
Adept at inventing illustrations for principles or ideas. Adept at using visual communications.	✓✓						
Coaching, advising, aiding people in making decisions.	✓✓		✓				
Consulting. — on financial investments			✓				
Mentoring and facilitating personal growth and development. Helping people make their own discoveries in knowledge, ideas or insights. Empowering.							
Clarifying goals and values of others. Puts things in perspective.	✓✓						
Fostering creativity in others. Showing others how to use resources.							
Group facilitating. Discussion group leadership. Group dynamics.							
Training. Designing educational events. Organizing and administering in-house training programs.							
D. Serving/Helping/Human Relations Skills							
Relating well in dealing with the public/public relations.	✓✓						
Helping and serving. Referring (people). Customer relations and services.							

	IR. Program						
	1	2	3	4	5	6	7
Sensitivity to others. Interested in/manifesting keen ability to relate to people. Adept at treating people fairly. Consistently communicates warmth to people. Conveying understanding, patience and fairness.			√				
Perceptive in identifying and assessing the potential of others. Recognizes and appreciates the skills of others.							
Remembering people and their preferences.			√				
Keen ability to put self in someone else's shoes. Empathy. Instinctively understands others feelings.			√				
Tact, diplomacy and discretion.	√√						
Caring for. Watching over. Nurturing.							
Administering a household.			√				
Shaping and influencing the atmosphere of a particular place. Providing comfortable, natural, and pleasant surroundings.	√√						
Warmly sensitive and responsive to people's feelings and needs in social or other situation. Anticipating people's needs.	√√		√				
Working well on a team. Has fun while working and makes it fun for others. Collaborating with colleagues skillfully. Treating others as equals without regard to education, authority or position. Motivates fellow workers. Expresses appreciation faithfully. Ready willingness to share credit with others.	√√		√				
Refusing to put people into slots or categories. Ability to relate to people with different value systems.	√						
Taking human failings/limitations into account. Dealing patiently and sympathetically with difficult people. Handles prima donnas tactfully and effectively. Works well in hostile environment.	√						
Nursing. Skillful therapeutic abilities.							
Gifted at helping people with their personal problems. Raises people's self-esteem. Understands human motivations, relationships and needs. Aware of people's need for supportive community. Aids people with their total life adjustment. Counseling.							

	IR. Program						
	1	2	3	4	5	6	7
Unusual ability to represent others. Expert in liaison roles. Ombudsmanship.	✓✓						
II. THE ENTERPRISING THEME (People, Idea and System Skills)							
A. Influencing/Persuading Skills							
Helping people identify their own intelligent self-interest.	✓✓						
Persuading. Influencing the attitudes or ideas of others.	✓✓		✓				
Promoting. Face-to-face selling of tangibles/intangibles. Selling ideas or products without tearing down competing ideas or products. Selling an idea, program or course of action to decision makers.	✓✓		✓				
Making and using contacts effectively. Resource broker.	✓✓						
Developing targets/building markets for ideas or products.	✓✓						
Raising money. Arranging financing.	✓✓						
Getting diverse groups to work together. Wins friends easily from among diverse or even opposing groups or factions.							
Adept at conflict management.		✓					
Arbitrating/mediating between contending parties or groups. Negotiating to come jointly to decisions. Bargaining. Crisis intervention. Reconciling.							
Renegotiating. Obtaining agreement on policies, after the fact.							
Recruiting talent or leadership. Attracting skilled, competent, creative people.	✓✓						
Motivating others. Mobilizing. Stimulating people to effective action.	✓✓						
Leading others. Inspiring and leading organized groups. Impresses others with enthusiasm and charisma. Repeatedly elected to senior posts. Skilled at chairing meetings.			✓				
Deft in directing creative talent. Skilled leadership in perceptive human relations techniques.	✓✓						
Bringing people together in cooperative efforts. Able to call in other experts/helpers as needed. Team-building. Recognizing and utilizing the skills of others.	✓✓						

	IR. Program						
	1	2	3	4	5	6	7
Directing others. Making decisions about others. Supervising others in their work. Contracting. Delegating.	✓✓						
Recognizes intergroup communications gaps. Judges people's effectiveness.	✓✓						
B. Performing Skills							
Getting up before a group. Very responsive to audiences' moods or ideas. Contributes to others' pleasure consciously. Performing.	✓						
Demonstrating. Modeling. Making presentations.	✓✓						
Showmanship. A strong theatrical sense. Poise in public appearance.	✓						
Addressing groups. Speaking ability/articulateness. Public address/public speaking/oral presentations. Lecturing. Stimulating people's enthusiasm.	✓✓						
Making people laugh. Understanding the value of the ridiculous in illuminating reality.							
Acting.							
Conducting and directing public affairs and ceremonies.							
C. Initiating/Risk-Taking Skills							
Initiating. Able to move into new situations on one's own.	✓✓						
Taking the first move in developing relationships.	✓✓						
Driving initiative. Searching for more responsibility.							
Excellent at organizing one's time. Ability to do work self-directed, without supervision.	✓✓		✓				
Unwillingness to automatically accept the status quo. Keen perceptions of things as they could be, rather than passively accepting them as they are. Promoting and bringing about major changes. A change agent.	✓✓						
Seeing and seizing opportunities. Sees a problem and acts immediately to solve it.	✓✓						
Dealing well with the unexpected or critical. Decisive in emergencies.							

	IR. Program 1	2	3	4	5	6	7
Adept at confronting others with touchy or difficult personal matters.							
Entrepreneurial.							
Showing courage. Willing to take manageable risks.	✓✓						
Able to make hard decisions.							
D. Planning and Management Skills							
Planning, development. Planning on basis of lessons from past experience. A systematic approach to goal-setting.	✓✓						
Prioritizing tasks. Establishing effective priorities among competing requirements. Setting criteria or standards.	✓✓	✓					
Policy formulation or interpretation. Creating and implementing new policies.	✓✓						
Designing projects. Program development.	✓✓						
Skilled at planning and carrying out well-run meetings, seminars or workshops.	✓✓						
Organizing. Organizational development and analysis. Planning and building. Bringing order out of chaos.	✓✓		✓				
Scheduling, Assigning, Setting up and maintaining on-time work schedules. Coordinating operations/details. Arranging.	✓✓						
Producing. Achieving. Attaining a goal.	✓✓						
Recommending courses of action.	✓✓						
Making good use of feedback.	✓✓						
III. THE ARTISTIC THEME (Idea Skills)							
A. Intuitional and Innovating Skills							
Having imagination and the courage to use it.							
Operating well in a free, unstructured, environment. Bringing new life to traditional approaches.	✓✓						

	IR. Program						
	1	2	3	4	5	6	7
Ideophoria; continually conceiving, developing and generating ideas. Inventing. Conceptualizing.							
Improvising on the spur of the moment.							
Innovating, Perceptive, creative problem solver. Willing to experiment with new approaches.							
Love of exercising the creative mind-muscle.	✓✓						
Synthesizing perceptions. Seeing relationships between apparently unrelated factors. Integrating diverse elements into a clear, coherent whole. Ability to relate abstract ideas.	✓✓						
Deriving things from others' ideas. Improvising, Updating, Adapting.	✓✓						
Relating theory to a practical situation. Theoretical Model development.	✓✓						
Generating ideas with commercial possibilities. Seeing the commercial possibilities of abstract ideas or concepts. Creating products or services.	✓✓						
Showing foresight. Recognizing obsolescence before it occurs. Instinctively gathering resources even before the need for them is evident. Forecasting.	✓✓						
Perceiving intuitively.	✓✓						
B. Artistic Skills							
Showing strong sensitivity to, and need for, beauty in the environment. Instinctively excellent taste.							
Expressive. Exceptionally good at facial expressions used to convey thoughts without (or in addition to) words. Using voice tone and rhythm as unusually effective tool of communication. Accurately reproducing sounds (e.g., foreign languages spoken without accent).							
Good sense of humor and playfulness conveyed in person or in writing.							
Aware of the value of symbolism and deft in its use. Skilled at symbol formation (words, pictures and concepts). Visualizing concepts. Creating poetic images.							

	IR. Program						
	1	2	3	4	5	6	7
Designing and/or using audiovisual aids, photographs, visual, spatial and graphic designs. Illustrations, maps, logos.	✓✓						
Perception of forms, patterns and structures. Visualizing shapes, graphs, in the third dimension.	✓✓						
Spatial memory. Memory for design. Notice quickly (and/or remember later) most of the contents of a room. Memory for faces.							
Exceptional color discrimination.							
Designing, fashioning, shaping, redesigning things. Styling, decorating.							
Writing novels, stories, imaginative scripts, ad campaigns. Playwriting. Assisting and directing the planning, organizing, and staging of a theatrical production.							
Musical knowledge and taste. Tonal memory. Uncommon sense of rhythm. Exceedingly accurate melody recognition. Composing, making music. Dancing, singing, expert at using the body to express feelings.							
IV. THE INVESTIGATIVE THEME (Data and System Skills)							
A. Observational Learning Skills							
Highly observant of people, data and things. Keen awareness of surroundings.							
Intensely curious about people, data, things.							
Adept at scanning reports, computer printouts or other sophisticated observational systems.	✓✓						
Hearing accurately. Keen sense of smell. Excellent sense of taste.							
Detecting, discovering. A person of perpetual curiosity. Delights in new knowledge. Continually seeking to expose oneself to new experiences. Highly committed to continual personal growth and learning. Wants to know why.							
Learning from the example of others. Learns quickly.							
Alert in observing human behavior. Studying other people's behavior.	✓✓		✓				

	IR. Program						
	1	2	3	4	5	6	7
Appraising, assessing, screening. Realistically evaluating people's needs. Accurately assessing public mood. Quickly sizing up situations and their political realities.	✓✓						
Intelligence tempered by common sense.	✓✓						
Balancing factors. Judging. Showing good judgment.	✓✓						
B. Investigating/Analyzing/Systematizing/Evaluating Skills							
Anticipating problems before they occur.	✓✓		✓				
Recognizing need for more information before a decision can be made intelligently. Skilled at clarifying problems or situation.	✓✓						
Inspecting, examining, surveying, researching exhaustively, gathering information.	✓✓		✓				
Interviewing people. Researching personally through investigation and interviews. Inquiring.	✓✓		✓				
Researching resources, ways and means.	✓✓		✓				
Dissecting, Breaking down principles into parts. Analyzing needs, values, resources, communication situations, requirements, performance specifications, etc.	✓✓						
Diagnosing. Separating "wheat from chaff." Reviewing large amounts of material and extracts essence.	✓✓						
Perceiving and defining cause-and-effect relationships. Ability to trace problems, ideas, etc. to their source.	✓✓						
Grouping, perceiving common denominators. Organizing material/information in a systematic way. Categorizing.	✓✓						
Testing an idea or hypothesis.							
Determining or figuring out, problem solving, troubleshooting.	✓✓						
Reviewing. Screening data. Critiquing, Evaluating by measurable or subjective criteria (e.g., programs, loans, papers, quizzes, work, staff, records, program bids evidence, options, qualifications, etc.).							

	IR. Program						
	1	2	3	4	5	6	7
Making decisions based on information gathered.	✓✓						
Reevaluating.							
V. THE CONVENTIONAL THEME (Data and Method Skills)							
A. Detail and Follow-Through Skills							
Following through, executing, maintaining.	✓✓						
Good at getting things done.	✓✓						
Implementing decisions. Providing support services. Applying what others have developed.							
Precise attainment of set limits, tolerances, or standards. Brings projects in on time and within budget. Skilled at making arrangements for events, processes. Responsible.	✓✓		✓				
Expediting, dispatching. Adept at finding ways to speed up a job.							
Able to handle a great variety of tasks and responsibilities simultaneously and efficiently.	✓						
Good at getting materials. Collecting things. Purchasing. Compiling.			✓				
Approving, validating information.	✓						
Keeping information confidential.							
Persevering.	✓						
Following detailed instructions. Keen and accurate memory for detail. Showing careful attention to, and keeping track, of details.	✓		✓				
High tolerance of repetition and/or monotony.			✓				
Checking, proofreading.	✓		✓				
Systematic manipulation of data. Good at processing information. Collates/tabulates data accurately, compares current with previous data. Keeping records. Recording (kinds of data).	✓✓		✓				
Facilitating and simplifying other people's finding things.	✓✓						

	IR. Program						
	1	2	3	4	5	6	7
Organizing written and numerical data according to a prescribed plan. Classification skills. Filing, retrieving data.	✓✓		✓				
Clerical ability. Operating business machines and data processing machines to attain organizational and economic goals. Reproducing materials.							
B. Working with Numbers							
Numerical ability. Expert at learning and remembering numbers.	✓✓						
Counting. Taking inventory.			✓				
Calculating, computing, arithmetic skills. Rapid manipulation of numbers. Rapid computations performed in head or on paper.	✓✓						
Managing money. Financial planning and management. Keeping financial records. Accountability.	✓✓		✓				
Appraising, economic research and analysis, Cost Analysis, estimates, projections. Comparisons, financial/fiscal analysis and planning/programming.	✓✓						
Budget planning, preparation, justification, administration, analysis and review.	✓✓		✓				
Extremely economical. Skilled at allocating scarce financial resources.			✓				
Preparing financial reports.	✓✓		✓				
Using numbers as a reasoning tool. Very sophisticated mathematical abilities. Effective at solving statistical problems.	✓✓						
VI. THE REALISTIC THEME (Thing and Method Skills)							
A. Working with Your Hands and Body							
Molding, shaping, making.							
Preparing, clearing, building, constructing, assembling, setting up, installing, laying.							
Lifting/pushing/pulling/balancing, carrying, unloading/moving delivering.							
Handling/feeling. Keen sense of touch. Finger dexterity, Manipulating things.							

	IR. Program						
	1	2	3	4	5	6	7
Precision working. Showing dexterity or speed.							
Feeding, pending.							
Controlling/operating, blasting, grinding, forging, cutting, filling, applying, pressing, binding.							
Using small or large tools, machinery. Operating vehicles or equipment.							
Fitting, adjusting, tuning, maintaining, repairing, Masters machinery against its will. Troubleshooting machine problems.							
Producing things.							
Motor/physical coordination and agility, Eye-hand-foot coordination. Walking, climbing, running.							
Skilled at sports.							
Physical recreation. Outdoor survival skills. Creating, planning, organizing outdoor activities.							
Traveling.							
Cultivating, planting and nurturing growing things. Skilled at planting/nurturing plants.							
Farming, ranching, working with animals.							

VICE PRESIDENT
OF SALES & MARKETING

Crandall Corporation, a medium-sized plastics manufacturer and anticipating a rapid growth rate over the next 5 years, is seeking a Vice President of Sales and Marketing.

This top position will coordinate the sales and marketing efforts of our 4 divisions, each serving a different market worldwide. Our newest division is experiencing rapid growth due to newly patented technology that has allowed us to position ourselves in the forefront of a niche market centered in the container/packaging field. Our other markets consist of office products, strip and impact doors and fence line products.

Qualified candidates should have a proven work history to the following areas:

- Strategic sales and marketing planning and implementation for existing and new product offerings.
- Leading a "multi-line" sales organization, preferably in the consumer packaging and retail markets.
- Container/Packaging concepts as it relates to new consumer products being introduced into the market places on a global basis.
- Must have strong managerial and team building skills in a TQM environment.
- Experience in small-to-medium sized companies preferred.

The successful candidate will join a highly capable and motivated professional team that is responsive, quality driven and committed to delivering innovation through marketing research and product development.

We offer a competitive salary and benefits program, including a relocation package to the beautiful mountain lakes region of northwest Alabama, where our facility is located, which provides for an environment of quality living. Qualified candidates should send resumes in confidence to:

C R A N D A L L
CORPORATION

**Human Resources Department 300
2600 E. Avalon Avenue
Muscle Shoals, Alabama 35630
(205) 261-3860
FAX (205) 261-3861**
Equal Opportunity Employer

you should address every one of the five bulleted items to have the best chance of landing an interview.

The fourth paragraph alludes to the company's corporate philosophy. It wants leaders who are team players, responsive to customer and company needs, driven by a dedication to quality and committed to the continual innovation of products. Referring to these more general, but highly important criteria in your resume will definitely win you some kudos.

Finally, the company expects you to move to Alabama if you want this position. Mentioning your willingness to relocate would be to your advantage as well.

While the preceding ad is pretty straightforward, others require some reading in between the lines. Let's take a look at one that will test your powers of observation and interpretation.

Strategy/Value Creation Consulting

Fast growing consulting firm seeks exceptionally bright, motivated, team-oriented individuals. Practice highly focused on assisting client companies achieve full financial and operating potential; create long-term value.

CONSULTANTS Required: Two years at leading corporate strategy consulting firm. MBA from top school. Operating experience or financial expertise a plus.

ANALYSTS Required: One year at leading corporate strategy consulting firm. Exceptional academic record. Financial modeling and computer skills.

Write to:

Stephens, Taylor & Associates, Inc.
Attn: Human Resources
21 Maple Street, Wellesley, MA 02181
Please, no calls

The company running this ad is a fast-growing consulting firm that wants people who will work hard, put in a good deal of overtime, travel extensively and get along with each other. It needs generalists who will look at the entire client operation and develop options to impact long-term results, rather than bottom line this quarter. Experience and education from leading businesses and academic institutions are very important to them.

If you want to impress their human resource professionals, be prepared to discuss high-profile projects geared to positioning your clients for long-term outcomes in organizational development, financial planning and analysis, management information systems, marketing strategies and other functions that affect the company as a whole. While specific experience in operations and finance would be useful, they are not looking for specialists, who focus only on one aspect of the business. And if your MBA is from a small, but proud regional institution, you can probably forget about this opportunity. You may have a fine education, but Harvard, Northwestern or University of Pennsylvania graduates will most certainly have the edge at this firm.

Resume Information on Companies Targeted for a Direct-Mail Campaign

Along with ads, networking and executive search firms, you may want to target some potential employers for a direct-mail campaign. Any direct-mail expert will tell you this type of communication is very much a numbers game. The usual response rate ranges between 1 and 5 percent. Consequently, if you want 10 replies to your mailing, you will have to send out between 200 and 1,000 resumes. When you consider the time, effort and money needed to mount this size campaign, it's apparent that papering the world with your resume is an exercise in diminishing marginal utility.

If you target potential employers very carefully, however, you can do a limited mailout and receive a reasonable return on your investment. To choose your best candidates, head for the Internet or to the business section of your nearest large library, where you will find an overwhelming abundance of reference material. If you visit the library, go directly to the librarian and ask for help. Believe it or not, librarians would much rather help you to find information than hide in the stacks. To facilitate their search, put together a list of demographics describing the types of employer you want to research. The company's industry, revenue, number of employees, geographical area, product or service, public or private ownership, profit or nonprofit status, years in business and contribution to the community are all attributes that might be useful.

If you can't find the librarian, or if she's busy or having a bad day, here are a few key resources that can provide data for writing cover letters and resumes designed to attract your target employers:

☆ *Ebsco.* This service searches for articles in thousands of periodicals. If you are using this database at a library, you can often e-mail what you find back to your home computer rather than having to stop and print it immediately.

☆ *Standard & Poor's Registry of Corporations, Directors, and Executives.* Listing thousands of corporations, officers, directors and trustees. This three-volume directory offers a plethora of information. Listings are indexed under a variety of headings that make it easy to search for company specialties. With a bit of sleuthing, you can also uncover background information on the "higher-ups" of a corporation, including where he/she was born or went to college.

☆ *The Thomas Register of American Manufacturers; Thomas Register Catalog File.* Look up a particular product or service, and you'll find every company that provides it in this 23-volume publication. Published annually, this reference also includes data on branch offices, capital ratings, company offices and, of course, addresses and phone numbers.

☆ *Moody's Complete Corporate Index.* If you are really interested in a lengthy description on a particular company, this publication is for you. If you want to know a company's history, Moody's provides the details—from financial information to when the company was founded.

☆ *The Million Dollar Directory.* This three-volume reference contains thousands of businesses, and the names of key personnel. Its listings are arranged alphabetically, geographically and by product classification to maximize the efficiency of your search.

☆ *Ward's Directory of Public and Private Companies.* As you might imagine, the directory lists both firms that are traded on stock exchanges and those that aren't. Each brief reference includes the company's name, address, phone number, officers, SIC code and products or services.

☆ *Annual Reports.* Publicly held corporations produce these handsome booklets to highlight their financial status, promote their products and services, and publicize their involvement in community and charitable activities. Because the firms author their own reports, they generally slant their presentation to be as positive as possible. However, they do provide a great deal of information and are worth using if you keep this intrinsic "spin" in mind.

☆ *Local Business Journals.* Many large cities also publish weekly business journals that specialize in reporting on the regional business scene. They can be especially useful for researching small to midsize companies that are privately owned and don't publish annual reports.

☆ *The Internet.* A connection to the Internet offers a world of information at your fingertips. Search engines such as Yahoo! and Excite will hyperlink you to corporate home pages, business magazine articles and a host of other sites that reference your targeted company.

Once you have your company's information at your fingertips, you will need a system for extracting the most valuable data in a reasonable amount of time. To write a tailored cover letter and resume, you'll need key facts and trends, not volumes of detail. The sample form on pages 42–43 shows how to gather the most salient information for an organization.

If the research to target direct-mail campaign companies is more work than you can abide, you might want to try the "send one resume and cover letter to everybody" approach. Just don't expect more than a 5 percent return. To increase your chances of getting a reply, do sufficient checking to be sure you have:

☆ The correct company name. Mergers and acquisitions continue to occur and names change as a result.

☆ The correct address. You would be amazed how often firms move.

☆ Your hiring manager's name and title, correctly spelled and proper gender identified. If you want to destroy an opportunity fast, misspell a name or call a man named Leslie, "Ms."

When you have determined that your names, addresses and phone numbers are correct, type them into your computer database. Then they will be easily accessible for mail-merged cover letters and follow-ups if you choose to do them.

Resume Information from Information Interviews

Information interviews with networking contacts can help you determine what a potential employer might require in a job candidate and uncover positions not typically advertised or filled through executive search firms. Larry, for example, made many appointments to learn about different industries and companies. Information interviews differ from employment interviews in several important ways:

☆ They're far less stressful because candidates are seeking information, not actual jobs.

☆ The interviewer is the person researching the job market. The interviewee is the company representative.

☆ Job hunters take the initiative in making the appointment, not employers.

Sample Form

Company/Agency Research

Name of Company | Synchronous Systems (not a real company)
Address | 2200 Wendover Road, Suite 1300, Palo Alto, CA 94303
Phone Number | 415-382-9900
Contact | Tom Watson
Title | Director of Client Services

1. **How old is the organization? How did it get started?**
   Company was founded in 1982 by Ben Johnson and Susan Stellerman.

2. **How has it grown: slowly, quickly, internally, by acquisition?**
   The firm has averaged an annual growth rate of 20 percent for the first five years and 8 to 10 percent since 1988. Growth has been entirely by targeting the niche market for more effective database management systems in the health care industry, especially large physician practices.

3. **What are its sales volume, annual budget, and number of employees?**
   Privately held company will not divulge this information. However, one trade journal article said the firm was in the $20 million range and employed about 100 people.

4. **What are its profit, return on investment, and market share?**
   Again, not specifically available, but the company is an acknowledged leader in its field, and I haven't found any information to indicate financial problems.

5. **Where are its plants, offices, stores, corporate headquarters?**
   Its base is in Palo Alto and it has small sales offices in Houston, Chicago, Boca Raton, and New York.

6. **What are its products and/or services; especially major areas of concentration and new developments?**
   The company provides both database management software and record-keeping services for large physician practices and medium-sized hospitals. It is currently working on increasing its usefulness to doctors by developing software and/or a service for billing insurance companies, HMOs, preferred providers programs, and medicare.

7. **Does it seem to be community spirited and/or profess an interest in cultivating its employees?**
   Based on an article I read in the *San Francisco Business Journal*, it is an avid supporter of the Ronald McDonald House and encourages its employees to

volunteer there on company time. While I didn't see any mention of specific training programs, a company that fosters voluntarism usually believes strongly in the importance of people. This is a good sign.

8. **What kinds of careers does it offer?**
   Obviously, it needs computer programmers, database managers, customer service representatives and salespeople. The customer service stuff interests me the most.

9. **What specific experience, personality traits or skills do I have that might interest this company?**
   My having been a physician's office administrator for several years should be of interest to them. I have managed the type of practice that represents their greatest market. I'm used to working with a variety of people in doctors' offices, including some real prima donnas. I enjoy organizing and coordinating projects, managing people, solving problems, dealing with disgruntled patients, and setting up new systems. Their expansion into medicare billing services should be a good match for my background because my office processed a lot of medicare claims for our patients.

Because this interview is a friendly conversation, not a mutual sales discussion, it doesn't carry the expectation of a job offer with it. Both parties can candidly discuss their requirements, goals, strengths, and challenges without worrying about revealing a "skeleton in the closet."

Many of your current contacts are likely to be invaluable sources of job-search information, even if their particular careers don't interest you. Relatives, friends, friends of friends, colleagues, members of your professional organizations, college alumni and participants in your church, health club, softball team, or continuing education class all can provide helpful insights into their companies or industries. And they can give you names of other contacts as well.

When you start networking, begin with these people. They know you. They like you. And they have your best interest at heart. While you may feel a little uncomfortable asking them for advice and contacts, your willingness to request help shows you trust them enough to risk being in their debt. The old cliche, "The best way to solidify a relationship is to ask for help" is only too true in a job-search situation. So give your friends the opportunity to nurture you a little, and everyone will benefit from the experience.

Aside from contacts who already know you, a variety of other people may prove to be valuable sources of information about companies, industries and jobs. Local college and university professors, continuing education course instructors, state employment office professionals, convention exhibitors and presenters and even potential employers whom you contact directly will give you their insights and advice if you ask for it. Why would they agree to spend valuable time with a perfect stranger? There are at least three good reasons:

☆ People like to talk about themselves, express their opinions, and bask in a listener's undivided attention. After all, how often do any of us have an opportunity to play the expert before a genuinely appreciative audience?

☆ Most people have a streak of altruism, even though it may be deeply buried in the context of their normal lives. If they feel your request for information is sincere and not a manipulative job-seeking ruse, chances are they'll be empathetic.

☆ Then there's enlightened self-interest. Few employers enjoy the task of finding new employees. It's time consuming, expensive, and fraught with potential misjudgment. Meeting with you on a purely informational basis is a very low-risk way to evaluate your potential. You make the appointment, do preliminary research, prepare a list of questions in advance, take the interviewing lead, and send an enthusiastic thank-you note following the meeting. In other words, you do all the work and the employer gets all the credit, and a relationship forms without the stress of a typical employment interview.

It's hard for potential employers not to admire your approach. Should they or one of their friends have an opening that matches your background, it's in their best interest to take advantage of your availability. If they recruit you themselves, they will have saved themselves the angst and expense of running an ad or hiring an executive search firm. If they discover you for a friend, that person will probably return the favor down the line.

Scheduling Information Interviews

Now that you're convinced people will respond positively to your requests, let's look at how to schedule information interviews. Keep in mind that your primary goal is gaining information, not a job. Since you're pursuing knowledge, not a position, contact the person who is best equipped to provide both. It's doubtful you'll find this individual in the human resources department, unless you want an HR position. Your best bet is to get in touch with the person who would logically be your manager if you were hired. After all, he or she knows the most about what's going on in the department, and he or she would be able to hire you if you both agree it makes sense to bring you on board.

When you call to schedule the appointment, your half of the conversation should go something like this, "This is Taunee Besson. Jim Beverly suggested I give you a call. (If you received a referral, mention your mutual acquaintance as quickly as possible. You'll gain credibility since your potential interviewee will assume his colleague wouldn't risk a friendship by recommending a loser.) I'm leaving Sears after a 15-year stint, and I'm trying to find out if the types of projects I handled there have any relevance to the world at large. Jim thought you'd be an excellent person to talk to because you left the company several years ago and have forged a successful career in a different industry. If you're willing, I'd like to meet with you at your office for about 30 minutes. Your answers to some key questions will give me important insights concerning my potential long-term career options. I'm available Wednesday, Thursday, or Friday afternoon. Would any of those times be convenient for you?"

After you've made the appointment, head to the library or Internet and use the techniques cited in the "Targeted Companies" section to learn about your interviewee's company and industry. Then prepare a list of questions based on your research about the company and your contact's background. Here are some issues you might want to address:

☆ How your interviewee made a successful transition from one industry to another.

☆ Your interviewee's career path and educational background.

☆ Where he hopes to go from here.

☆ What he most enjoys and dislikes about his job, company, and industry.

☆ Your contact's view of his most pressing current and future challenges.

☆ The skills, personality traits, backgrounds of the most successful people in his department, company, industry.

☆ Where he envisions his department, company, industry heading in the future.

☆ Other people he thinks you should contact. Usually interviewees enjoy referring you to others. In fact, if you network wisely, there's a good chance you won't have to make cold calls or send your resume to a stranger. If people who know you receive your resume, it's less likely to be thrown into the round file. You'll also have the tremendous advantage of being able to tailor your documents to the specific needs of your recipients.

Your questions will help you draw out your recipient and develop rapport. At this point, you should talk a little about your background, goals, skills, and values. To be concise during this initial discussion, practice describing your ideal job to yourself ahead of time. This will help you develop a two- to three-minute "commercial" about yourself, such as the one below.

During my career I've been a senior manager in banking involved in activities such as creating, building, reengineering and downsizing departments, designing management information systems, supervising and negotiating deals, mentoring high potential employees and serving as an expert witness in contract litigation.

Most recently I've taken a sabbatical to get my Master of Management degree in Human Resources, which I've chosen to add to my original MBA in finance. While I think it's important to keep an eye on the bottom line, I'm fully convinced that people are a company's most valuable assets.

I'm looking for a management role that will combine my background and interests in human resources, finance and law. Depending upon the size and growth stage of the company, it could be as an executive assistant to a CEO, a Chief Operating Officer, a Chief Administrative Officer, a CFO, or an HR Director.

I see myself working most effectively in a small to mid-sized company. What's most important to me is that I be able to create an environment that brings out the best in people. This requires a company to be efficient, creative, growth-oriented, financially successful and market-driven.

Repeat this commercial to your contact so he can augment your job search by brainstorming with you, suggesting people and companies to target, and providing a ballpark range for a compensation package. He may even consider hiring you himself. If your contact especially admires certain elements of your experience, skills, or personality, you'll know to include them if you follow up with your resume.

To keep track of your thoughts, take notes while talking with your contact. Jot down his perspective of your qualifications, industry or company trends, the correct spelling of other contact names, compensation estimates and position requirements for available openings. As your job search progresses, you'll appreciate having these facts stored on paper rather than in the remote recesses of your already overloaded brain.

As soon as possible after the interview, write down the more subjective bits of knowledge you gathered from your conversation. Include how you felt about the interviewee, the company and its policies, and your potential for moving into a satisfying position there. Also note the best way to follow up on the appointment. Keep these notes in a binder, on cards, or in your computer for future reference. If you conduct the 20 to 30 networking discussions typical of most job seekers, you'll need this informal reminder of each of your interviewee's specifications. Your record might look like the completed information interview evaluation form on page 48.

It's easy to determine how to use the information gained from a networking appointment as background for a tailored resume. If a position is available that you and your interviewee have discussed, you already know what key experiences, skills, and personality traits to include in your resume. In fact, you've likely already noted these descriptors on your Information Interview Evaluation form. Should your contact ask for a resume after your appointment or you choose to send one when a position becomes available, you can easily match your most useful experience with the requirements of the job. The inside information you gathered will propel you head and shoulders above your competition and automatically reserve you a position in the "interview" stack.

By the way, don't feel duty-bound to take a resume with you on an information interview. If you bring one, you'll send a mixed message—"I say I'm here for information, but what I really want is a job"—to your interviewee. And you'll waste a unique opportunity to tailor your resume specifically to his needs.

INFORMATION INTERVIEW EVALUATION

Person Interviewed: Susan Schmidt
Title: Manager, Marketing Support
Name of Company: Tabor Information Systems
Address: 332 Marlboro Drive
                       Fort Worth, Texas 76118
Phone Number: 817-387-2242
Secretary's Name: Melinda Daniels
Name of Person
Who Can Hire: Susan Schmidt
Date of Interview: July 3, 1999

What was my general feeling about the interview?

Susan was very accommodating. . . .

How did the interviewee respond to questions about herself?

Susan was very candid about her transition from IBM to Tabor. She said the cultures were very different, and it took her a while to adjust. She also mentioned that her *commitment to customer service* and *the many hours of training from IBM* have served her well at Tabor. She seemed very open to answering questions about her past and future, and she enjoyed musing over the state of her company and industry.

How do I feel about the company and its policies?

Tabor is a *very entrepreneurial company.* The success of the individual is *predicated on her ability and willingness to adapt to changing market demands,* while keeping *customer service at the top of her priorities.* "If these customers would leave me alone, I could finish this paperwork," is an attitude that won't fly there. I like that. *Individual ideas* are encouraged. *Teamwork and empowerment* are not just cliches. . . .

Which of my skills, personality traits, experiences mesh with what this company needs and wants?

I have the commitment to customer service and the desire to serve the client even if my quota suffers for it this quarter. I like the fact that Tabor doesn't require specific industry experience, because I consider myself to be more of a customer service generalist than a specialist. It seems *my constant ideaphoria* will serve me well here, where it has caused me problems in the past. I particularly *enjoy working with small to medium-sized businesses, which are a major target market for Tabor.*

Can I fit into the current structure? Can I create a new job for myself? Does this company have opportunities that meet my requirements?

While the Marketing Support area is currently at full staff, Susan says her budget calls for a *new position to be added next quarter.* Given what I've seen of the company so far, I think this job would suit my skills, personality and goals. While Susan won't be leaving her job soon, she says there will be *other opportunities to move into manager slots as the company expands across the United States and into Mexico. I speak Spanish* and the *chance to live in a foreign country is very appealing.*

What should I do to follow up on this information interview?

Of course, I'll send a thank-you note and resume. . . .

Resume Information from Executive Search Firms

As part of your job-search strategy, you'll probably send resumes to headhunters. To target the recruiters best suited to your needs, go to the library and review search-firm directories categorized by industry or job function. If you plan to stay in your current location, you might only wish to contact firms that specialize in your geographical area. It's also worthwhile to ask friends and colleagues to refer you to particularly responsive firms. Contacting these companies, along with any you already know, should get your credentials listed in several executive search databases.

Although search firms match people with jobs, they work for corporate clients, not for you. Don't expect a headhunter to get all excited about your resume and start calling potential employers on your behalf. Their allegiance is to the party who foots the bill. In a fee-paid situation, this isn't you.

Even though you can't get a search firm to work for you, you can facilitate how they work with you. Before sending a recruiter your resume, call the firm to ask how applicant resumes should be formatted. Also, ask if any types of experience in your industry or career are particularly marketable. Check to see if the firm is working on any search assignments for which you're qualified. If it is, tailor your resume to parallel the requirements of these positions. While accommodating a firm's preferences won't significantly improve your chances of being placed, it may stack the deck in your favor just enough to move your resume into the "deserves further review" category.

Once you've gathered key information from your newspaper ad, library research, networking contact, or search executive, combine it with your most relevant accomplishments to produce a tailored resume that entices the recruiter/interviewer to ask for more. Chapters 3 and 4 show how to do this.

"I must say, I'm particularly impressed with the coffee rings and eraser crumbs on your resume."

3

Resume Guidelines

Now that you have organized your office and job-search system, developed your accomplishments history and gathered information on possible employers and job openings, you're ready to write your resume. While you can use a number of different formats or approaches (described in detail in later chapters), all resumes should adhere to the basic guidelines described in this chapter.

Tailor Your Resume to Employer Needs

Customize as much as you possibly can. This advice may seem redundant by now, but customizing your resume is the single most important thing you can do to make it successful. In fact, the reason most job hunters aren't more effective when mass-mailing resumes is that they don't address each potential employer's specific needs.

ROBERT HALF'S RESUMANIA

It's fine for job seekers to include strengths on their resumes if they involve work-related skills. This Las Vegas job seeker didn't quite succeed in making a good connection. "I have an amazing memory. Once I read or hear something, I never forget it. As evidence of this, I have the ability to beat the house here in Las Vegas at 21, even if they use as many as eight decks of cards. In fact, two of the largest casinos here have prohibited me from playing."

To derive the greatest benefit from your resume, consider how your past experience pertains to the position you want. Then, exclude all information that isn't relevant. Don't feel compelled to use extraneous items on the off chance that they might be remotely interesting to a prospective employer. Using a scattergun approach forces employers to hunt for experience parallel to their requirements and gives them good reasons to reject your resume altogether. If you want to land an interview, make it easy for recruiters. Provide them with what they need to know, nothing more.

By now, you may be asking, "All this tailoring is fine if I know what job I want. What if I don't know? What if a friend wants to distribute my resume to her network of contacts? Or, suppose I'm contemplating a career change and haven't decided on my new vocation? How can you expect me to customize anything under these circumstances?"

There are two answers to this question. First, if you're planning a career change, don't construct a resume until you decide what your next career will be. One of the quickest ways to guarantee your resume a spot in the reject pile is to cover a variety of unrelated bases or simply list your work history in chronological order. If you've been an accountant and you want to be a people influencer, distributing a resume that labels you as a number cruncher is deadly. Before you start your resume, conduct your research and choose your next career. Don't begin writing until you have a clear idea of your new direction. In other words, use the same process outlined in Chapter 2, but wait until you have made some important career decisions.

If you have an enthusiastic friend who wants to give your resume to lots of people, ask her if you can talk to them instead. Then you can meet with them, ascertain their needs, and tailor a resume for each contact who asks for one. If this approach is fraught with political potholes, go ahead and give her the resume she requested. But tailor it, too. Since you have no benchmark description, you'll have to create your own, and write your resume to parallel it. Granted

ROBERT HALF'S RESUMANIA

A Boston man devotes most of his resume to what he has called "Strengths." Under that heading, he stresses that he is a hard-nosed, demanding manager whose eyes never left the bottom line. That isn't necessarily bad in these lean-to-mean times. But he concludes the section with the following: "I'm willing to take on the nasty tasks that others shun. For instance, I have no trouble calling employees in, looking them in the eye and telling them they're fired. In fact, I suppose you could even say I enjoy this aspect of management. It gives me gratification to know that I'm weeding out the chaff and keeping the wheat. Not only am I comfortable in this role within the company, I don't hesitate to get rid of vendors who aren't up to snuff. In the first six months of my present job, I fired the law firm, the accounting firm and the advertising agency."

your idealized version may not match everyone's needs, but it will mesh with yours. If you customize your resume to your own criteria, it will speak to jobs you'll enjoy and eliminate those you won't.

Rachel had been in sales for a number of years and was anxious to move into fund-raising for a large nonprofit agency. She had a friend with contacts in the nonprofit community who wanted to hand-deliver her resume to some likely employers. Because Rachel had done a lot of development work for her local Jewish Community Center, she decided to feature it on her resume instead of stressing her background in computer sales. But she was concerned about this approach. What if her resume was reviewed by someone who was anti-Semitic? He obviously wouldn't want to hire her. She would be taking herself out of the running for positions at his organization.

But, Rachel's career counselor asked—Wouldn't losing out on such opportunities be better for her? What if she weren't eliminated? Suppose this type of employer hired her, then learned of her propensity for working with "those people." How would Rachel feel about collaborating daily with a bigot? Would she want to divide her priorities between raising money for a good cause and raising his consciousness? Or would she prefer to confine her battles to just one productive front? Rachel decided to describe her experience with the Center and let the chips fall where they might. If any of her friend's contacts had a problem with her choice of volunteer assignments, both she and they would be better off not exploring the possibility of working together.

To develop your ideal job description, list the following elements:

- ☆ Your top 10 skills from your skills inventory.
- ☆ The specialized knowledge you have enjoyed developing in your paid positions, volunteer work, hobbies or classes.
- ☆ Your strongest personality traits.
- ☆ The elements you most value in your work setting such as intellectual freedom, opportunity to help others, a substantial income, teamwork, project or operations orientation, chance for advancement, variety, independence and a fast or slow pace.
- ☆ The salary, benefits, perks, bonuses, stock options, commissions you expect.
- ☆ Your intermediate and long-term career goals.

Once you have listed these criteria, synthesize them into a paragraph or two describing the activities and environment best suited to your talents, background and needs. Then, using this ideal job description as your benchmark, tailor a resume that illustrates how exquisitely qualified you are for your perfect position. Probably your ideal position won't be an exact fit with any available openings, but it should be close enough to a few opportunities to get you a courtesy interview, especially if you're recommended by a mutual friend. An example of a typical Ideal Job Description follows.

IDEAL JOB DESCRIPTION

My overriding motivation is to make a positive difference in other people's lives. I most enjoy doing this through counseling individuals, facilitating workshops and speaking on personal and professional development issues.

I'm people-oriented, goal-directed, creative and a quick thinker, so I need to move forward with cutting-edge programs that fulfill people's needs. Bureaucracy, fuzzy thinking and indecisiveness, when the well-being of people is at stake, drive me wild.

I'm best in a leadership or coaching role where I can call my own shots. I like to develop pioneering projects and use my planning, motivating, synthesizing and analytical skills to create new programs or solutions. There's nothing more fun than a successful team effort, especially when I'm the leader.

Having control over my schedule will give me the opportunity and flexibility to spend time with my family and exercise on a regular basis. A successful career is an empty triumph without good health and a happy personal life.

ROBERT HALF'S RESUMANIA

"SKILLS: Possess the needed ingredients for a successful manager: One cup of ambition, a pinch of aggressiveness, two pounds of determination, one touch of integrity, one ounce of intelligence, a bit of reliability and a sprinkle of humor."

Use Humor Sparingly

Unless you have credentials as a stand-up comic or joke writer, be careful about including jokes in a resume. Humor is an art form best left to professionals, who, even with their experience and polish, don't always achieve the results they want.

Be Brief and Concise

Have you ever received a resume that droned on for four incredibly detailed and boring pages? The person who wrote it wanted to ensure that he included everything you needed to know about his job experience. He didn't understand that resumes are similar to advertisements or brochures. Their purpose is to highlight experience and entice the potential "buyer" to get better acquainted with the

ROBERT HALF'S RESUMANIA

I'm looking at a resume right now from a gentleman whose background is solid, but who chose to use a cover sheet featuring a cartoon he drew of himself training an automatic weapon on three other cartoon characters, who are backed up against a wall, their hands raised, a look of abject terror on their faces. I think those three characters are supposed to represent wasteful spending in business, and our candidate is attempting to graphically illustrate how capable he is of holding them in check. No matter. Cartoons not only are inappropriate when seeking a job, this one happens to be offensive.

product. If your resume is longer than two pages, you're not just hitting the high points—you're telling your life's story.

Picture yourself sitting at your desk, wading through a stack of resumes sent in response to a recent newspaper ad. Because this project is using valuable time that you should be spending on more immediately productive activities, you're already feeling hostile about finding a new employee. Halfway through the stack you spy a resume, heavier than most, that begins with a half-page, single-spaced dissertation on John Smith's current assignment. You're peeved that John has the audacity to assume you would be interested in the intricacies of his daily routine. With more than a little righteous indignation, you pitch his resume into the wastebasket.

On the other hand, don't become overzealous in your need to be concise, or fall for the old myth that employers won't read resumes that exceed a page. For most seasoned professionals, one page isn't enough. To list your most important accomplishments may require two pages.

To keep from running long, pretend you're composing an executive brief of two pages or less describing salient points about a complicated deal. First write your rough draft, then critique it for extraneous material. Be relatively ruthless, but don't omit key elements that play an important role in substantiating your position. You want your resume to be lean, not anorexic.

Write Your Own Resume

Many resume readers scan thousands of these documents each year. They're intimately familiar with formats, typefaces and buzz words. And they can readily spot a professionally written resume. When they see one, they often question its credibility, either because it sounds too slick or they recognize its fill-in-the-blanks formula.

A resume should be a personal expression of who you are. It should represent you in a way that's both comfortable and accurate. If you think you're incapable of writing such a document, get help, but maintain control over the final product. When you're facing your interviewer, you must sound as if you wrote your resume and be conversant with everything in it. Cyrano de Bergerac won't be hiding in the bushes to coach you with optimal answers.

If the thought of writing a resume sends you into an intellectual paralysis, take heart. Chapter 4 includes a primer on how to find a professional who'll help you create a resume that highlights your best achievements, sounds as if you wrote it and prepares you to tell a potential employer in person why you're the right candidate for the job.

Be Neat and Error Free

Everyone knows that even one resume typo can destroy a candidate's credibility, yet recruiters continue to find unbelievable bloopers that serve as a continual source of black humor. These come from Robert Half:

> A young lady actually sent out her resume with the following statement about herself: "I am very consiensous about my acurecy when I work."

> "STRENGTHS: I am very detail oriented, and i believe in doing things wright the first time threw."

The writers who produced these gaffes, while probably literate, are nonetheless careless or lack good proofreading skills. If you read what you're thinking instead of what's actually written, don't trust yourself to proofread your own resume. Give it to other people to look over as well.

Typos aren't the only glitches job seekers neglect to fix. Certain errors in grammar, sentence structure or word meaning would be laughable if they didn't have serious consequences, as you can see from the Resumania items on page 58.

Prioritize Everything

Your resume should be a document that Mr. Spock would be proud to present to Starfleet Command. Its logic should be impeccable, and its ideas should flow easily from one to another in descending order of importance. What are the most critical pieces of information an employer needs to know about you? Your name, address, phone number, fax number and e-mail address. That's why they always appear at the top. What's the next most significant item? Your job objective, because it establishes the premise for everything else in your resume.

The order of your education, experience, personal qualifications and employment history will depend on what's most important to your potential employer. Most businesses are more concerned about your work background than your education. Consequently, it makes sense to put career accomplishments before educational credentials. However, if you're applying for a position in academia, you should emphasize your academic background, because education is an educator's bread and butter.

If you don't know who will receive your resume, prioritize according to your own preferences. Suppose you're justifiably proud of your recent MBA and certification in Total Quality Management. List these educational credentials

ROBERT HALF'S RESUMANIA

"MOST RECENT JOB: Accounting cleric."

"PERSONAL STRENGTHS: I am loyal, hard working, and have plenty of patients."

"DUTIES: Handled all faces of account receivable and payable."

"DUTIES: Responsible for oversight on all aspects of the internal and external systems."

"REASON FOR LEAVING: Left position to rum family business. Have now had to close the office due to circumstances beyond our control."

directly under your objective. If doubling territory sales to $10 million from $5 million in the past two years is your most outstanding accomplishment, don't bury it. Put it right at the top where it grabs readers' attention.

As you plan your resume, decide first on the order of the main headings: Objective, Professional Summary, Applicable Experience, Work History, Education, Awards and Honors, and Personal or Other Facts. Then prioritize the items under each of these major components. When finished, the information on your resume should descend logically from the most to the least important elements.

Make Your Resume Easy to Read

Sometimes well-written resumes are difficult to read because they are poorly formatted. Like a candidate during an initial interview, the impression your resume makes during the first 60 seconds will color readers' attitudes about its total content. To encourage a reader to scan your resume completely, use a format that's easy to follow.

Allowing enough white space on the page is an excellent formatting technique. Make your margins wide enough so the body of your resume won't look crowded. Leave a line of space between main headings and each of the elements below them.

Use bullets instead of long, complicated paragraphs to emphasize key points. Four lines of single-spaced text is about all a recruiter can read without getting restless. More copy can make her feel as if she's slogging through the dismal swamp. Notice the difference between the following long paragraph versus the bulleted list that presents the same information:

IS Director   7/93 to present

Create, administer and enhance information systems for international widget manufacturer/distributor with $40M in annual sales. Direct information systems supporting financial, manufacturing and distribution functions; system supports 60 users with three locations nationwide. Manage staff of four in coordination with multiple outsourced contracts. Executive management team member with involvement in strategic planning for cross-functional business areas. Skilled in MRP, MRPII and ERP.

IS Director   7/93 to present

- Create, administer and enhance information systems for international widget manufacturer/distributor with $40M in annual sales.
- Direct information systems supporting financial, manufacturing, and distribution functions; system supports 60 users with three locations nationwide.
- Manage staff of four in coordination with multiple outsourced contracts.
- Executive management team member with involvement in strategic planning for cross-functional business areas.
- Skilled in MRP, MRPII and ERP.

Another way to add interest and readability is by varying typefaces, using two or three versions at most. Bold type can emphasize headings. Italic type adds punch to key words or phrases. Just be judicious when selecting typefaces. Some resumes look as if their writers have suddenly discovered a new toy. They're such a hodgepodge of type styles their message gets lost in a confusion of letters.

Probably the most important advice on format concerns the use of readable language. The KISS Principle (Keep it Simple, Stupid) is critical to a successful

ROBERT HALF'S RESUMANIA

"While I am open to the initial nature of an assignment, I am decidedly disposed that it be so oriented as to at least partially incorporate the experience enjoyed heretofore and that it be configured so as to ultimately lead to the application of the more rarefied facets of financial management as the major sphere of responsibility."

resume. Write as if you were talking, and leave the 50-cent words to the William Buckleys of the world who use them regularly.

Omit Negative Information

While it's always advisable to be truthful on your resume, soul baring isn't mandatory. If you aren't particularly proud of something in your job history, don't mention it until the interview stage.

Imagine that you're scanning resumes in search of a new employee. How anxious would you be to meet the candidate who wrote the following Resumania item?

PERSONAL—I am the most accurate and knowledgeable information systems expert in the company I work for. I turn out more work than any two of my colleagues put together. However, I have a time phobia that has existed since childhood. I can never get to work on time regardless of when the starting time is. But that shouldn't matter. Why should anyone care when I do my work?

ROBERT HALF'S RESUMANIA

"OBJECTIVE: Post as data communicative expert in which coordination as an administrative responsibility in pertinence to my related background in relevance to."

"OBJECTIVE: Where the need for the ability to relate abstract concepts to clear understandable examples exists."

"EXPERIENCE: The major projects with which I have been involved include a heuristic approach to solving a three variable function to within some arbitrarily defined error using a nine point matrix, determination of the effect on next period forecasting using an exponentially weighted moving average when time periods of data are aggregated and the separate period forecasts are used to develop the next period forecast, and the method to find optimal clusters from a machine/component matrix by modifying the Direct Clustering and Bond Energy algorithms."

Curb Your Anger

It's understandable for many job seekers to be angry and frustrated with former employers. However, it's neither fair nor wise for them to vent their feelings on future ones. This behavior falls into the "go home and kick the dog" genre of misplaced emotion.

Sometimes anger develops from anxiety and disappointment over the results of the job-search process. Having received several rejection letters, or, worse, no response at all, an unsuccessful candidate may decide to paint all potential employers with the same negative brush. Certainly, we can empathize with the disgruntled resume writer's righteous indignation. But we can't admire his negative attempt at selling himself.

No employer wants to hire a professional who hates the world. If you were looking to fill a key position in your firm, would you pick a hothead? Anger has no place in cover letters or resumes, no matter how justified it may be. Don't forget: One brief moment of self-serving vitriol can sabotage all your efforts to gain long-term satisfaction.

Don't Make Demands of the Employer

When seeking a position, it's important to know whether a potential opportunity can meet your needs. But don't mention what you want until after the recruiter has determined what you can do for him. If you make demands in your cover letter or resume, you're likely to be labeled as a malcontent primarily interested in what you can squeeze from the company.

Put yourself in the shoes of a potential employer who has never met the writers of the following resume excerpts. How would you feel about hiring a candidate who demands concessions before you've met him or her? If you're like most recruiters, you'll put these job seekers' resumes in the reject pile:

OBJECTIVE: Easy work, pleasant surroundings, large expense account, high wages and close to home.

OBJECTIVE: To find a job in which my education and experience will be put to optimum use, and that will appreciate the fact that I am happily married, and that my wife comes first.

ROBERT HALF'S RESUMANIA

"After careful consideration, I regret to inform you that I am unable to accept any refusal to offer me employment with your organization. I have been particularly fortunate this year in receiving an unusually large number of rejections. It has become impossible for me to accept any more, and your rejection would not meet with my needs at this time. Therefore employ me as soon as possible. Best of luck in employing future candidates."

"CURRENT EMPLOYMENT STATUS: At the present time I still have pending litigation against individuals, newspapers and financial firms for invasion of my privacy, harassment, criminal conspiracy, fraud, and other violations of state and federal laws that have resulted in severe damage to my personal and professional life."

"My boss is a tyrant, has no compassion at all, and has an intelligence slightly above the level of an idiot. I have a list of all our customers and suppliers, which I will bring to my new employment. I also have the home phone numbers of more than a hundred of the best employees who are anxious to join me to leave this intolerable garbage dump."

"Is this position really available or is this just some come-on to get me in your office? I don't have time for that. I also question some of the qualifications you list as being necessary. Life experience should be ranked a lot higher than education."

To Whom It May Concern:

I am not available for many job interviews because I have very little leisure time, so any interview must be with a company that is already interested in me. In addition, the company must offer me what I am looking for. I must have in any new employment medical insurance coverage that is effective on my first day of work, and a salary to exceed what I am currently making.

I am mainly interested in working in Brooklyn, and my second choice is downtown Manhattan. If a position is offered me in Manhattan, the company will have to be a very good one and offer me no less than $10,000 more than I am currently making.

I am not a typist. I do not take shorthand. I have no experience or interest in word processing.

ROBERT HALF'S RESUMANIA

THE RESUME FROM HELL

Occasionally, an entire resume is bad enough to be considered for this column. This resume was written by a gentleman from Toledo, Ohio, who sought a job as a plant accountant. His resume ran on page after page, and ended with the infamous Reasons for Leaving section:

"My first job was with the XYZ Corp. I was hired to do the procedures and programming for converting their P/R to EDP. This was quite an assignment and it took two years to complete. To my amazement, when the new machine came in it was an IBM, and I had programmed the job for a Burroughs. I say this was not my fault since the memorandum from the controller advising me that they had ordered the IBM instead of the Burroughs was never received by me.

"When I left XYZ (they got awfully stuffy about the incident), I took a position with ABC Services, Inc. as a tabulating supervisor. Here I had experience in production control and inventory on EAM (had enough EDP). Their procedures were very straight forward and did not show imagination or use of the more involved aspects of machine work, so I revised them. At the end of the first year I gave them a real inventory job for a change. They never had as much information before. Naturally since it was the first year with a new system, there were some problems and the results weren't too exact. I didn't realize then how inventory and taxes are related so when the President and Chairman of the Board were both put under Federal Indictment for embezzlement, I didn't wait around. I could see the old handwriting on the wall again and started scouting around for a new position.

"I next had four or five jobs as supervisor or assistant supervisor which were not too interesting so I won't go into them.

"On my last assignment I was manager of a three-shift operation. I gained experience in time-recording and machine utilization and if they had given me time to complete my re-organization I could have whipped up a crackerjack outfit there. See, what happened was this. I was going at it one shift at a time and I shaped things up on the 1st and 2nd shift and was just starting on the 3rd. I only just then started to notice that the third shift utilization was low and this surprized me because there were always an awful lot of people leaving when I came on each morning. I was going to investigate this but unfortunately the police beat me to it. It seems that my third shift supervisor was running an open craps game and taking horse bets. It seems only two of the people [I] saw leaving were employees. Well, you know how management is always looking for a scapegoat and they picked me.

"I gained a lot of experience and I am sure you will agree I am the man for you."

IN YOUR DREAMS!

"Just out of curiosity, was there any part of
my resume that you *did* like?"

4

The Parts of
Your Resume

Keeping in mind the guidelines from Chapter 3, let's take a look at how to prepare the various components of your resume, starting with the most important ones.

Your Name, Address and Phone Number

Putting your name, address, phone and fax numbers and e-mail address at the top of your resume seems simple enough, but it may be more complicated than you think. You'll want to use an address where you can receive correspondence from employers and search firms. Should it be your home, post office box, out-placement office or an executive suite? Probably the most convenient place makes the most sense.

Should your phone number be connected to your home answering machine, place of work, outplacement office, executive suite or a temporary voice mailbox? The best option is probably the most businesslike one.

Conversing with a cacophony of barking dogs or crying children in the background tends to cramp a person's professional style. Talking in a whisper or in code so your boss won't find out you're job hunting can be awkward. And then there's the 30-second message on your answering machine that greets all callers with your imitation of Jimmy Stewart. Your friends may love your sense of humor, but will it amuse the CEO of Cyber Industries, especially when he's cut off in midsentence?

To enhance your professional image, arrange for a real person to answer your phone, saying "Mr. [or Ms.] _____'s office," if you can. Outplacement and executive suites do this automatically. If you have a private office, phone line and secretary whom you trust implicitly at work, list your work number on your resume. If these options aren't available, rent an unlimited-message voice mailbox for three months. Record a businesslike greeting and check for calls at least twice a day. You also can use your home answering machine, but give Jimmy Stewart a rest.

Giving potential employers your fax number and e-mail address is also a good idea. It shows you are comfortable with using technology and communicating electronically. However, offering these forms of contact can cause major problems if they are not secure from prying eyes and gossiping tongues. If your fax and e-mail don't come directly to you, omit them from your resume. If you feel like a Model T without them, buy yourself a fax machine and spend the $19.95 per month to connect your home computer to an Internet provider.

Your Resume Objective

Below your contact information, state a concise and specific objective. If you're applying for a position as controller of A&J Mechanical, use that job title as your objective. There are several reasons this makes sense:

☆ Using a specific job title forces you to tailor your resume. Many job seekers think a generic objective gives them a lot of latitude, rather than restricting them to a particular position. The problem with this philosophy is that an ill-defined goal leads to an ill-defined resume. To secure an interview, your resume must speak directly to the needs of each recipient. Trying to be all things to all people usually results in not being much of anything to anyone.

ACCOUNT EXECUTIVE

Motorola's new Position and Navigational Systems Business' next generation of components will provide superior navigational and communications technologies to manufacturers and consumers. To service and develop new and existing accounts, we are now seeking a sales professional.

Incumbent will manage own territory of direct commercial accounts, manufacturer's representatives, provide staff and customer training, develop sales forecasts and plans, and participate in trade shows. Extensive travel is involved. Candidates need at least 5 years electronic sales experience and a record of meeting or exceeding sales goals. Strong technical background and a BS in Electronic Engineering or Navigation is preferred. Ability to close long- and short-term sales, train and motivate others, and service a large territory under remote management is also vital. Knowledge of GPS radio communications and /or navigational markets a plus.

Motorola provides a work environment that supports the highest quality, excellent salaries and attractive fringe benefits. To be considered, send your resume to: **Manager of Staffing, Dept. J/511, Motorola, Position and Navigational Systems Business, 4000 Commercial Avenue, Northbrook, IL 60062.**
Equal Opportunity/Affirmative Action Employer.

MOTOROLA
Automotive & Industrial Electronics Group

☆ An employer likes to see the name of his job opening and company at the top of your resume. It makes him feel special. He appreciates the extra effort it took to prepare a resume just for him. Think about the little shiver of pleasure you experience when, in conversation, someone addresses you by name, or the maître d' at your favorite restaurant says, "So good to see you this evening, Ms. Myers." Potential employers feel the same spark of recognition when you mention their name. Don't underestimate this simple, powerful tool. It rarely fails to make a positive impression.

Another effective technique when writing an objective is to include key skills that mirror important requirements mentioned in an ad or conversation with a potential employer. For instance, the Motorola ad from the *National Business Employment Weekly* says the firm is looking for a candidate who can:

☆ Develop and service new and existing accounts.

☆ Close long- and short-term sales.

☆ Train and motivate others.

☆ Service a large territory under remote leadership.

If your experience includes doing any or all of these things, your objective might say:

OBJECTIVE: Account Executive for Motorola's Automotive & Industrial Electronics Group where developing and servicing new and existing accounts, closing long- and short-term sales, training and motivating others and handling a large territory under remote leadership are key elements.

By using this technique, your objective becomes a summary of the most important accomplishments listed on your resume. You give the potential employer an easy and explicit bridge between what she wants in a candidate and what you offer. If you don't have bona fide background in some of the listed areas, leave them out of your objective. Otherwise you'll only serve to spotlight your deficits.

If you've had a networking appointment with a manager who has a job opening you would like to pursue, use your completed Information Interview Evaluation Form to provide ideas for enhancing your objective. In the evaluation form in Chapter 2, the italicized phrases offer excellent clues as to what Tabor Systems wants in its employees.

After identifying the key issues of importance to Tabor, your objective might read something like this:

OBJECTIVE: Marketing Support Representative for Tabor Information Systems where a commitment to customer service, enthusiasm for adapting to changing market needs, and a desire to contribute new ideas in a team environment are prerequisites.

ROBERT HALF'S RESUMANIA

"OBJECTIVE: To work with real people again."

"OBJECTIVE: To have something to do."

"OBJECTIVE: To work for a strong, prosperous company in a professional environment as an internal auditor with opportunities for advancement and the potential of creating a union on inculcated academic ideals with practical and tangible objectivity."

"OBJECTIVE: Cash for talent."

"OBJECTIVE: A management position in which I can make order out of chaos and evil."

"GOAL: Get out of a rut."

"OBJECTIVE: To inject Faith, Hope and Charity into the American workplace."

"OBJECTIVE: A position in which I can run the whole shootin' match."

"OBJECTIVE: I am anxious to work for your company."

"OBJECTIVE: To make money and have fun."

"GOAL: It's my ambition and challenge, just to summarize my position, to simultaneously confirm and formulate a consistently profitable, coherent and emotionally rewarding career."

By recognizing the cornerstones of Tabor's corporate culture, and stating them at the top of your resume, you've grabbed the company's attention and put yourself in a position to reinforce mutual philosophy with tangible experience.

Objectives for executive search firms and direct mail campaigns are a little more difficult to formulate because you don't have a specific job title. However, if you have done your homework, you'll know the types of skills or personality traits they most appreciate. An objective for one of these potential job sources might read:

> OBJECTIVE: A Financial Management position (for Baker Foods) where experience in developing new information systems for a fast-growing environment, coordinating IPO activities, troubleshooting with a number of divisions and supervising a rapidly expanding staff would be useful.

If you have no idea who will be receiving your resume, (remember the friend who has decided to become your personal agent), it's probably best to omit your objective altogether. While this approach certainly isn't ideal, it's better than using such a conglomeration of pablumlike phrases as:

> OBJECTIVE: Seeking an opportunity for advancement in a dynamic, growth-oriented company where my hands-on management style will produce bottom-line results.

> OBJECTIVE: Contribute leadership experience, acquired skills and education background to a position offering opportunities for growth and advancement based on merit and initiative.

Robert Half's quotations illustrate the principle that a poorly-conceived objective is far worse than none at all.

The Professional Qualifications Brief (Summary of Qualifications)

This part of your resume summarizes the most important skills, experience and personality traits you have to offer a prospective employer. For maximum impact, you must tailor it to the specific job you seek and provide a unique commentary on who you are and what you can do. This four-to-six phrase section should capture your professional essence. It is your 30-second commercial. Lavish on it all the attention and care General Motors Corporation would put into a Super Bowl ad.

Go back to the drawing board, though, if your first attempt at a summary sounds like this:

> PERSONAL QUALIFICATIONS: A demonstrated record of achievement, leadership and hard work.
>
> A dedicated, highly motivated team member.
>
> Work well under pressure.
>
> A people person.

ROBERT HALF'S RESUMANIA

"PERSONALITY PROFILE: Gemini-Mercurial personality, extremely witty, charming, kind, loving, sociable and with a light, easy-going disposition. I'm a super salesman, as well as a wonderful executive who creates systems that work. I am determined to succeed. I work hard. I have sound judgment and a ton of common sense and drive. I believe in action, and positive thinking. I do business best with Aquarius and Aries personalities."

"AREAS OF COMPETENCE: Demonstrated responsibilities to plan, direct, develop, evaluate and expedite all operations. I possess the ability to make sound judgments, influence people, organize, persuade and motivate them to produce and achieve their goals. I am ambitious, self-motivated and industrious. Besides being trustworthy, honest and diplomatic, I communicate well with others, and plan and present ideas. Some of my older attributes are assertiveness, consistency and tenacity. Dominance, achievement, autonomy, intraception and heterosexuality are my many traits."

"My most attractive qualification is the ability to get to the heart of a problem. I have a mind that most people say is highly analytical. One person I worked with even called my mind a steel trap. When you combine my personal appearance and communication skills with my ability to analyze a problem and solve it in record time, you'll agree that I am a very attractive find for any employer looking for the cream of the crop."

"QUALIFICATIONS: No, I am not the typical job seeker you deal with on a regular basis whose resume fits perfectly into the expanding global strategy of a well-oiled, competitive multinational corporate leader."

If you can't say something special about yourself, omit this section and move directly to "Experience."

The two Qualifications Briefs that follow work well with their job objectives because their authors have carefully customized them to a specific position or career. While the briefs are quite different, they speak volumes about their writers in just a few short phrases.

OBJECTIVE

Top-ten market videotape editor position.

PERSONAL QUALIFICATIONS

- Fifteen years of experience in editing for both network and public stations.
- Enjoy coordinating complicated logistics such as incoming/outgoing satellite feeds and facilities and schedules for remote crews.
- Known as the "go-to guy" for quick, high quality story production.
- Particularly adept at troubleshooting technical problems.
- Strong knowledge of a variety of broadcast/production editing equipment.

OBJECTIVE

Director of Development for the Save Our Forest Foundation.

PERSONAL QUALIFICATIONS

- Many contacts in the academic, social service and corporate communities, cultivated over the past 15 years.
- Expert in designing and presenting proposals and training programs.
- Easily establish rapport with people of all ages, cultures, and philosophies.
- Skilled in organizing events.
- Active member of the Sierra Fund for the past 10 years.

Experience

There are many ways to put together an experience section. However, the following tips are essential.

Talk About Your Accomplishments Rather Than Your Responsibilities

If a company employs three people with the same job description, one may be exceptional, another may be only mediocre and the third may be downright incompetent. If all three listed only duties or responsibilities on their resumes, a recruiter wouldn't be able to detect any difference among them.

You can spotlight your capabilities by selecting and expanding on specific achievements that reflect your initiative, creativity, follow-through, problem-solving and management skills. The following are before-and-after versions of an IS Director's accomplishments:

Before

- MIS director/systems analyst and administrator for worldwide drip irrigation manufacturer and distributor.
- Responsible for management information systems and administration of financial, manufacturing and distribution package.
- Developed multiple custom applications for system enhancement. Currently implementing world class ERP to drive strategic plan.
- Managed staff of four in coordination with multiple outside consultants.

After

- Built state-of-the-art corporate data center capable of supporting company's aggressive growth mode with a projected doubling in revenues to $85M over the next three years. Project manager accountable for budgeting, facilities design, space configuration, installation planning and physical relocation.
- Initiated successful internal change management programs supporting technology advances, modifications to existing work processes and realignment of technology/support teams; initiatives promoted growth in annual sales from $18M to $40M.
- Led initiative to implement world-class ERP system to drive strategic plan; wrote technical specifications for project, eliminating $55,000 in consulting fees and negotiated a hard dollar savings of $90,000.
- Developed multiple custom applications for system enhancement.
- Delivered order processing cost reductions of 38% through process simplification.
- Tenure with company distinguished by rapid advancement through increasingly responsible IS assignments.

Which do you find more impressive: the basic job description or the summary of key accomplishments?

Always Use Action Verbs to Begin Each Achievement

Action verbs add sizzle and punch to your resume. When you review your completed skills inventory from Chapter 2, you'll note that it's full of these verbs.

Use them when formulating your Experience section. The accompanying list of examples should help you get started:

Administered	Designed	Negotiated
Advised	Developed	Organized
Analyzed	Directed	Persuaded
Appraised	Edited	Planned
Arranged	Established	Presented
Budgeted	Estimated	Recruited
Chaired	Evaluated	Represented
Coached	Explained	Researched
Collaborated	Facilitated	Reviewed
Contacted	Improved	Sold
Cooperated	Instructed	Supervised
Coordinated	Investigated	Updated
Counseled	Lead	Visualized
Created	Learned	Wrote
Decided	Managed	

Remember: Too much of a good thing is too much, as shown by a Santa Fe, New Mexico resume writer who took the action verb idea to the extreme. The first page of his resume listed these items: *Catapulted* sales of new product . . . *Captured* multimillion dollar contract . . . *Slashed* expenses . . . *Sparked* large increase in revenue . . . *Propelled* profitability . . . *Spearheaded* projects . . . and *Pioneered* the development of . . .

This description sounds more like Attila the Hun's battle plan than the activities of a typical account executive.

Do Not Use the Pronoun "I"

Refrain from using the pronoun "I" or referring to yourself as "the candidate" when listing your achievements. The reader knows whose resume she's reading.

Quantify Your Accomplishments Whenever Possible

There's something about numbers that catches people's attention and helps them to understand the scope of your work. Items to be quantified include sales revenue, inventory turns, worker hours or dollars saved, clients or other employees served, states covered by your region, percentage reduction in plant accidents or claims filed, widgets produced, funds raised and so on. Here are some examples:

- Managed a program that trained 120 adults per year for competitive employment.
- Supervised a staff of 60.

- Developed proposals for funding that resulted in 100% increase in program funds.
- Sold and serviced approximately 100 wholesalers, manufacturers, major retail chains and independent stores throughout the Southwest.
- Administered an annual budget of $2.6 million.

If your achievements don't easily translate into numbers, try mentioning names instead. Listing projects where you worked with the CEO, an important political figure, a VP or a well-known sports personality may score you some points. If your company's or clients' names are particularly impressive, use them unless it would be unethical or inappropriate to do so. For instance, you might say:

- Worked in collaboration with all of Nabisco's regional managers to formulate a new long-range management incentive plan.
- Managed all public relations activities for the Byron Nelson Golf Classic.
- Provided customer service for Midwestern key accounts including Xerox, GM, the Post Office, WR Grace, and Exxon, among others.

Use Appropriate Jargon

Using the correct jargon for the industry and company you are courting is especially important for career changers who might be unclear about the meaning of relatively esoteric words.

A good illustration of how the wrong jargon can sabotage you: What is the term that describes speaking to impart knowledge in front of a classroom full of attendees? In elementary schools and high schools, the activity is known as teaching. In a social service setting, it's called facilitating. At a college or university, it's instructing. And in a business environment, it's training. Don't ever confuse a teacher with a trainer (the teacher may tell you that trainers work with animals, not children). And, when businesspeople hear the word facilitator, they think of a bleeding-heart social worker, not a savvy, profit-oriented professional.

Don't Separate Volunteer or Other Unpaid Experience from Paid Achievements

In your accomplishments history, you included all the experience you deemed satisfying and worthwhile. Regardless of whether your experience is paid, volunteer, hobby, professional organization or daily life activity, it deserves a place on your resume if it relates to your job objective.

Unfortunately, money and value seem to be synonymous in our culture. This attitude is wrong, but must be dealt with nonetheless. Getting credit for your unpaid work may require using a functional rather than a chronological format. Here's how a teacher included volunteer accomplishments as well as paid ones among her relevant experiences:

Project Management

- Chaired seven receptions honoring retirees and volunteers. Approximately 200 people attended each event.
- Served as Chairman of the Public Relations committee that organized and implemented a charity softball game for the Kent Waldrep National Paralysis Association. Players included members of the Dallas Cowboys and the Dallas media.
- Organized a field day for 300 people that required working with staff and volunteers, finding in-kind services, planning games, logistics and an awards ceremony.
- Facilitated or found speakers for over 50 training programs for administration, staff and parents of the Richardson Independent School District.
- Developed a variety of volunteer programs for parents who helped with field trips, field days, classroom activities and parties.
- Created and taught a pilot kindergarten program for RISD. Designed the physical environment, planned curriculum, started a parent volunteer program, budgeted and ordered supplies.

Hobbies are valid achievements, too, especially if they enhance your job objective. Suppose you're an art teacher who has been belly dancing for years to stay in shape. After careful thought, you decide to make belly dancing a career (yes, this is a true example). You realize that having a resume that describes your educational credentials won't inspire confidence in your ability to amuse a crowd of partying adults. Instead of concentrating on your paid career, you list a variety of venues where you danced in front of groups. Toward the bottom of your Experience section, you allude to your ability to hold a group's attention and foster its enthusiastic participation based on your years of working with teenagers. However, you don't list this skill first.

Use Dates If They're in Your Favor

Some job seekers have "perfect" employment records that show progressively increasing responsibilities. They have never been laid off or worked at home to raise children, and have stayed at each job for three or more years. For these candidates, listing employment dates in reverse chronological order works nicely. However, a growing number of people have gaps in their employment history, have held numerous jobs or need to list their previous positions in order of importance instead of putting their most recent jobs first. If you're one of them, consider stating the number of years you held the job instead of employment dates, or omitting employment dates and length of employment altogether.

Unfortunately, some employers discount candidates whose resumes show that they've stayed at one company for an extended period, or whose work histories portray them as seasoned veterans (in the workforce 20 years or more, 40 years old or older). If you're in either of these categories, providing specific dates may not be to your advantage.

There are several ways to categorize experience without focusing on dates. Older professionals may decide to omit the first few jobs on their resumes, thereby reducing their employment histories. This technique isn't likely to force them to omit their most important accomplishments. Nor will it reveal their ages.

Older candidates also can list their experience by job title, giving the number of years worked for each position instead of the dates of employment. If you choose this method, put your employment time span in a relatively inconspicuous place. For instance, you might try this approach:

Purchasing Manager   Crawford Technologies   Omaha, NE   Five years

Using a functional format also allows you to catalog your most important accomplishments without marrying them to specific job titles and dates. The following functional experience module pulls together related activities:

Project Management and Administration

- Developed and implemented companywide employee survey for corporate office and three manufacturing plants.
- Researched the market and selected a consultant to do communications workshops based on the above survey results.
- Coordinated innovative programs to encourage productivity, including:
  —Monthly bonuses to plant with the best safety record.
  —Quarterly bonuses to plant with highest productivity of board feet of foam insulation.
  —Plant employee of the year.

Education

Education may be listed before experience if:

☆   Your objective requires a specific credential.

☆   Your educational background is stronger than your work history.

First-time job seekers often have freshly minted degrees, but not much applicable experience, to offer potential employers. They should focus on their education by listing it near the top of their resumes.

Professionals applying for careers in academia also need to give priority to their educational credentials because credentialing is the main purpose of their industry. They should also include references to ongoing coursework in their field of expertise. If they're seeking instructor or professor positions, they'll want to mention research papers, speeches to professional groups and other accomplishments generally not included on a typical resume.

Most other workers can assume that experience is more important to potential employers than education. Consequently, education usually follows experience in most resumes.

Your education section may include formal degrees, noncredit courses at colleges or universities, in-house training programs, or informal learning experiences such as travel, tutoring or extensive reading in a subject. The following example of a typical education section mentions all these qualifications:

Education

MBA, Northwestern University, 1989

BSBA, The Pennsylvania State University, 1982

Continuing education courses in Total Quality Management, Covey's Leadership

Training, Negotiating for Win-Win Results

Extensive reading on global socioeconomic issues

If you're planning to change careers and your major has little to do with your new objective, list only the degree level and omit your field of study. If your degree is more than 10 years old, leave out the graduation date. In many instances, your level of education tells more about your ability to persevere than your expertise in a given subject. If your degree has become obsolete or doesn't relate to your career, there's no need to emphasize it.

Organizations

Potential employers look favorably on candidates who are active participants in organizations. Your involvement in such activities as PTA, church, social service agency board of directors, professional association, alumni club, ecological society or city commission shows your willingness to participate in a worthy cause or help your profession. It also demonstrates that volunteer groups trust you to follow through on your commitments. Businesses need professionals who want to pursue a common mission, are capable and interested in assuming leadership roles, and know how to gain the respect and cooperation of their peers. Your organizational activities speak to your skills in all these areas.

Companies also realize they can bask in your reflected glory when you're chosen for a responsible position in a community or professional group. Your high profile and superb leadership only serve to reinforce what a good decision they made in hiring you. These associations also can provide you and your company with the valuable contacts needed to develop business opportunities and gain greater visibility within your industry, profession and community.

If you've played an active role in any worthwhile organization, don't hesitate to include it on your resume or use your fellow participants as references. Employers regard your ongoing commitment and contribution to these groups as both a confirmation of your competence and a proving ground for your talent.

Awards

Writing a resume gives you a mandate for talking about how wonderful you are. If other people have already honored you by selecting you for a Who's Who directory, Woman of the Year, the President's Award or other kudo, tell your potential employer about it. This is no time to be modest.

If your award is for an accomplishment within the context of your job, put it in your experience section instead of toward the end of your resume. Sales Associate of the Year is too important a distinction not to be read early on.

Personal Data

Experts offer conflicting advice about whether to include personal information on a resume. Many say to omit it altogether. Some think that listing hobbies and volunteer work gives employers a better picture of a candidate. Others suggest mentioning personal information only if it improves your chances of landing an interview. All typically agree that references to age, marital status, number of children, health, physical characteristics, as well as other types of demographic data, rarely belong on a resume unless they are a bona fide occupational qualification (BFOQ).

If you decide to include personal facts, always put them at the bottom of your resume. Even if you share a love of sailing with the recruiter, it can't be as relevant to the job as your experience or education, unless you'll be running a marina.

ROBERT HALF'S RESUMANIA

"PERSONAL: I had two children by my first wife, both live with me, but she also had two children by her second husband. One lives with his former wife, and one with my first wife. My second, and present wife, had one child by each of her first two husbands, and we had two kids together. All of those are living with us. That presently makes a total of six, but my wife is now pregnant with twins."

"PERSONAL: Married for 26 years, quit smoking 11 years ago, never had a drink, have been a gambler all my life."

"PERSONAL: 34 years old, one daughter, 9, currently entering bankruptcy proceedings."

"WHO AM I? I am 43, married for the third time and have a two-day-old son who remains nameless."

"HEALTH: I am healthier than most men half my age. I do, however, wear two hearing aids. To some, this may be considered a disadvantage. On the contrary, because I am a workaholic, I simply remove both aids when I am in the middle of a difficult project."

"Interests include: universalism, pacifism, humanism, longevity, open-minded, liberal-thinking people, lectures, meditation and any other personal growth experience. I'm allergic to smoke and wiseguys."

Salary History

Including your salary history on your resume isn't a good idea. If it's too high or too low, you'll automatically be eliminated from consideration. Even if it's in the ballpark, a salary amount mentioned early in the get-acquainted process can inhibit your ability to negotiate for what you want later on. Salary is one of those subjects best discussed face-to-face once you and your potential employer are almost ready to close the deal.

ROBERT HALF'S RESUMANIA

The individual who sent this resume hails from Milwaukee and was looking for an internal auditor job. His background included having worked for a wine company in California, and a brewery in Milwaukee. Under SALARY HISTORY he listed the following: "Abe Wine Company—$40,000 plus 20 cases of wine. XYZ Brewery—$43,000 plus 25 cases of beer."

Fair enough, but then he went on to list areas of the country to which he'd consider moving, "First choice—Milwaukee or Minneapolis/St. Paul area. Relocation to other areas considered on a *case-by-case* basis."

"SALARY NEEDED: I have one kid in college now, another one to enter next year, and two more coming up a few years after that. This translates to $56,000 this year, $80,000 next year and who knows after that. In other words, I can't work for peanuts."

"SALARY DESIRED: $100,000, which is what my wife currently earns."

If an ad requests that you send a salary history with your resume, but you believe that including one will jeopardize your candidacy, don't send it. You may be rejected anyway for not following instructions, but you won't be any worse off. If an employer is genuinely interested in you, excluding salary information usually won't stop you from getting an interview.

Reason for Leaving

As noted in an earlier chapter, being laid off or fired because of a hostile takeover, downsizing, acquisition or difference in management philosophy will or has already occurred to most people at one time or another. You needn't be embarrassed or defensive about it.

ROBERT HALF'S RESUMANIA

"When they recruited me, it was red carpet all the way. Then they pulled the rug out from under me."

"Gunned down in a political crossfire."

From a person who had left a position with a City Opportunity Council: "No Opportunity."

"Didn't know what I was doing."

"To escape this terrible town, where a beer bust is considered a big evening. Nobody plays bridge and I am bored stiff. I do not want to work for any division of this company because their accounting practices are different from concepts that let me sleep at night. Help! Get me out of here."

"Embezzlement." (He worked for a bank, and was on probation.)

"My complete mastery of the software interface was undermined by jealous peers. You can see the whole story when I sell the screenplay."

"REASON FOR LEAVING: It had to do with the IRS, FBI and SEC."

"So my ex-wife couldn't attach my wages in our divorce settlement."

"The company made me a scapegoat, just like my three previous employers did. This company would be out of business if it weren't for me. Nobody here seems to know what is going on, and I am the only one who does. Despite that, they treat me like an alien, and I am fed up with it. I think I'd better get out of here before they ask me to turn water into wine."

"NOTE: Please do not misconstrue my 14 jobs as 'job-hopping.' I have never quit a job."

ROBERT HALF'S RESUMANIA

"REFERENCES: Don't take their comments too seriously. They were unappreciative beggars and slave drivers."

But no matter how you explain it in a resume, you may put yourself in a no-win situation because potential employers tend to identify with former ones. Unless an ad specifically asks you for this information, don't offer it. Delay the subject until you have built some personal rapport with your interviewer. Then he will be more likely to combine this part of your conversation with his overall perspective, instead of making it the focus of a preconceived opinion.

References

Don't include references on your resume unless they're famous and admired. People's names, addresses and phone numbers take up a lot of space and usually have little meaning to a potential employer.

Only when you become a finalist for an opening should you give your list of references to an employer. But before you do, call your references to explain the position for which you're being considered and what the interviewer will probably want to know about you. By using this technique, you will be tailoring your references' responses to the job you're seeking and giving them some valuable time to think about what they want to say.

When choosing references, include people who know you from other walks of life besides work. In our litigious society, many employers instruct managers not to discuss your record even if it's exemplary. This means that if you only use former managers or colleagues as references, they may not be able to say anything about you, good or bad.

Other excellent references include colleagues you've worked or volunteered with, friends, bankers, ministers, golf partners, or anyone who knows you well and can articulate why you would be a welcome addition to an organization. Under no circumstances should you list people who might disparage your reputation.

How to Find Resume Help

If thinking about tackling your resume and cover letters all by yourself gives you a severe case of writer's block, don't despair: Professional help is available—lots of it, representing a continuum from truly awful to sublimely perfectionistic. To find a good service and protect yourself from incompetent and unethical ones, rely on the same techniques that characterize a successful job search:

☆ Ask your friends, fellow job seekers, volunteer colleagues, church members and so forth if they can recommend a good resume service. Review a resume produced by their resource and ask how effective it was.

☆ Call the continuing education departments and community counseling services at local colleges to inquire about resume-writing courses or person-to-person counseling for nonstudents. If they provide these services, make sure they use a tailored, businesslike approach. You don't want a warmed-over, fill-in-the-blank version of a student resume, or a 5- to 10-page academic vitae.

☆ Check out nonprofit agencies such as the YMCA, YWCA, church-sponsored job club, state employment commission or private industry council job-training program to see if resume help is provided. At many nonprofits, volunteer professionals provide assistance for free or on a sliding scale based on your ability to pay.

☆ Call resume services and career counselors listed in the phone book, and ask them the following questions:

—How does your service work? Do you tailor resumes to individual positions or careers, or do you write one resume and make multiple copies?

—How do you obtain client information and prepare resumes? Does the client work with you? Do you use an accomplishments form and extrapolate from it? Do you have a fill-in-the-blanks computer program?

—How do your resumes look? Do you have a specific format? Do you customize fonts? Can you send me a couple of examples? Do you use a laser printer?

—What other services do you offer? Do you prepare envelopes and cover letters? Can you mail the resumes for me? Can you do a mail merge if I need one?

—What is your turnaround time? Will you give me the computer disk containing my resume if I request it? What is your price schedule?

—How would you approach writing a resume for clients who don't have specific career goals?

Many services can give you the resume support you want, but be finicky. Shop around until you find a resource that produces tailored, professional-looking resumes at moderate prices in a reasonable time frame, only makes promises it can keep and treats you like a valued client. You deserve nothing less.

"Just drop your resume into the slot and we'll be in touch."

5

The Chronological Format

The chronological resume is the type most people use. It's the traditional format that lists last position first, then rolls back in time until the final job mentioned is the first one out of school. The assumption, and rationale, behind this approach is that you'll be given increasingly responsible positions as you move through your career. Consequently, your most recent job should be your highest level one.

The main difference between the chronological format and other types of resumes is the Experience section. Chronological resumes always use job titles, company names, locations and dates as the framework for discussing your career. As with any format, this method has it pros and cons.

The Good News

Chronological resumes are readily accepted by everyone. This traditional, conservative format is comfortable for all employers. In fact, some professionals in executive search, human resources and technical fields discount any other type of resume when they seek candidates. They want to see dates because they assume that job hunters who don't include them are trying to hide something. From their point of view, good, solid candidates don't need to disguise their employment history.

A chronological resume makes an excellent showcase for someone with a perfect career, who has been promoted with every move, whose work history has no gaps and who has changed firms enough to develop a broad perspective, but not enough to be classified as a job-hopper. In this format, the last position—placed at the top of the resume—is the premier experience. The dates march smartly down the page and are sequential from one assignment to the next. And there's evidence of sufficient movement among employers to show ongoing marketability and adaptability to different corporate cultures.

The chronological format is easy to follow because it's structured on a job-by-job basis. You don't have to do much synthesizing to put it together.

The Bad News

Unfortunately, not everyone looking for a job has a perfect work history. The following types of candidates will have significant problems with this format because of their backgrounds:

☆　Parents who have taken time off to raise children.

☆　Individuals whose job searches have dragged on for months or even years.

☆　Workers who have spent time recovering from an accident or illness or caring for a sick child, spouse or parent.

☆　Those who take a year off to see the world before increasing responsibility prohibits it.

☆　Professionals who have had to make frequent job changes because their employers went bankrupt, closed offices or departments to cut overhead, or were devoured in mergers or hostile takeovers.

☆　People who transfer to lower-level jobs to stay with their companies.

☆　Job seekers who are forced to take lower-level positions to survive, because they couldn't find better opportunities before their savings or unemployment expired.

☆ Career changers who have chosen to leave long-held professions to start over in different fields.

☆ Seasoned professionals who have worked continuously for one corporation but were terminated to improve the bottom line.

The chronological format may do these job seekers more harm than good because it spotlights career steps they would like to ignore. A functional or hybrid approach will probably work better for them unless they decide to rely primarily on ads, search firms, personnel departments and conservative thinkers to help them secure new positions. If candidates with nontraditional career paths use only traditional methods of finding employment, they will, out of necessity, back themselves into a chronological corner, whether the format suits them or not.

Before-and-After Examples

This section includes some examples of good resumes that, with a little revision, became outstanding ones. Take a look at the "before" and "after" versions of each one and think about how you might apply the same suggestions to your resume.

David Scott

David Scott isn't unemployed, but you wouldn't know it from his original resume. After a successful career with RJC Corporation, he began consulting in 1996. Because David continued to look for a senior management position, he didn't think of consulting as actual work, even though he was being paid for it. Many seasoned executives don't acknowledge a job as real unless it comes with a semi-monthly paycheck.

To bring his resume into the electronic age, David started with a keyword summary listing the major venues where he had significant experience. Computer resume scanners love these summaries, and human resource and executive recruiters are becoming accustomed to them.

David then talked about his accomplishments in reverse chronological order, putting them under the appropriate job titles. Breaking his Group VP accomplishments up by functions makes the section more readable and calls attention to phrases recruiters look for, such as cost reduction and information technology.

Because few companies care much about employment history longer than 15 years ago, David deleted his experience before 1975. He also left the date off his degree to de-emphasize his over-50 status.

DAVID L. SCOTT
5674 Church Street
Roswell, Georgia 30076
(770) 663-6204 658-8323 fax

PROFILE: RJC Corp., a NYSE-listed international company, provided an opportunity to manage in a very entrepreneural environment. The co-management of an RJC Subsidiary, comprised of seven multi-level direct sales divisions with over 700 employees and the participation in numerous acquisitions and startups, resulted in the development of a broad range of cultural adaptability. The use of my vision, planning and cross-functional team-building experience resulted in long-term stability and sales and profit growth. I am confident that my knowledge and skills would be of enormous value to any company in that our group consistently exceeded the corporation's percentage of profit by 50%.

PROFESSIONAL EXPERIENCE

Group Vice President, Pipemaster (1985–1996)
- Full P&L responsibility for seven Pipemaster divisions.

Selected Accomplishments:
- Expanded retail brands into the Home Center market, i.e., Home Depot, Lowe's, Hechingers, achieving a 122% sales volume increase.
- Consolidated inside sales and customer service, resulting in a $12MM sales increase.
- Reduced administrative expense by 34% through the post-acquisition consolidation of accounting credit/collections, purchasing, and through ongoing cost control efforts in other key areas.
- Saved $4.5MM through establishing volume discounts, offshore packaging and outsourcing in the U.S., Japan, Taiwan, Canada, Mexico, China, Thailand, Hong Kong and El Salvador.
- Focused on the use of new technologies to reduce cost:
  - EDI established a direct link for order processing and invoicing with 5,400 customers.
  - Document imaging provided instant response to customer inquiries on orders, resulting in improved cash flow due to same day mailing of duplicate invoices and increased productivity.
  - Caller ID facilitated instant identification of an account, contract name and purchase history and hand held data units. Implementation resulted in a $1.4MM productivity savings.

Vice President of Operations, Pipemaster (1978–1985)
Responsibilities included: general administration, accounting, IS, purchasing, manufacturing, distribution and acquisitions for five divisions of Pipemaster.

Selected Accomplishments:
- Established strategic planning, P&L tracing including trend proformas and statistical reporting for all companies, resulting in 20 years of profitability.

David L. Scott   Page 2

- Established an international procurement and quality control group including a manager and staff based in Taiwan resulting in a 17% reduction in cost of material.
- Maximized profit margins by developed pricing programs that considered type of demand, market share, cost and source of the product.
- Achieved the benefits of economies of scale through the consolidation of sales and marketing communication materials for all companies.
- Established new company to sell the wholesale market and acquired a brass valve distributor to complement the product line.
- Established distribution facilities and expanded retail and institutional brands into Canada.
- Established a manufacturing unit to produce hard-to-find plumbing specialties.

Operations Manager, Creech Co., Division of Pipemaster (1975–1978)

General Manager, Power Systems (RJC) (1974–1975)

Projects/Operations Manager, Divisionmaster (RJC) (1973–1974)

Industrial Engineering, RJC Corp. (1971–1973)

CAPTAIN USMC (1968–1971)
Served as Logistics Officer in the U.S. and Vietnam.

RJC CORP. (1978–1996)
Completed a nine month management training program prior to joining the USMC.

ESSEX PRECISION, Marietta, Georgia (1965–1967)
Production Planner (worked second shift while attending Emory University).

H.P. ORDONIO & CO., Atlanta, Georgia (1959–1965)
Production, administration and sales (summers and while attending Emory University).

EDUCATION
B.B.A., Emory University, Atlanta, Georgia (1967)
Held various student government, fraternity and club offices.
Attended numerous seminars and courses.

AFTER

DAVID L. SCOTT
5674 Church Street
Roswell, Georgia 30076

Phone: (770) 663-6204   Email: consultscott@aol.com   Fax: (770) 658-8323

SENIOR MANAGEMENT PROFILE

- Strategic Planning
- Global Sales & Marketing
- Team Building & Leadership
- New Market Assessment

- Global Manufacturing Operations
- Information Applications & Systems
- Corporate Administration
- Product & Market Development

- Sourcing & Distribution
- Acquisitions
- Logistics & Materials
- Finance & Analysis

PROFESSIONAL EXPERIENCE:

SCOTT CONSULTING CORP. - Roswell, Georgia   1996–present

Executive Consultant specializing in profit planning, organizational development and change management for start-up, turnaround and emerging organizations. Key engagements include:

- Developed business plan and market strategy for new concept placing high-end European, Asian and South American products into exclusive retail markets nationwide.
- Structured sourcing plan to import products from Pakistan and Thailand into the U.S. market.
- Positioned business plan for start-up national association targeted to niche health-care sector.
- Authored business plan for start-up acquisition company marketing unique professional services. Post positioned company for rapid growth and excellent cash flow.

RJC CORP. - Irving, Texas

NYSE listed industrial manufacturer and supplier with $767 million in revenue and worldwide distribution.

Group Vice President - Pipemaster - Philadelphia   (1985 to 1996)

One of two senior operating executives with full P&L responsibility for $80 million stand-alone company and its seven operating divisions. Focused efforts on accelerating growth and diversification while redesigning and strengthening existing operations. Held full management responsibility for strategic planning, finance, operations, manufacturing, distribution, human resources, administration, regulatory and safety affairs, quality and productivity. Led a work force of 400+. Controlled $21+ million in operating and capital budgets.

Revenue & Market Growth

- Launched retail brands into the home-center market, captured key accounts (e.g., Home Depot, Lowe's, Hechingers) and drove sales growth 122%.
- Consolidated inside sales and customer service, integrated core competencies of each and increased sales an additional $12 million annually.
- Led two successful acquisitions (Hardware Junction, Futty) through a strategic initiative to expand market penetration and increase market share.

David L. Scott   Page 2

Operations Improvement & Cost Reduction

- Reduced administrative expense by 34% through the post-acquisition consolidation of accounting credit/collections, purchasing, technology implementation and ongoing cost control efforts.
- Delivered $4.5 million savings through negotiation of volume discounts, offshore packaging and outsourcing in the United States, Japan, Taiwan, Canada, Mexico, China, Thailand, Hong Kong and El Salvador.
- Expanded distribution facilities by 175,000 sq. ft., acquired material handling equipment and achieved a $600,000 productivity savings.
- Utilized cross-functional task groups to achieve P&L objectives during rapid growth of retail division.

Information Technology

- Spearheaded acquisition of advanced information technologies to enhance operations, increase sales/productivity, improve customer service delivery and reduce operating costs. Implemented:
  –LAN/WAN to integrate warehouse operations. Delivered $1.4 million in productivity savings.
  –State-of-the-art integrated business solutions software.
  –EDI links for order processing and invoicing with 5,400 customers.
  –Document imaging for instant response to customer billing inquiries and cash flow improvement.
  –Call ID for instant identification of account, contract name and purchase history.

Vice President of Operations - Pipemaster - Philadelphia   (1978 to 1985)

Promoted from Division to Headquarters as the most senior Operations Executive in the corporation. Held full planning, operating and decision-making responsibility for general administration, accounting, IS, purchasing, manufacturing and distribution for five operating divisions. Concurrent responsibility for directing acquisition/integration projects. Led a team of 200+. Managed $10+ million budget.

- Established the strategic plans, P&L management systems, statistical reporting processes and trend budgets/proformas for the corporation and all operating units. Resulted in 10 years of profitability. Developed manufacturing operation to produce hard-to-find plumbing specialties and position Pipemaster as a "single source" provider. Established competitive position against major industries.
- Launched new venture to penetrate the wholesale market, acquired Specialty Products Company, manufacturer/distributor of new construction products to complement existing product line, and built new $5 million revenue center. Penetrated Canadian and French markets.

EDUCATION: Bachelor of Business Administration (B.B.A.), Emory University.

   While I would have recommended he put a specific objective at the top of his resume, it's pretty evident that a high-level management position in international business is what he wants to land.

John Rugiero

John Rugiero, a human resources professional with strategic vision, had developed a reputation for innovative HR initiatives with an eye on the bottom line. Yet, his "before" resume damns him with faint praise over four long pages.

   Why doesn't his resume belie his outstanding record? John uses many more words than is necessary to explain what he has done. Consequently, the reader gets lost in his verbiage. Because his phrases are too general, he doesn't capture the essence of his accomplishments. As he moved through his career, Jack undertook similar projects at increasingly higher levels, yet his experience section seems to repeat itself instead of showcasing his growing responsibilities.

   In his much shorter "after" resume, John cut the fat from his phrases and made them much easier to read. He talks about specific achievements instead of general HR responsibilities. And he spotlights accomplishments only in earlier positions that are different from ones he's already mentioned at higher levels.

Before

JOHN RUGIERO
10 Parchment Dr., Carrollton, TX 75024
Res: 972-555-0130
Bus: 972-555-8700
jrugiero@mci.net

OBJECTIVE

Provide senior level leadership comprised of HR excellence and strategic business focus for organizational impact.

EXECUTIVE SUMMARY

Human Resources executive with extensive experience in all aspects of the human resource functions, balanced blend of generalist and functional experience with excellent leadership, communication and interpersonal skills. Placed on 1993–1996 top talent list (10% of officer group) and maintain the highest performance ranking in the system. Promoted four times since August, 1990 along with a significant performance bonus/achievement award each year. Proven accomplishments in the areas of:

- *Merger/acquisitions*
- *Employee relations*
- *Management consulting*
- *Strategic planning*
- *Union avoidance*
- *Organizational transitions*

- *Team building*
- *Management training and development*
- *EEO/AAP compliance*
- *Recruiting*
- *Compensation and benefits*
- *Corporate re-engineering and downsizing*

PROFESSIONAL EXPERIENCE

United HealthCare Corporation
Vice President, Human Resources
Customer Services Group
Dallas, TX

Lead the human resources organization in support of six business groups (customer administration, small group, national accounts, medical case installation and claim operations) Key responsibilities include:

- *Directing a high performing HR organization of 60 people (30 generalists) covering 49 facilities and 9,000 employees.*
- *Strategic business consultation to Senior Vice President-Customer Services Administration, eight Vice Presidents, 40 Directors and 400 Managers.*
- *Creating and implementing of corporate business-driven policies and practices for the organization.*
- *Senior level staffing and leadership enhancement initiatives for workforce focus and improvement.*
- *Developed culture tied to high performance and self-directed-cross functional teams and skill-pathing-competency base pay.*

John Rugiero   **Page 2**

United HealthCare Corporation   10/95–9/96
Divisional Vice President, Human Resources
Claim Services Administration
Dallas, Texas

Full accountability for leading the human resources organization in support of the field claim services division (5,000 employees). Position involves direct responsibility for the following:

- *Directional support to 50 HR professionals located in 29 cities in the United States.*
- *Strategic consultation to the VP-Claims and 12 field directors and 200 business managers.*
- *Development and implementation of new HR policies, practices and programs for the organization.*
- *Defining new culture for the merging of two large health care organizations.*
- *Transitioning of two HR organizations into one highly effective, cost efficient operation.*
- *Operational results directly tied to workforce enhancement and overall upgrading of employee effectiveness.*

MetraHealth Insurance   1/95–10/95
(Health care merger of Travelers and Metropolitan Life)
Regional Vice President, Human Resources
Field Claim and Customer Service
Dallas, Texas

Field wide responsibility for building and leading the human resources organization service division of MetraHealth. Senior level direction of 25 human resource generalists who provide consulting/partnering services to 7,000 employees in 31 sites throughout the United States. This position is accountable for the following:

- *Defining "new" culture for the merger of Travelers and Metropolitan Life claim operations.*
- *Providing strategic leadership while building a world class HR organization.*
- *Creating human resource leverage/value to impact the business results of MetraHealth as a new and large entrepreneurial organization.*
- *Essential cost reduction results associated with streamlining merged organizations.*
- *Infusion of critical senior level leadership through effective recruiting strategies.*

Travelers Insurance Company, Hartford, CT   8/90–12/94
(A $55 billion multi-line financial services company employing 35,000 people in 65 U.S. locations)

Regional Director, Human Resources, Managed Care (Sales & Claim)   9/92–1/95
Dallas, TX

Directly responsible for human resource services supporting sales and claims in the southwest and western regions serving 2,600 employees in 13 states. Revenues of $908 million in 1992. Report to President of southwest home office for managed care and employee benefits operations.

- *Directed HR team consisting of six professionals and seven support people to include innovative leadership centered around "partnering" with seven district business groups.*

John Rugiero   Page 3

- *Formally recognized as outstanding HR team for effective servicing of the managed care division in 1993.*
- *Provided strategic counsel and guidance to VP-Field Claim, RVP-Field Sales and Field Management.*
- *Developed and piloted major job objectives for HR professionals which link accountability/risk with business groups serviced. Concept now used corporate wide.*
- *Pioneered HR partnering concept which is being driven throughout the organization.*
- *Lead role in re-engineering claim organization to include major consolidation of officers (eight) and deploying field structure for cost elimination/FTE reductions. Produced annual savings of $400,000.*
- *Developed customized HR site audit.*
- *Performed active role with VP-Human Resource in Hartford.*
- *Consulted with regional staff and managers to coordinate manpower planning, diversity objectives, and position elimination initiatives.*
- *Established as central source and in developing the HR role in the team environment.*
- *As "mentor" in conjunction with focused staff development plans and meaningful performance reviews allowing for HR expertise to be fully leveraged on our business priorities.*
- *Prepared position statements on 16 EEOC charges. All resulted in dismissal.*

The above initiative assisted in leading the southwest region to a record year in 1993, exceeding goals, new business sales of $100 million/135% of target, 207% of profit after tax target and 300% of plan margin target.

Regional Manager, Human Resources, Managed Care (Claims)   9/91–9/92
Dallas, TX

Accountable for the development and support of all aspects of Human Resources, serving 750 employees in five office locations (southwest region).

- *Built and managed the HR team, (two staff and three support people) and established site specific HR business plans within the region, linking HR to the "Line of Business."*
- *Served as senior consultant to Regional Vice President-Operations and his senior management staff (12 managers) on employee relations issues.*
- *Conducted extensive training for managers and supervisors in officer/exempt compensation philosophy, progressive discipline, grievance procedures, employee relations and recruiting.*
- *Participated in quality improvement teams and other total quality management initiatives.*
- *Created and implemented internal job posting procedures, perfect attendance program and absence management policies.*
- *Analyzed workforce and implemented staff adjustments within region in response to cost cutting and increased efficiency initiatives.*
- *Established link between performance management and compensation practices to include procedural check points to insure timely completion of performance appraisals and the practice of "pay for performance."*
- *Established officer management succession plan to include peer ranking and individual development plans.*

John Rugiero   Page 4

- *Conducted "Excel" training (Introspect model) with regional staff which drives new principles of management and changes organizational behavior for increased efficiency. Implemented competency based training which followed leadership analysis (Praxis model) of supervisory staff.*
- *Worked with consultant to establish and facilitate team building seminar for senior management staff.*
- *Conducted regional HR site assessments, including a climate assessment of one office experiencing employee relations problems.*

Travelers Heath Network, Corporate Offices, Dallas, TX   8/90–9/91
(Subsidiary of The Travelers - Managed Care Division)
National Director, Human Resources, Dallas, Texas

Corporate and field responsibility for providing human resource services and leadership to 100 people in eight divisions (Dallas based) and 650 field and sales/network operations employees in seven regions with a total of 60 sites represented.

- *Provided daily HR counsel to president, eight corporate division heads, seven regional vice presidents and 28 executive directors.*
- *Employed and directed a staff of one HR professional and four support people while administering a salary and non-salary budget of $24 million and $1.5 million, respectively.*
- *Worked with consultant to prepare and facilitate a "Powerful Business Presentation" program for all senior officers.*
- *Influenced corporate and regional business strategies along with quality service initiatives and offered HR perspective on key operational decisions.*
- *Administered officer management review process, succession planning, and the management incentive program for officers throughout the United States.*
- *Coordinated manpower assessment and recruiting initiatives for the seven regions to include monitoring of authorized employee census levels for all field sites. Employed 25 professionals for corporate finance group.*
- *Conducted HR site assessments at troubled field sites, recommended changes on staffing and proposed employee relations initiatives to the president.*
- *Facilitated employee opinion poll process for corporate and field to include summary of results and site specific action plans.*

Travelers Insurance Company   1973–1990

Associate Manager - Dallas, Texas
Assistant Manager - Little Rock, Arkansas
Administrative Asst. - Oklahoma City, Oklahoma

EDUCATION
Wichita State University, Wichita, KS   BBA - Business - 1973

John Rugiero   Page 5

TRAINING

CCL Senior HR Leadership Workshop (1996)

Certified Employee Relations Law Specialist (1993)

Certified Total Quality Management Team Leader (1992)

Participated in Collaborative Consultation Workshop (1992)

Participated in Powerful Business Presentation Seminar (1991)

Certified "Managing Personal Growth" Instructor (1990)

Participated in Leadership, Power and Influence (1990)

Certified in Positive Employee Relations Program (1989)

Completed Effective Management Program (1988)

ASSOCIATIONS/AFFILIATIONS

CCL Resource for Executive HR Development

Texas Council Director for SHRM

Director - Senior HR Executive Conferences

Dallas HR Management Association

Richardson Board of Higher Education

SHRM Texas Council Director of HR Executive Development

Founding member of Dallas HR Boardroom which includes 25 senior HR leaders in the metroplex.

After

John Rugiero
10 Parchment Dr., Carrollton, TX 75024
(h) 972-555-0130
(o) 972-555-8700
jrugiero@mci.net

Objective

Corporate or business group leader of Human Resources requiring partnering with senior management to set company strategic direction and subsequently develop objectives and action plans for success.

Executive Summary

Promoted four times since August, 1990 while performing leadership role through three restructures, one merger and two acquisitions. Placed on top talent list 1994–1997 (10% of officer group) while maintaining the highest performance ranking in the system. Proven results in the following areas:

• *Mergers/Acquisitions*	• *Compensation and Benefits*	• *Staffing*
• *Consolidations and Downsizing*	• *Team Building*	• *Employee Relations*
• *Management Consulting*	• *Succession Planning*	• *Process Improvement*
• *Organizational Transitioning*	• *Management/Employee Development*	• *Union Avoidance*

Professional Experience

United HealthCare Corporation - Dallas, Texas
Vice President, Human Resources - Customer Services Group   9/96–Present

Senior leader of the Human Resource organization consisting of 60 people (30 generalists) covering 49 service centers across the United States totaling 8,500 employees. Leverage strategic partnership with six business groups. Serve on Corporate Senior HR Leadership Council for UHC to develop, implement and administer policies and practices for 28,000 employees. Key accomplishments include:

- Provided consultation to senior vice president, eight vice presidents, 40 directors and 400 managers.
- Led recruiting initiative to staff three senior level positions, eight directors, and 33 business managers.
- Created new HR structure which eight regional HR coaches partnered with eight field vice presidents.
- Exceeded HR business plan by restructuring the organization, increasing generalist expertise/breadth of focus and strategic staffing (six new hires/seven managed terminations).
- Established seven core metrics tied to customer service to benchmark and measure human resource performance.

John Rugiero Page 2

- Created and implemented a skill-based pay and business/team incentive plan (all employees), volunteer relocation program for non-exempts, associate manager staffing program, and college recruiting plan.
- Revamped culture to emphasize high performance results, self-directed/cross-functional teams, and skill pathing/competency-based pay.
- Reduced workforce by 600 employees through performance management and process improvement while maintaining high morale.
- Led HR work team on job/salary grade review which eliminated 400 positions, created organizational consistency and streamlined positions for career pathing.
- Co-directed corporate HR job family review to create new competencies, job descriptions, career pathing and subsequent market analysis for salary grade assignments.

United HealthCare Corporation - Dallas, Texas

Divisional Vice President, Human Resources -
Claim Services Administration   10/95–9/96

Full accountability for leadership of the Human Resources organization supporting the field claim services division totaling 5,000 employees. Accomplishments include:

- Created and directed a new HR organization (25 HRG's/23 HRA's) out of three merged organizations that reduced expenses by $500,000 and increased operational effectiveness.
- Consolidated business operations through eight service center closings. Increased efficiency by eliminating 2,000 jobs from a 9,000 employee workforce at 43 locations.
- Upgraded workforce through development of a sophisticated testing process, new interviewing/hiring model and managerial training, (15% reduction in unmanaged turnover).

MetraHealth - Dallas, Texas
(Merger of Travelers and Metropolitan Health Operations) - 20,000 employees

Regional Vice President, Human Resources -
Field Claims and Customer Service   6/94–10/95

- Led Human Resources organization (20 HR generalists) providing consulting and field services to the claim/services division (7,000 employees in 31 sites across the U.S.).

Travelers Insurance Company - Dallas, Texas
(A $55 billion multi-line financial company employing 35,000 people in 65 U.S. locations)

Regional Director, Human Resources - Field Sales and Claim   9/92–6/94

- Managed Human Resources supporting sales and claims in the Southwest and Western regions (2,600 employees in 13 states). HR performance assisted in leading southwest region to a record year in 1993. New business sales exceeded $100 million and were 207% of profit target and 300% of plan.

John Rugiero   Page 3

Regional Manager, Human Resources - Southwest Region
Field Claims   9/91–9/92

- Developed and delivered HR services for five offices and 750 employees. Conducted extensive training for site managers (15) and supervisors on compensation strategy, performance management, grievance procedures and recruiting/selection skills.

National Director, Human Resources - Corporate Offices,
Travelers Health Network   8/89–9/91

- Managed corporate and field HR services for 100 officers in eight divisions (Dallas based) and 650 field sales/network operations employees in seven regions, 60 sites. Led HR staff to conduct site assessments, opinion surveys, manpower assessments, succession plans, and pay for performance reviews to improve workforce effectiveness.

Travelers Insurance Company (cont.)

Manager, Human Resources - Dallas, Texas	1984–1989
Associate Manager, Human Resources - Dallas, Texas	1979–1984
Assistant Manager, Human Resources - Little Rock, Arkansas	1976–1979
Administrative Assistant, Human Resources - Oklahoma City, Oklahoma	1973–1976

Education

BBA-Business, Wichita State University - Wichita, Kansas
CCL Senior HR Leadership Workshop (1996)
Certified Employee Relations Law Specialist (1993)
Certified Total Quality Management Team Leader (1992)
Participated in Collaborative Consultation Workshop (1992)
Participated in Powerful Business Presentation Seminar (1991)
Certified "Managing Personal Growth" Instructor (1990)
Participated in Leadership, Power and Influence (1990)
Certified in Positive Employee Relations Program (1989)
Completed Effective Management Program (1988)

Organizations

CCL Resource for Executive HR Development
Texas Council Director for SHRM
Director - Senior HR Executive Conferences
Dallas HR Management Association
Richardson Board of Higher Education
SHRM Texas Council Director of HR Executive Development
Founding member of Dallas HR Boardroom (1994) which includes 20 senior HR leaders in the metroplex

Success Stories

The resumes in this book represent real people. Some of them have interesting stories that they're willing to share.

Camille Russu

Camille Russu is an insurance pro and a relocating spouse, who recently left a position she loved. With this resume and some savvy networking, she quickly started a new job created for her at a large insurance agency a few minutes from home.

Kenneth Myers

Kenneth Myers decided to be a police officer when he was a Boy Scout riding on patrol with his local police force. When he graduated from high school, he enrolled in a community college to get his two-year degree. As he began to look for a full-time job, he soon discovered that an associate's degree just wasn't viewed as sufficient in today's workplace. Kenneth returned to school to pursue his bachelor's degree in Criminal Justice while working his way through college.

Only two months after graduation, he landed a full-time position with Trophy Club, a fast-growing municipality, which was in need of a drug education officer. Kenneth really enjoys combining his education, experience in law enforcement and medical settings with his natural talent for interacting with teenagers.

Camille Russu
2212 Random Lane
Des Moines, IOWA 50312
515-435-3636
crussu@aol.com

Objective:

Seeking a position with an established insurance company where my professional knowledge relating to producing, customer service, and underwriting skills are required.

Professional Qualifications:

- Possess a unique combination of accuracy, speed, attention to detail, and a photographic memory
- The "go to" person for difficult or complicated projects
- Jack-of-all-trades. If it needs to be done, I will do it.
- Enjoy teamwork where camarderie produces a sum greater than its parts

Experience:

| **Producer/Agent, Personal Lines** | **McCart Insurance, Inc.** | **1996–1998** |
| | **Norcross, GA** | |

- Manage current book of business for over 700 accounts relating to renewals, endorsements, new coverages, invoicing and claims. A vast majority of these accounts are considered "large accounts."
- Know underwriting procedures for Chubb, Fireman's Fund, Atlantic Mutual, C.N.A., Travelers, Ohio Casualty, Mercury and various other companies.
- Produce and write new business coming into the agency.

| **Producer/Agent, Personal Lines** | **Jim Anderson & Co.** | **1984–1996** |
| | **Lawrenceville, GA** | |

- One of the top producers of new business sales for three consecutive years
- Manage current book of business for over 600 customers relating to renewals, endorsements, new coverages, invoicing and claims.
- For the entire agency, handled all computer transactions for Safeco applications, endorsements, claims, billing inquiries, pre-approvals, and retrieval of e-mail.
- Know underwriting procedures for Aetna, Cincinnati, Continental, Cigna, Great American, Southern Heritage, Safeco, Westfield, Progressive and Atlanta Casualty.

| **Customer Service Representative** | **A.A.A. of Michigan** | **1979–1982** |
| | **Dearborn, MI** | |

- Served as a Customer Service Representative for a large metropolitan branch office with 30 personal line agents.
- Processed paperwork for five agents and data entry in this totally automated company.

| **Customer Service Representative** | **State Farm Insurance** | **1974–1977** |
| | **Dearborn, MI** | |

- Responsible for all customers' files, new business, endorsements, claims, loans, filing for the top Metro producer for four years.

Education:

Henry Ford Community College, Dearborn, MI

- Associates of Arts - Major: Business Administration
- Licensed Georgia Property & Casualty Agent

Kenneth A. Myers
226 Blue Lane
Arlington, TX 76011
817-349-0066
kenmyers@erols.com

Objective: Police officer for Trophy Club.

Business Experience:

The Kroger Co.   Keller, Texas   1996–Present
Security Investigator covering 83 stores in the Dallas/Fort Worth Division for the
  nation's largest grocery store chain with annual sales of $26 billion
  • Perform employee background investigations
  • Conduct internal/external civil and criminal investigations and lawsuit research
  • Provide supervision of contract security companies
  • Implement multiple safety, risk management and security projects
  • Control access in corporate office, distribution warehouse, and all stores in the
    division utilizing locks, electronic card access, and video systems

Careflite   Dallas, Texas   1995–1996
Emergency Medical Technician for a private ambulance service operated by three major
  hospital systems in the area
  • Transferred injured, critically-ill and neonatal patients between healthcare facilities
  • Provided comfort and stress-reduction to both patients and family members
  • Trained and oriented new employees as an Emergency Medical Technician Field
    Trainer
  • Obtained Level Two ranking as an Emergency Medical Technician

Methodist Hospital   Dallas, Texas   1995–1996
Security Officer in a major trauma hospital located in metropolitan Arlington
  • Provided a safe and secure environment for patients, staff and visitors
  • Assisted **Careflite** helicopters with loading and unloading of critical patients
  • Responded to high-stress calls involving a need for quick resolutions
  • Conducted internal and external investigations relating to the hospital

Denton County Sheriff   Denton, Texas   1992–1995
Detention Officer/Deputy Sheriff for a county with a population of more than 250,000
  citizens
  • Promoted from Detention Officer to Deputy Sheriff
  • Operated both a conventional and direct-supervision jail
  • Processed in new inmates, including warrant service, and processed out inmates
    according to court orders
  • Responded to calls for service which included some investigations

Kenneth A. Myers   **Page 2**

Related Volunteer Positions:

City of Rhome   Rhome, Texas   1996–Present

Police Corporal/Patrol Supervisor for a small town with a population of approximately 1,500 citizens

- Supervise 8–12 patrol officers
- Investigate misdemeanor and felony crimes
- Respond to calls for service from the community
- Participated in the implementation of and provided assistance in the starting of the police department
- Awarded Community Service, Certificate of Merit, and Good Conduct awards

City of Ovilla   Ovilla, Texas   1995–1996

Police Officer for a small community with a population of approximately 2,500 citizens

- Provided police protection and investigations
- Investigated in-progress or reported felony and misdemeanor offenses
- Became acquainted with citizens, businesses and the community through community policing
- Received commendation from the Chief of Police for new procedure regarding the filing of cases with the District Attorney's Office

City of Trophy Club   Trophy Club, Texas   1993–1994

Police Officer for a small community with a population of approximately 2,500 citizens

- Provided police protection and investigations
- Helped provide supervision of local Police Explorer Program

Education:

University of Texas at Arlington	Bachelors of Arts Criminal Justice/Criminology Major	May 1998
Richland College, Dallas	Business Administration	1991–1992
Texas Tech University, Lubbock	Business Administration	1990–1991

Certifications and Licenses

Texas Intermediate Peace Officers license (TCLEOSE)
Texas Jailers License (TCLEOSE)
Emergency Medical Technician (TDH)
American Heart Association CPR Instructor
*Numerous specific job related training courses

Other Good Chronological Resumes

Because so many people sent in excellent examples of chronological resumes, here are some others representing a variety of careers and industries. Feel free to use them as models, but be careful about resorting to a fill-in-the-blank approach. The main reason these resumes stand out from hundreds of others is that they contain a compelling message about individual achievements. For your resume to be equally powerful, it must be uniquely yours.

BENETTA L. RUSK, CCIM
222 Redbird Ave.
Tulsa, OK 45454
(h) 918-387-2567
(w) 918-392-4000
blrusk@mailbag.com

Experienced real estate professional with a diverse background in acquisition, disposition and finance of retail, industrial and office properties.

PROFESSIONAL EXPERIENCE

INTERSHOP REAL ESTATE SERVICES, Tulsa, OK   1994 to 1998
  Manager Acquisitions/Dispositions
- Involved in disposition of entire U.S. operation of Intershop Real Estate Services, totaling 5.1 million square feet of commercial real estate assets.

Acquisitions
- Prior to the divestiture, was directly responsible for or assisted with purchasing more than $100 million in over 1.3 million square feet of shopping centers and institutional quality single tenant properties for Intershop and third-party clients.
- Evaluated new deals and developed packages involving power retail centers and single tenant triple net properties for review by Intershop investment committee in Zurich, Switzerland; screened unsolicited offers to determine if they met Intershop's investment criteria; worked broker network; marketed the firm by networking with members of ICSC, CCIM, CREW; researched, analyzed, and evaluated targeted markets; monitored investment rates; performed detailed analysis of projects under consideration using ARGUS; coordinated and managed due diligence process and closing.

Dispositions
- In addition, was responsible for disposing of portions of non-strategic assets, selling 35 properties with an aggregate value of $65 million.
- Negotiated purchase and sale agreements, letters of intent, listing agreements; responded to broker and principal inquiries on properties for sale; evaluated offers based upon company objectives, then recommended the best deals; developed flyers and sales packages for direct dispositions; researched and selected brokerage firms for properties throughout the U.S.; managed broker marketing material to assure it met seller's standards; set up and monitored marketing process internally and with each broker; coordinated and managed the information necessary for purchaser's due diligence.

AETNA INVESTMENT GROUP, Tulsa, OK   1991 to 1994
  Assistant to Managing Director in charge of sales
- Managed sales by coordinating principals, brokers, attorneys, asset and property managers, surveyors, and title companies to perform disposition activities for a commercial real estate portfolio of approximately 90 properties worth over $370 million.
- Managed 60 property closings for the Southwest Region totaling 7.5 million square feet.
- Disposed of assets using the same process detailed under Intershop.

TRAMMELL CROW COMPANY, Dallas, Texas   1988 to 1991
  Assistant Asset Manager/Analyst
- Planned, coordinated and reviewed initial PRO-JECT modeling for approximately 200 properties in the $500 million Equitable Refinance Transaction.

Benetta L. Rusk   **Page 2**

- Managed property information for a combined $800 million portfolio.
- Interacted with field partners to analyze problem areas for strategic planning purposes.
- Performed individual project and portfolio analysis for management action.
- Developed operating performance reports for use in portfolio analysis.

Audit Senior
- Managed and coordinated financial and property management audits.
- Presented audit reports to all levels of management, including partners and controllers.
- Recommended improvements in operating efficiency/effectiveness for divisional administration.

TEXAS SAVINGS AND LOAN DEPARTMENT, Austin, Texas   1984 to 1988
   Examiner
- Planned, coordinated, and set scope for audit examinations.
- Reviewed and analyzed overall condition and lending procedures.
- Reviewed and analyzed appraisal assumptions and conclusions.
- Performed credit analysis.
- Prepared examination reports for supervisory action.
- Performed special investigations.

W.M. MURRAY & ASSOCIATES, INC., Austin, Texas   1981 to 1984
   Gross Sales Auditor
- Conducted gross sales audits of tenants on percentage rent leases.
- Reviewed and generated reports of audit field work.

COMPUTER SKILLS
ARGUS; PRO-JECT; Microsoft: Excel, Word

EDUCATION/CERTIFICATION
Certified Commercial Investment Member (CCIM) - #6489
(Educational equivalent of 240 hours of graduate-level curriculum in real estate finance and investment plus documentation of actual market experience.)

The University of Texas at Austin
Bachelor of Business Administration in Finance, 1981

Texas Real Estate Broker License No. 0338326

Federal Home Loan Bank Board
- Finance I and Senior Finance Schools
- Real Estate Appraisal Schools I and II, incorporates SREA Course 101 and 201

PROFESSIONAL & CIVIC AFFILIATIONS
Tulsa CCIM Chapter
Commercial Real Estate Women (CREW)
International Council of Shopping Centers (ICSC)

Susan G. Komen Foundation, Tulsa Chapter Treasurer
Tulsa Ninety-Nines (International Women's Pilot Organization)
Tulsa Junior League volunteer

PERSONAL ACHIEVEMENTS
Two Year Letterman, University of Texas Cross Country & Track Team
Private Pilot License ~ Instrument and Multi-Engine Rated
United States Parachute Association ~ C (Advanced) Licensed

WILLIAM C. MICHALAK
14630 N. Canard Lane
Chicago, IL 60620
312-305-5614
312-777-6236
wcmichalak@mci2000.com

OBJECTIVE

Vice President of Human Resources.

CAREER SUMMARY

Sixteen years of Human Resources experience including department management, policy writing, staffing, AAP/EEO, counseling, training and development, compensation/benefits, HR database development and implementation. Extensive work in management development, succession planning and linking human resource activities to the business plan.

PROFESSIONAL SUMMARY

Since 1991   **Amoco Production Company,** General Office   Chicago, IL

Consultant, Human Resources Planning & Development

Succession planning and management development responsibility, focusing on top 130 positions, replacement candidates, and high-potential employees. Significant accomplishments include:

- Resurrecting the succession planning process after a two-year moratorium, leading to senior management's understanding and effective use of human resource planning systems throughout the organization as a source of competitive advantage.
- Providing leadership and technical support for a global cultural diversity initiative, focusing management's attention on the strategic imperatives around diversity, and developing a process to help in achieving the desired results.

1987–1991   **Amoco Corporation,** Corporate Headquarters   Chicago, IL

Consultant, Management Development

Responsible for succession planning and management development with a focus on the top 60 positions, replacement candidates and high potential employees. Significant accomplishments:

- Designed, developed and implemented a succession process to focus attention on executive management replacement and development.
- Consulted with operating companies on a replacement planning and management development process to include middle management levels.
- Supported an executive development program targeting the top 100 executives and a corporate university targeting the top 3,000 managers.
- Provided leadership and support to a task force of senior line managers that resulted in a new companywide performance management process.

1983–1987   **Borg-Warner Corporation,** Corporate Headquarters   Chicago, IL

Corporate Manager, Human Resource Development

Responsible for succession planning/management development processes with a focus on corporate and subsidiary officer level positions (150 executives from a population of 88,000).

WILLIAM C. MICHALAK - Page Two

Significant accomplishments:

- Refined and institutionalized succession planning/management development system in a highly decentralized environment leading to a better strategic fit between executives, replacement candidates, executive development and the business plans.
- Refined and administered individually focused assessment and development workshop aimed at high-potential middle managers. Evaluated their management/leadership style and versatility in dealing with situations typical of general management or senior level staff positions.

1976–1983   **Borg-Warner Financial Services, Inc.**   Chicago, IL

Compensation Manager (1983)

Compensation responsibility for salary administration, analysis of competitor and industry pay practices and recommendation of pay policy. Significant accomplishments:

- Designed, developed and implemented a revised manager bonus program with front-end input by incumbents and a direct link to performance.
- Developed and designed a performance appraisal system, emphasizing individual contributions and accountabilities with direct linkage to the job evaluation system, resulting in clarification of performance expectations.

Manager Employee Relations (1980–1982)

Managed human resource department providing support to a 300-branch office, multinational operation. Responsible for clerical staffing, benefits administration, policy development and implementation, career/personal counseling, APP/EEO, program planning and automation of department. Significant accomplishments included:

- Enhanced stature of the department from maintenance type personnel function to a visible, proactive, human resource function.
- Automated HR database, AAP reporting and unemployment claim reporting.

EDUCATION
University of Chicago, Chicago, Illinois
Various graduate level courses through <u>Returning Scholar Program</u>

St. Joseph's Calumet College, Whiting, Indiana
BA Psychology, 1976

PROFESSIONAL & COMMUNITY AFFILIATIONS

St. Coletta's School and Training Center	Chairman of the Board
Catholic Charities	Advisory Board Member
Human Resource Planning Society	Member
Human Resource Management Association of Chicago	Member

"Thanks for the offer, but I really don't want to work here . . . I just wanted a second opinion on my resume."

6

Functional Resumes

Functional resumes are the "new kids on the block." Instead of highlighting experience by job title, they group accomplishments by functional area or overall job objective. The following sections show examples of these two approaches.

Experience by Functional Area

BUSINESS DEVELOPMENT/SALES
- Developed and managed $13 million loan portfolio for 175 customers composed of corporate executives, doctors, attorneys, CPAs, wealthy individuals, and private companies.
- Built a $3 million life insurance practice in 1½ years serving 100 upper-income clients.
- Recruited, trained and developed a unit of five life insurance agents producing over $5 million in insurance sales in a 12-month period.

- Planned and implemented new business development program for S&L branch; awarded President's Trophy for top production.

COMMUNITY INVOLVEMENT
- Served on Board of Urban Services for the YMCA and as Division Leader of Annual Campaign, 1998.
- Active on Board of the Way Back House and on its fund-raising committee.
- Participated as Administrative Board member and teacher, Highland Park Methodist Church.
- Contributed many hours as coach and leader for YMCA Youth Sports and Indian Guides.
- Active Dallas native with numerous contacts developed in civic, business and educational sectors.

Experience by Job Objective

EXPERIENCE HIGHLIGHTS
- Managed the development and sale of a wide range of highly profitable financial and computer-based services to thousands of corporations and financial institutions worldwide.
- As Senior Vice President and Deputy Department Head of the International Division of EurAm Bank, directed and administered its lending operations in Europe, the Asia/Pacific region, and Africa.
- Played a major role in opening the London branch of the bank.
- Cultivated relationships with companies and financial institutions in the London market.
- Served as liaison with the Head Office in New York.
- Established the branch's Credit Department.
- Coordinated facilities preparations from working with the architects to choosing the chef.
- Spearheaded and supervised the largest syndicated loan in EurAm history.
- Planned and conducted a road show for potential U.S. lenders featuring presentations by the borrowing country's Finance Ministry, Central Bank, and Treasury.
- Pioneered a new loan pricing concept aimed at attracting regional banks into the syndicate.
- Cultivated continuing relationships with high-level contacts in commercial and central banks, government agencies, and corporations all over the world, particularly in Europe.

Aside from not listing experience by job title, the functional resume differs from the chronological one by rarely using dates of employment or an employment history. Job titles and company names may appear in the text of the achievement per se, but they do not dictate the structure of the Experience section. For instance, an accomplishment in a functional resume may be described in the following style:

- Managed the production of seven brochures, four 10-minute videotapes, and a variety of PSAs and press releases as Director of Community Relations for the Metropolitan YMCA.

As with any format, the functional resume has its good and bad points. Review them to see whether they apply to your situation.

The Pros

This approach to resume writing is an excellent vehicle for putting together paid and nonpaid experience without the confusion of conflicting dates and titles. It's particularly useful when volunteer assignments or life experience support your job objective more effectively than your paid work. It assumes that your performance of a task had value even if you weren't paid for doing it.

It allows you to place your most relevant experience at the top of your resume, even if it's several years old. This feature is especially useful if your career has veered off its intended path, or a new direction hasn't met your expectations.

The functional resume doesn't focus on dates. Consequently, job gaps, job-hopping and staying too long in one place aren't issues for concern.

For career changers, who need to concentrate on functional rather than specialized skills, this format emphasizes what they can do rather than where they did it. Example: "Devising a system to increase customer contact by 50%" is a worthy accomplishment wherever you achieve it. Attaching it to a particular company or industry isn't as important as the fact that you know how to do it.

The Cons

Many people don't like functional resumes. Unfortunately, these individuals often are important to your search. They include personnel recruiters, executive search professionals and technical managers. They screen candidates for many openings that might interest you and become nervous when they don't see dates and job titles in reverse chronological order. They tend to think functional resume writers have something to hide. If you send a functional resume to one of them, you risk being rejected. On the other hand, if this approach tells your story effectively, don't abandon it in favor of a more traditional, chronological format, which will likely focus on the very things you want to minimize.

Another problem may be that you're uncomfortable with this style. A cardinal rule of resume writing is to produce a document that represents you personally. If you don't buy this approach, don't use it. Only a believer should play with the new kid on the block.

For individuals who are not adept at synthesizing data into functional categories, this format can be a real challenge. While it's relatively easy to list achievements by job title, it takes a little more creativity to group them into clusters of activities. If you are having difficulty visualizing what some typical functions might be, refer to the resumes in this chapter or start with the following categories:

		Purchasing
Production Planning	Project Management	Public Speaking
— Training	⌐ Financial Management	Event Planning
Sales/Marketing	Consulting	Troubleshooting
Customer Service	Administration	— Inventory Control
Fund Raising	Quality Management	⌐Human Resources
International Business	Public Relations	— Leadership

Don't assume that this list includes every function you should mention. Rather, it represents only a few of the myriad types of tasks that many professionals perform daily.

Example of a Personal Profile

T. C. Browne

Quoting a recent Exec-U-Net newsletter, "When it comes to resumes, most of us are very aware that the norm is a standard, crisp chronological format. There are, however, many occasions when you need something different because your purpose is to convey information in a more concise, yet powerful fashion. The one-page functional resume, or Personal Profile, is an excellent resume to leave behind after a one-to-one meeting and smaller networking sessions, where it is important to get your needs across quickly and clearly.

"As you look over T. C. Browne's profile, notice how he immediately shows you where his focus lies, the types of results he has produced and the expertise that has driven those results. Note, too, how he leaves his position titles to the end. The positioning is, I think, very clever and strategic, because all that precedes them help to spotlight the skills T. C. has and continues to use. Very smart."

T. C. Browne
27 Ridge Road, Greenwich, Connecticut 06820
203-656-4000 (office); 800-282-1234 (fax mail); tcbrowne@erols.com

FOCUS

Operating executive skilled in sales, marketing, P&L management, strategic development and leadership of growth and turnaround communications businesses.

RESULTS

Business Leadership - Led restructuring of a 400+-person, eight-unit business group. Grew revenues from $75 million to a $110 million run rate in 15 months, in spite of a $30 million drop in sunset revenues, in businesses focused on next-generation Internet, wireless mobile networks, secure electronic commerce, Web software, and outsourced network engineering and operations, for corporate and federal customers.

Multi-Channel Sales Management - Guided 50-person key account sales force in seven U.S. regions through a multi-channel, multi-product shared-P&L organization. Direct and indirect sales grew to over $200 million, corporate account revenues grew 40%, gross margins gained two points and sales productivity nearly doubled.

Corporate Account Marketing - Developed and implemented relationship marketing programs to expand sales and executive access in major multinational corporations, with customers such as Anheuser-Busch, AT&T, CocaCola, Dow, IBM and JCPenney. Implemented a cross-company marketing program which tripled consumer electronics sales to the corporate market. Achieved share dominance in two key segments.

Technology Marketing - Managed introduction of technologies in gigabyte routing, low power wireless, digital signature management, videoconference systems, satellite scrambling and control systems, and helped introduce portable CD-ROM multimedia products. Introduced videoconferencing, satellite television, computerized process control and high-speed fiber networks to major corporations and helped plan early EFT network. Organized first intercontinental HDTV satellite conference. Built a multicontinent videoconference network and created a desktop video product.

New Business Development - Established a $30+ million joint U.S./Japanese project to develop an ultra-high speed Internet router. Developed strategy, business plan and offering for a multimedia communications company. Solicited early stage investment and content partners for business video-on-demand networks. Assisted in business planning and market strategy formulation for a personal security system. Developed requirements plan and brand name for a Cellular 911 emergency locator.

EXPERTISE

Internet, wireless and multimedia communications, satellite television networks, videoconference systems, database and analysis software, systems integration, computerized process control, remote computer services, training and aviation.

EXPERIENCE

Senior Vice President & Group Gen. Manager - **BBN Corporation/GTE Internetworking**
President - **Technology Marketing Associates**
Vice President, Strategic Development - **Sony Electronics Inc.**
Vice President, Corporate and Government Marketing - **Sony Electronics Inc.**
Vice President & General Manager - **Sony Video Conference & Satellite Systems**
Director of Marketing and Director of Sales - **Private Satellite Network, Inc.**
Senior Sales Executive - **US Sprint/The Meeting Channel/ISACOMM**
Area Manager - **Measurex; Branch Manager and Sales Representative - Tymshare**
Lieutenant Commander, Naval Aviator, Executive Officer, MIS Project Mgr. - **U.S. Navy**

EDUCATION

The College of William and Mary, Williamsburg, Virginia
B.S., Physics

The George Washington University, Washington, D.C.
M.S.A., Management & Operations Research

Success Stories

Bonnie Sampson

Bonnie Sampson is a very savvy, self-made business woman who, throughout her career, was chosen for increasingly responsible positions because of her common sense, people skills and quick grasp of new information. In her recent job search, Bonnie couldn't decide whether she wanted another office manager position or to specialize in human resources. To give herself a broader range of options, Bonnie decided to do a resume for each of these jobs.

Because Bonnie's career history had a lot of extraneous responsibilities having little to do with either of the positions she wanted, she opted to put together two resumes that highlighted her applicable experience and deleted the rest. Both of her resumes are good examples of the flexibility of the functional format. While Bonnie mentioned some job titles, they have no chronological order or dates attached. Instead, Bonnie zeroed in on specific accomplishments that will interest an employer looking for either an office manager or an HR professional. She uses the same experience as a basis for both resumes, yet they look very different, don't they?

Lisa Brady Gill

Lisa Brady Gill was an elementary school teacher for 10 years before deciding to switch to a career that would allow her to interact more with adults. Because she still had a strong desire to serve people, she opted to look at careers in the nonprofit area, particularly those linking business with education.

Since then Lisa spent several years as the education coordinator for the *Dallas Morning News* and the *Dallas Times Herald*. In 1995, Lisa joined Randy Best in getting the Voyager Expanded Learning program up and running. Voyager is a program that motivates students to learn after school and during the summer. The firm partners with public schools, community colleges and universities to provide extended-time programs for K-6 children. While it started in Dallas, Voyager now employs several hundred individuals and works with educators across the country. As regional director, Lisa collaborates with school administrators to sell, develop and implement programs in their districts.

Other Good Functional Resumes

Some examples of good functional resumes are on pages 124–128.

BONNIE SAMPSON
87 Bridgeton Terrace
St. Louis, MO 45789
314/252-8789
bsamp@mailbag.com

OBJECTIVE

An office management position where a caring supervisory style, commitment to customer satisfaction, and the ability to maximize system effectiveness can be used in any of the following areas:

- Office Administration
- Total Quality Management
- Training and Development
- Human Resources
- Customer Service
- Sales Support
- Public Relations/Promotions

EXPERIENCE

OFFICE MANAGER—5 YEARS
Silver Nail Building Products
Overland Park, KS

- Reorganized the budgeting process for a four-state district office, including the sales support, customer service, and administrative departments. Actual expenses of district office consistently below budget, sales forecasts on target each year plus or minus 5%.
- Facilitated a corrective action team to eliminate obsolete/slow moving inventory in thirteen plants. Team consisted of district, office, national account, plant, and corporate level managers who first initiated a quick fix, then brought the process up to benchmark level in two years.
- Trained customer service representatives one-on-one and in groups to facilitate their own corrective action teams.
- Served as a member of two other CATs to improve products and office procedures.
- Won a TQM award for my work on various CATs especially in the application of principles and continuous commitment to zero defects.
- Developed an order entry system that reduced the customer deduction list from $100,000 to $1,000.
- Established and facilitated training programs for office procedures, TQM, and product knowledge.
- Wrote cross training and procedure manuals for secretaries, customer service, and sales representatives.
- Hired and trained a staff of customer service representatives who did telemarketing and handled all orders for 500 customers.
- Accompanied CSRs to construction sites to see how products were used and meet their customers face-to-face. Trained them that the customer always comes first.
- Won the "Customer Is King" award for service above and beyond expectations.

ADMINISTRATIVE ASSISTANT TO THE PLANT MANAGER—6 YEARS
Jameson Distributors
Lorina, KS

- Took orders and solved complaints for customers including Pepsi, Coca-Cola, Shasta, and R.C.
- Served as the assistant to the National Quality Control Manager as well as the Plant Manager.
- Kept track of plant inventory using Lotus spreadsheets.
- Monitored shipping to assure on time delivery at customer plants.

EDUCATION

Quality Education System (Total Quality Management) by Phillip Crosby.
Platt College - Accounting
Johnson County Community College - Management Seminars

OTHER FACTS

Train horses and give riding lessons. Starting a saddle club.

BONNIE SAMPSON
87 Bridgeton Terrace
St. Louis, MO 45789
314/252-8789
bsamp@mailbag.com

Objective: Human Resources position where excellent interpersonal skills and a background in handling multiple tasks simultaneously, dealing with all levels of employees, and working on a team would be useful.

Experience:

Human Resources:

Interviewed and hired administrative, clerical, and customer service representatives of all ethnicities.

Terminated employees, being very careful to document each case and conform to EEO guidelines.

Conducted and monitored performance appraisals for office staff at Gold Bond Building Products and the Private Industry Council of Kansas.

Wrote training programs and conducted workshops for employees on the following issues:

- Orientation to the company, its philosophy, and policies
- Total Quality Management
- Customer Service
- Product Knowledge
- Human Resources Policies
- Supervisory Techniques
- Cross Training for Several Jobs
- Order Entry Systems
- Inside Sales
- Office Policies

Prepared a handbook for all PIC employees and specific manuals for secretaries, office and telemarketing policies and procedures at Gold Bond.

Wrote ads and job descriptions for MIS director, college liaison, secretary, and customer service representative positions.

Wrote justifications for promotions and salary increases.

Other Applicable Experience:

Facilitated a corrective action team to eliminate obsolete/slow moving inventory in thirteen plants. Team consisted of district, office, national account, plant, and corporate level managers who first initiated a quick fix, then brought the process up to benchmark level within two years.

Won a TQM award and a "Customers Is King" award for application of principles, continuous commitment to zero defects, and service above and beyond expectations.

Reorganized the budgeting process for a four state district office, including the sales support, customer service, and administrative departments. Actual expenses of district office consistently below budget, sales forecasts on target each year, plus or minus 5%.

Employment:

Office Manager	Silver Nail Building Products	5 years
Human Resource Mgr.	Private Industry Council of Kansas	less than 1 yr
Administrative Assistant to the Plant Manager	Jameson Distributors	6 years

Education:

Quality Education System (Total Quality Management) by Phillip Crosby
Platt College - Accounting
Johnson County Community College - Management Seminars

Other Facts:

Train horses and give riding lessons. Starting a saddle club.

LISA BRADY GILL
9930 Grovenor Circle
Middletown, NY 12205
(phone) 518-683-9999
(fax) 518-683-9172
6542@compuserve.com

OBJECTIVE   A Community Relations position with the Middletown Independent School District.

PERSONAL QUALIFICATIONS

Many contacts in the corporate, academic and social service communities, cultivated over the past 15 years.

Easily establish rapport with people of all ages, cultures and philosophies.

Adept at selling ideas and programs to decision makers.

Expert in designing and presenting proposals and training programs.

Skilled in organizing events.

TEACHING EXPERIENCE

Taught kindergarten and third grade for Middletown Independent School District for 10 years.

Created and taught a pilot kindergarten program for MISD. Designed the physical environment, planned curriculum, started a parent volunteer program, budgeted and ordered supplies.

Facilitated or found speakers for over 50 training programs for administration, staff and parents of the Middletown Independent School District.

Developed a variety of volunteer programs for parents who helped with field trips, field days, classroom activities and parties.

Organized a field day for 300 people that required working with staff and volunteers, finding in-kind services, planning games, logistics and an awards ceremony.

Chaired 7 receptions honoring retirees and volunteers. Approximately 200 people attended each event.

LISA BRADY GILL   **Page 2**

PUBLIC RELATIONS/SALES

Promoted and demonstrated products for Developmental Learning Materials at a national convention for educators.

Initiated and conducted over 35 information interviews with members of Middletown corporate and social service communities.

Contacted numerous members of the Middletown business and education communities in pursuit of starting an Adopt-a-School type program for MISD.

Consulted on the media campaign for Carolyn Corbin, Inc.

Served as chairman of the Public Relations committee that organized and implemented a charity softball game for the National Paralysis Association. Players included members of the Middletown Flyers and the local media. Contacted radio and television personalities about participating in media softball game.

Selected as Staff Advocate to present proposals to the MISD School Board.

Wrote public service announcements and press releases for National Paralysis Association.

Wrote monthly educational newsletter for parents and early childhood staff throughout MISD.

Served as my school's representative on the Faculty Advisory Committee, REA, and RATPE, all forums for MISD employees that develop and present ideas to the Board on topics such as career ladders, model programs and teacher evaluation.

EDUCATION

BS in Elementary Education, University of Texas at Austin, graduated with honors.

MEd in Early Childhood Education, East Texas State University, graduated with honors.

LIZ WALLY
3320 Kaiser Boulevard
Dallas, TX 75268
214-249-7166
ewally@city-net.com

OBJECTIVE   Project management in an entrepreneurial organization where initiating new programs or changes, visualizing the big picture, creative problem solving, organizing tasks, ideas and people and monitoring follow-through are prerequisites.

QUALIFICATIONS

- Fifteen years of executive and Board experience with diverse nonprofit organizations.
- Founder of several professional and civic groups geared to meet specific community needs.
- Coordinator and catalyst for events that both educate and bring together representatives to share information and ideas.
- Small business/agency consultant specializing in strategic planning, marketing, operations and personnel.

EXPERIENCE

Project Design and Management

Developed and managed the Loretto Auction, the largest fund-raiser in this private school's history. (3 years)
— Recruited and managed the volunteer services of over 40 people.
— Created, built and maintained the donor base.
— Developed and refined systems for processing items.
— Marketed event to the public.
— Designed the PR materials.

Planned a national computer-use conference for over 20 Junior Leagues across the country.
— Handled logistics of catering, rooms, transportation and materials.
— Organized programs and social events.

Arranged two regional conferences for educators, a pilot program in Kansas City and another at Greenhill School in Dallas, featuring John Rassias, of Dartmouth College who is recognized nationally for his unique method of teaching foreign languages.

Served six years as Regional Chairman for the Stanford University Annual Fund, a biannual drive.
— Recruited volunteers
— Put together a phone bank

Organizational Development

Founded the Kansas City chapter of Who's Who International, a social and charitable organization for single people.

LIZ WALLY

- Recruited members.
- Designed programs.
- Managed the budget for four years.

Created and coordinated the Independent School Group of Kansas City, a coalition of headmasters and development officers from all the city's private schools.
- Designed and distributed a brochure, used primarily by realtors, describing each private school.
- Coordinated calendars and shared strategies and information.

Built a broadly representative team to study citywide issues and produce yearly reports (adapted from the Citizen's League in Minneapolis). Once formed, the Board:
- Hired an executive director, research assistant and secretary.
- Formed three study groups (the first year).
- Approved and publicized the "white papers" resulting from the study groups.
- Evaluated, improved and continued the process.

Finance and Budget

Served as Vice-President of the Junior League of Kansas City, with a budget of over $500,000. (2 years)
- Served as bookkeeper for one year, handling employee taxes, W-2 forms and insurance.
- Generated monthly financial reports using Peachtree General Ledger software.
- Chaired Finance Committee, acting as chairman of Thrift Shop (gross over $250,000).
- Produced new cookbook (three printings in first year).
- Negotiated contract dispute with printer.
- Reviewed projects for financial feasibility.
- Prepared and administered yearly budgets and audits.
- Worked on personnel policies, benefits and reviews.

Consulting

Performed consultant services for The Best of Kansas City, a firm with two retail locations and mail order business. (2 years)
- Interviewed and evaluated personnel.
- Reviewed financial and organizational systems.

EDUCATION

Stanford University, Palo Alto, California. BA 1965.

Continuing education courses in small business management and financial record keeping.

OTHER

Fluent in Spanish.
Willing to travel.

WILLIAM R. THURSTON

OBJECTIVE

To obtain a sales/marketing position in the insurance industry.

Qualifications

- Exceptional sales/marketing skills
- Innovative and creative management talents
- Strong written and oral communication ability
- Excellent computer skills

Work experience

- 10 years negotiating contracts with national and local insurance sales organizations producing $50 to $100 million in premiums
- Successfully hired, trained and motivated salespersons that increased sales by 35%
- 20 years organizing and conducting weekly and monthly sales training seminars
- Designed sales presentations that consistently for 20 plus years won high praise from the sales force and the clients for "easy to understand"
- Consistently produced from $5 to $75 million in premiums as an overriding Special General Agent
- 9 Years opening and organizing new regional offices in Texas, Oklahoma, New Mexico, Arizona
- Managed a Marketing Department with a staff of five and budget of $250K reporting to Sr. Marketing VP
- Created computerized proposals for efficient and effective sales presentations and tracking system
- Spearheaded new policy development and regulatory approval in record time of 8 months from conception to marketing campaigns
- Worked closely with upper management designing and creating sales and marketing projects
- Designed and created slide rule rate calculator that was used nationally and increased sales by $50 million

Work History

- OfficeMax, Arlington, Texas - Corporate Direct Representative
- AlphaGraphics, Dallas, Texas - Account Representative
- Stream International, Inc., Dallas, Texas - Technical Support Representative
- IMA Brokerage, Dallas, Texas - Owner/Manager
- Western States Administrations, Fresno, California - National Sales Director
- American Bankers Life Insurance Company, Waco, Texas - Sales Manager
- California Pacific Insurance Services, San Rafael, California - Divisional Manager
- Financial Reserve Life Insurance Company, Tulsa, Oklahoma - VP Sales

EDUCATION

- Southern Methodist University, Dallas, Texas
  Graduate: Institute of Life Insurance Marketing
- Tulsa University, Tulsa, Oklahoma
  Major: Business
- Richland College, Dallas, Texas
  Computer courses—PageMaker, Corel Draw, Windows, Internet
- Additional courses—Desk Top Publishing, Excel, PowerPoint, MS Word, Windows 95, WordPerfect, MS Office 97, Publisher 97

66225 Skillman, #202
Phoenix, AZ 85044
602-424-3535
602-424-3772 (fax)
wrt@mci.com

George Wisdom
2100 Cameron Road
Kansas City, KS 66111
(phone) 816-241-7273
(fax) 816-241-7278
gwisdom@aol.com

POSITION OBJECTIVE
Management Consultant

BACKGROUND SUMMARY

Over 15 years' experience in all aspects of mine operation, contributing to an historic safety record. Five years of supervisory experience promoting high levels of production while building and maintaining a good safety attitude.

MAJOR ACCOMPLISHMENTS

Supervision

○ In 1997 helped department to exceed production goals and deliver coal at 10% under budget. Motivated and trained employees to switch from conventional to spoil side dragline stripping.

○ Supervised 24 employees, two draglines, coal loading and reclamation. Skilled at resolving day-to-day crises on the job.

○ Helped to achieve the highest years of production in the history of the mine in 1995–1998. Able to build a sense of pride in the work group and create opportunities for employees to improve performance.

○ Worked on special projects that included haul road construction and creek reroutes.

Heavy Equipment Operator

○ Skilled at the operation and overall management of 100 cubic yard dragline. Also helped erect these draglines.

○ Experienced in the operation of shovels, track dozers, haulers, scrapers and front-end loaders.

○ Able to operate cable and hydraulic cranes, also rig and determine equipment limits. Knowledge of wire rope, slings and capacity charts.

○ Operated and maintained over-the-road trucks for three years.

○ Drove a city truck for three years.

Safety

○ Assisted work unit to achieve two million manhours without a lost-time accident in 1995. Personal perfect safety record spanning 15 years.

George Wisdom
Page 2

○ Conducted monthly safety meetings and trained employees in safety practices.
○ My crew has not had a lost-time accident in over four years.
○ Trained over 150 employees in handling hazardous materials.
○ Capable in handling dangerous and emergency situations.
○ Skilled at identifying and removing safety and health hazards.
○ Certified for MSHA safety audits for surface mines, First Aid, CPR and industrial fire fighting.

EDUCATION

Baylor University—Waco, Texas	BA—Psychology
Brownfield High School—Brownfield, Texas	
Athens Training Center	Basic Mining

PERSONAL

Fire Chief—Gause Volunteer Fire Department
School Board President—Gause Independent School District
Board of Directors—Rockdale Roping & Cutting Club
4-H Leader Milam County

MARK SLAGLE
373 Copeland Drive
Addison, TX 75248
214-779-2650
mark.slagle@micron.net

OBJECTIVE   Property management position with Carter-Crawley where I can use my experience in dealing with people and managing a large facility.

QUALIFICATIONS AND EXPERIENCE

WORKING WITH TENANTS
- Sold memberships by showing prospective members the facilities and explaining the amenities at Twin Timbers Country Club.
- Planned functions for both members and nonmembers such as wedding receptions, Christmas parties, and golf outings attended by 50–1,000 people.
- Negotiated contractual arrangements for the above activities.
- Handled member complaints with speed and diplomacy.

OFFICE ADMINISTRATION
- Purchased over $100,000 of supplies for clubhouse each year.
- Supervised a staff of 5–10 people.
- Held general management responsibility for a 650-member club including food and beverage, monthly newsletter, accounting, pay roll and membership.

PROPERTY MAINTENANCE
- Scheduled and delegated daily maintenance for a 40,000-square-foot clubhouse and its surrounding grounds.
- Assured that two commercial kitchens met health department standards.
- Contracted with 20 vendors who provided service for electricity, plumbing, pest control, air conditioning, etc.

EMPLOYMENT EXPERIENCE

10 years   Clubhouse Manager, Twin Timbers Country Club, Dallas, Texas.

3 years   Manager & Sales for Curtis Mathis Store, Dallas, Texas.

EDUCATION   BA Economics, Southern Methodist University, graduated cum laude

"I'll have to agree with you . . . it's not exactly your run-of-the-mill-resume."

7

Hybrid Resumes

A hybrid resume combines elements of the chronological and functional formats. Separate sections often are used to describe accomplishments and work histories, but this rule isn't "poured in concrete." In fact, one of the advantages of the hybrid format is its versatility.

The Pros

Another advantage is its logical blend of the functional and chronological features. This format does the following:

☆ Concentrates on achievements rather than job titles. This is a real boon to career changers and people whose last jobs weren't their most responsible.

☆ Puts dates toward the end of the resume where gaps in employment, job-hopping and long periods at one company aren't so obvious.

☆ "Hedges your bets" if the chronological format is too rigid and the functional one too avant-garde.

Many hiring executives like this approach because it focuses on what you can do for them rather than what you have done for someone else. If a job requires several main functions, composing your resume to correspond with them delivers a uniquely explicit response to a potential employer's needs.

The Cons

Some human resources recruiters and executive search specialists are purists. They want chronological resumes. Nothing else will do. Even though job titles and dates are listed in a hybrid format, they probably won't be in the spot where these screeners expect to find them. This small break from tradition may be sufficient reason to preclude you from getting an interview.

Writing a resume that gets results is both an art and a science. Your judgment is the most critical factor when choosing between two potentially conflicting factors: how you want to present yourself versus what a potential employer expects from you. Even if your choice of format lands you in the reject pile, it's important to be true to your convictions. An employer who doesn't like your resume probably won't appreciate you either.

The examples in this chapter illustrate the variety of ways job seekers have chosen to employ this approach.

Using the Same Experience in Chronological and Hybrid Formats

Linda Oshman

For several years, Linda Oshman had considered leaving accounting and moving into investment banking. Having positioned herself as an independent contractor, which allowed the flexibility needed to investigate a new field, she spent a good bit of time networking with professionals in her chosen arena. One of her contacts introduced her to the CEO of Venture Capital Partners, who was building a new branch of a Houston-based firm. He liked Linda's financial background and

LINDA S. OSHMAN
2510 HAVERWOOD
FLOWER MOUND, TX 75022
(h) 972-355-3908
(o) 972-492-4800
(e-mail) 8647@compuserve.com

OBJECTIVE

Financial professional with MBA and CPA seeking an opportunity in financial management, utilizing the following skills: profitability analysis, problem identification and resolution, budgeting and planning, management reporting, and systems development and implementation.

PROFESSIONAL EXPERIENCE

PRICE WATERHOUSE, Dallas, TX • 1995–1998 • *Tax Manager*
Reviewed federal and state tax accounts to determine refund opportunities for Fortune 500 companies or companies with $50 million in annual revenue; managed the status and monitored workflow of all projects in the department. Independent Contractor from 1995–1996, preparing federal and state income tax returns for corporations, partnerships and individuals.

OMEGA FINANCIAL CORPORATION, Dallas, TX • 1994 • *Investment Reporting Manager*
Supervised staff of five and managed the administration of over 30 limited partnerships; reviewed tax and legal implications in structuring these entities. Managed investor reporting department; coordinated and improved timeliness of quarterly client statements. Directed review of in-house systems to improve productivity and eliminate reporting inefficiencies.

TRI-RING CIRCUS, Vienna, VA • 1992–1993 • *Senior Tax Accountant*
Prepared consolidated federal income tax returns for large multi-national corporation with 19 subsidiaries; prepared and reviewed state income tax returns filed in over 50 states and localities. Designed tracking system to monitor hundreds of tax filings for all jurisdictions.

1ST NATIONAL BANK, N.A., Washington, D.C. • 1990–1992 • *Assistant Vice President-Financial Planning*
Analyzed profitability and presented financial performance results of $3 billion bank representing the Greater Washington Region to senior management and bank directors. Coordinated Region's preparation of annual budget. Identified and recommended opportunities for profit improvement to regional executives. Proposed and coordinated implementation of a local area network which significantly improved productivity.

LINDA S. OSHMAN

FINEBERG AND HALPIN, CPA's, Washington, D.C. • 1989 • *Tax Accountant*
Reviewed and prepared accounting and financial reports and related income tax
returns for corporations, partnerships and individuals. Developed business plans,
cash flow models and pro forma financial statements.

REPUBLIC BANK, Houston, TX • 1983–1988 • *Assistant Vice President-Financial
Planning*
Reviewed and presented financial results of $11 billion bank to senior
management; designed analytical and reporting mechanisms to facilitate
profitability analysis. Developed annual budgets and strategic plans. Managed
numerous projects, including reorganization of all lending departments; set goals,
established procedures and timetables, and directed 25 departments to modify all
supporting information systems.

COOPERS & LYBRAND, Houston, TX • 1981–1983 • *Staff Accountant*
Supervised up to 18 professionals on banking and governmental audits; prepared
auditors' reports and recommended policy and procedural improvements to
management.

EDUCATION & PROFESSIONAL LICENSES

The University of Texas, Austin, Texas • M.B.A. in Accounting/Finance, 1981

Tulane University (Newcomb College), New Orleans • B.S. in Psychology, 1977

Certified Public Accountant (Texas, August 1983)

After—Hybrid Resume

LINDA S. OSHMAN
2510 HAVERWOOD
FLOWER MOUND, TX 75022
972-355-3908 - res
972-492-4800 - bus
8647@compuserve.com

OBJECTIVE

Financial professional with MBA and CPA seeking an opportunity in financial management, utilizing the following skills: profitability analysis, budgeting and planning, management reporting, problem identification and resolution, systems development and implementation, and project management.

SKILLS AND QUALIFICATIONS

- Analyzed profitability of company performance and identified strategies for profit improvement, including development of loan pricing guidelines and enforcement of service charge policies for a bank. Analyzed real estate department customer base and determined most profitable relationships.
- Coordinated and prepared multimillion-dollar budgets for financial institutions; evaluated reasonableness of projections in achieving corporate goals. Developed and presented strategic plans for real estate department to senior management.
- Reviewed and presented monthly financial performance results to senior management and designed analytical and reporting mechanisms to highlight performance and analyze variances. Developed and implemented a report reflecting composition of performing vs. non-performing loans to assist a bank in management of portfolio.
- Identified weaknesses in productivity and proposed and coordinated implementation of local area network which reduced processing time by 75%.
- Managed reorganization of all lending departments for $20 billion bank: set goals, defined procedures and timetables, and directed over 25 departments to modify all supporting information systems.
- Supervised staff of five and managed investor reporting and partnership administration for small investment management firm. Reviewed and monitored legal and tax compliance issues.
- Prepared audit reports and recommended policy and procedural improvements to management.
- Prepared federal and state income tax returns for corporations, partnerships and individuals.

EMPLOYMENT HISTORY

Independent Contractor, Dallas, TX, Present
Price Waterhouse, Dallas, TX: Tax Manager, 1996–1997
Independent Contractor, 1995–1996
Omega Financial Corporation, Dallas, TX, Investment Reporting Manager, 1994
Tri-ring Circus, Vienna, VA, Senior Tax Accountant, 1992–1993
1st National Bank, N.A., Washington, D.C., Assistant Vice President-Financial Planning, 1990–1992
Fineberg and Halpin, CPA's, Washington, D.C., Tax Accountant, 1989
Republic Bank, Houston, TX, Assistant Vice President/Project Manager-Profit Planning, 1983–1988
Coopers & Lybrand, Houston, TX, Staff Accountant, 1981–1983

EDUCATION AND PROFESSIONAL LICENSES

MBA in Accounting/Finance, The University of Texas at Austin
BS in Psychology, Newcomb College (Tulane University)
Certified Public Accountant (Texas)

her enthusiasm for learning the art of deal making. Linda is now an associate in this fast-growing organization.

On pages 137–138 is Linda's "Before" chronological resume. It has accounting and tax literally written all over it. No wonder investment bankers were having a hard time understanding how Linda would fit into their milieu.

Using a hybrid resume (page 135) gave Linda the opportunity to highlight her experience that relates to her desired career instead of the details that would relegate her to another tax job. While she may not sound like a bonafide investment banker yet, her "After" resume reflects a well-rounded savvy business professional who is capable of doing a lot more than corporate tax returns.

Jacqueline Terrara

Jacqueline, college-educated, moved from a recruiting position in academia to become a law firm's receptionist. Unfortunately, her new employer didn't understand the marketability of a liberal arts degree or its efficacy within a legal environment.

But Jacqueline didn't let her management's tunnel vision discourage her from becoming a law firm recruiter. She started building her credibility by volunteering to help the recruiting department plan events for summer law clerks. She gave the recruiters tips on how to be more competitive in attracting college students. Gradually, they began to count on her help and advice.

Jacqueline also started actively networking with recruiters in other law firms. As they got to know her, she became a colleague. Not too surprisingly, when a recruiting director's position came open at a fast-growing branch of a national firm, the managing partner called her to see if she was interested. She was and took the job.

Before—Chronological Resume

JACQUELINE A. TERRARA
55 Redbird Lane
Dallas, TX 75123
214-666-5555
terrara@erols.com

EXPERIENCE: **Minich, Hauer & Beldon, Dallas, Texas**

Receptionist, September 1990 - May 1992; February 1993 - Present
Responsible for initial contact with clients and others over telephone
and at the firm. Maintain staff time records and data base for files
stored off-site. Organize facility schedule. Periodically assist with
data entry, special mailings and client billing. All Firm Committee
member: All Firm Meeting planner and master of ceremonies; spring
and summer firm social event coordinator.

Assistant Paralegal, June 1992 - January 1993
Assisted attorneys with real estate closings. Drafted a variety of
foreclosure documents and coordinated sale day activities. Filed and
recorded legal documents.

Texas Woman's University, Denton, Texas

Admissions Counselor/Recruiter, October 1987 - July 1990
Provided guidance for potential students. Coordinated special
recruitment events. Developed regional recruitment strategy.
Maintained counselor contact at secondary school and junior college
levels. Wrote and directed production of publicity brochures and
reports. Redesigned and managed an expanded student phonathon.
Implemented new Alumnae Admissions Recruitment Program.
Traveled extensively.

Culwell and Son, Dallas, Texas

Sales Associate, July 1986 - October 1987
Provided personalized service and attention, identified and defined
customer profile, and tracked new and special request inventory.

Dallas Museum of Art, Dallas, Texas

Registrar's Office Assistant, July 1986 - May 1987
As a volunteer, duties included logging object receipt and shipping
orders, completing certificates of insurance and loan agreements,
and developing and organizing exhibitions.

JACQUELINE A. TERRARA   Page 2

ACTIVITIES: Community Activities:

> R-MWC: Alumnae Chapter Secretary, Area Admissions
> Representative, Communication Coordinator for Young Alumnae
> Gatherings
>
> The 500, Inc.: A charitable group which supports Dallas' cultural
> arts.
>
> Dallas Museum of Art: Professional Members League
>
> Ronald McDonald House: Wednesday Dinners

Continuing Education:

> Southern Methodist University, Dallas, graduate studies in Art
> History
>
> Southeastern Paralegal Institute, Dallas, Post-Baccalaureate
> Certificate, May 1992, ABA approved

EDUCATION: **Randolph-Macon Woman's University, Lynchburg, Virginia**
Bachelor of Arts: May 1986
Major: Art History   **GPA:** 3.25   **Minor:** English

University of Reading, Reading, England
Selected as one of thirty-five students to participate in Junior Year
Abroad. Studies concentrated on British history, culture, literature,
and art. Traveled through eight European countries.

After—Hybrid Resume

JACQUELINE A. TERRARA
55 Redbird Lane
Dallas, TX 75123
214-666-5555
terrara@erols.com

OBJECTIVE: **A recruiting position for a large law firm**, which may also involve client development, community relations and special event coordination.

EXPERIENCE: *Recruiting Activities*

Assist with the administrative aspects of lawyer recruitment by maintaining the applicant data base, soliciting attorney volunteers to participate in the interview process, making logistical arrangements, serving as a greeter and information resource for the interviewee, and coordinating new attorney orientation activities.

Facilitate on-campus recruitment efforts by coordinating the campus interview schedule, serving as a liaison between the law school representatives and the firm's on-campus recruitment team, and assisting with the day-long call-back interview program. Participate in the planning and execution of the summer program.

Implemented new Alumnae Admissions Recruitment Program which involved coordination of training workshops, representation at college fairs, and alumnae-sponsored receptions. From 1987 to 1990, alumnae assistance with college fairs increased by 170% and contact with prospective students increased by 263%.

Public Relations and Marketing

Facilitate the client development activities of the law firm director of client relations by assisting with public relations and business development events. Assist with the design, production and distribution of public relations materials. Maintain firm's client mailing list and communicate firm profile to on-line information services.

Developed university's regional marketing strategy for student recruitment by reviewing statistical information from regional and feeder schools; targeted both undeveloped and well-defined areas to establish, maintain or improve relations. Initiated and maintained contact with key personnel at secondary schools and junior colleges.

Maintained communications for alumnae admissions program through a periodic newsletter. Highlighted volunteers' efforts and encouraged new participation by writing articles for the nationally circulated alumnae magazine. Wrote and directed production of publicity brochures for prospective students.

Redesigned and managed telephone campaign which gave prospective students personalized attention and encouragement to enroll. Calls increased 62% within three years.

JACQUELINE A. TERRARA   **Page 2**

Event Planning

Aid law firm director of client relations by researching and scheduling venues for meetings and special events. Assist with all communications and logistical arrangements.

Coordinated special on and off campus university recruitment events by planning and evaluating the program strategy, agenda, budget, inviting key faculty and staff members, making physical arrangements, and preparing written communications.

As a selected member of The All Firm Committee, planned and served as master of ceremonies for The All Firm Meeting 1993 & 1994. Perform as a social coordinator for firm wide spring, summer, and holiday events.

As alumnae association chapter president, coordinated general membership meetings, social parties, prospective student recruitment functions, and young alumnae gatherings.

Technical

Use software programs: WordPerfect 6.1, MicroSoft Office Suite '97, Outlook, Internet Explorer, Windows 3.1, Perfect Office 4.0 (including WordPerfect 6.1, GroupWise 4.1, InfoCentral), WordPerfect Office 4.0a, & WordPerfect 5.1 for DOS.

EMPLOYERS: Minich, Hauer & Beldon
Dallas, Texas, 1990 - Present
Marketing and Recruiting Assistant
Receptionist
Assistant Paralegal

Texas Woman's University, Denton, Texas, 1987 - 1990
Admissions Counselor/Recruiter

EDUCATION: Randolph-Macon Woman's College, Lynchburg, Virginia
Bachelor of Arts: 1986

University of Reading, Reading, England
Selected for Junior Year Abroad program. Traveled in eight European countries.

ACTIVITIES: Dallas Junior League
Active Member

Dallas Museum of Art
Docent

Ronald McDonald House
Volunteer Hostess

Randolph-Macon Woman's College Alumnae Association, Dallas and Fort Worth Chapter
President (1995 - 1997), Secretary (1994 - 1995)
Area Admissions Representative, Young Alumnae Coordinator
(1994–1997)

Matching Functions to Objectives

Elise Starrett

After 17 years of increasing responsibility at a national hospitality firm, Elise was ready for a new challenge. Having recently completed her MBA, she was in a quandary about whether to pursue a high-level operations position or one in marketing. She decided to consider both.

Before developing her two main resumes, she put together an accomplishments history according to her most successful and satisfying job functions, as listed below. Some functions contain similar achievements, proving there is more than one way to slant experience.

Notice how Elise tailored her functional categories in her resumes to reflect each of their objectives. The marketing resume stresses her company's market and its needs, while the operations resume focuses on revenue, profit, customer service and management. Yet both reflect the same experience, albeit through different filters.

GROWING REVENUE AND PROFIT

In the two following roles, my areas of responsibility exceeded sales and profit targets every year. In addition, many new accounts in other parts of the country as a result of potential client visits to my accounts.

As a District Manager

- Increased number of accounts from 8–17, sales from $12 million to $23 million in 4 years.
- Progressed from one of the smallest to one of the largest districts in the country.
- One of the first district managers to achieve profit of over $1 million.

As an Account Director

- Went from $2 million to $4 million in sales in 3 years, with profit increasing $270,000 between the first and second years under my direction at ABC University.
- At XYZ University, sold so many off campus meal plans the university had to impose a waiting list.
- Achieved a profit margin of well over 20% at QRS College in Charlotte.

As Vice President of Marketing

- Division experienced unprecedented growth during my second tenure leading the Marketing Function.

BUILDING STRONG CLIENT RELATIONSHIPS

Possess a natural talent for understanding current and potential clients' spoken and unspoken needs.

As a Regional Vice President, District Manager and Account Director

- Communicated regularly with client management to integrate strategic plans, discuss progress and operations, seize opportunities and prevent problems.
- Participated in activities and influenced company relations with client regional and national professional associations, such as Central Association of College and University Business Officers, National Association of College Auxiliary Services, National Association of Student Personnel Administrators.

As a District Manager

- Instituted yearly Client/Director Workshops.
- Easily negotiated Win/Win contracts (some in excess of $20 million) and yearly rate changes.

As a Regional Vice President

- Coached District Managers in building stronger, well rounded relations with their clients.

As Vice President of Staff Support

- Sent by President to approximately 30 accounts across the United States, which were hampered by poor relationships.
- Participated in extensive client satisfaction research across all businesses of the corporation during reengineering project.

ENHANCING CUSTOMER SERVICE

Have always believed in striking a strategic balance between Customer and Client needs. Happy Customers keep Clients happy.

As an Account Director

- Instituted active feedback/response processes.
- Kept satisfaction survey scores on an upward trend.

As a District Manager and Regional Vice President

- Taught and coached management on how to improve satisfaction trends.
- Instituted standards for formalized two-way communication process.

As Regional Vice President and Vice President of Marketing

- Planned competitive shopping events with District Managers and Marketing Managers to teach them to have a customer's eye and to instill a need to incorporate the latest trends into our business.

- Used Socratic methods to teach District and Marketing Managers to evaluate their roles and operations from the perspective of customers.

MANAGING PEOPLE

Hired, trained and empowered hundreds of management and hourly employees of whom

- Six are now Vice Presidents.
- Six went on to become District Managers.
- One is our company's top recruiter.
- Another is a key sales executive in another division.
- And, yet another is now President of a regional competitor.

Built and motivated teams through developing common goals and recognizing each individual's role in achieving them. At the same time, did not hesitate to remove people who were not adding value to the team.

Successfully negotiated union contracts at four campuses. Created a positive environment where one group of employees chose to decertify their union.

Replaced by two people when I was promoted from a District Manager.

During a merger, successfully integrated teams and accounts from three companies into one harmonious district.

SETTING TRENDS AND INNOVATING PRODUCTS/SERVICES

As a District Manager and Account Director, insisted on establishing and maintaining high operational standards while satisfying customer needs. Turned many accounts into benchmarks used by other teams, including Sales.

As an Account Director

- Created and adapted food concepts never before seen in any resident college market place.
- Developed and implemented five new, innovative retail food concepts in one year. Initiatives included menus, recipes and employee training tools.

As a District Manager

- Took a risk and installed the first Nationally Branded Food concept in the division.
- Operated the first convenience store on a college campus.

As Vice President of Marketing

- Led company/vendor team that designed industry's first flexible (computer generated), graphic menu board system giving managers cost-effective control through in-unit creation of strips and item identifiers.

- Instituted a mystery shopper program that expanded from the Collegiate Division to other company businesses.
- Initiated division promotions that were adapted and used throughout the corporation. "Cool Burgers" was the first corporate-wide promotion that ever sold out!

INNOVATION

Led the company/vendor team that designed a flexible, graphic menu system giving managers cost-effective control through in-unit creation of menu strips and item identifiers. This innovation was an industry first.

Instituted a mystery shopper program that expanded from the Education Division to other divisions in the company.

As a Food Service Director, created and adapted food concepts never before seen in any contract marketplace, including a stuffed baked potato format and made to order burritos.

Initiated division promotions that were adapted and used throughout MMS. "Cool Burgers" was the first promotion that ever sold out!

SPEED TO MARKET

Developed and implemented five new, innovative retail food format concepts in three months before the school year started. Initiatives included menus, recipes and employee training tools.

Collaborated with an outside creative agency and an architectural sign company to develop and present the "original" Crossroads project (a customer area and food identification system for resident dining) within five months. The project included:

- Creating format names, logo designs, signage, menu board designs and software for strips and identifiers.
- Designing and developing a brochure for use as a sales or a training piece.

Managed a cross function team that developed a sales building initiative and trained four hundred division people at all levels in seven months:

- Two four hour training sessions.
- Training modules to allow operators to segment and size campus markets and identify common market needs.
- Delivered tools to meet those needs including an inexpensive mobile food sales cart, a self-contained, portable convenience store for use in resident dining operations, a meal package (marketed to parents) for non-meal plan holders during exam week.

- A program, geared to managers and hourly staff, designed to promote enviable customer service.

UNDERSTANDING MARKET NEEDS

Constantly comb new restaurants, trade journals, consumer food magazines and supermarkets to learn what is hot, what is turning into a long run trend and what is no longer popular.

Recognize we must be using a cooking style or offering a product before it is introduced into supermarkets.

Understand how trends move across the country. I know where to find new ideas.

Know how to glean information from potential and current customer surveys to obtain directional guidance for promotional opportunities.

Skilled at extracting and synthesizing accurate information from qualitative sources such as focus groups and customer intercepts.

OPERATIONS MANAGEMENT

As a District Manager, increased number of units from 8 to 17 and sales from $12 million to over $23 million. Progressed from one of the smallest to one of the largest districts in the country.

As a Food Service Director:

- Went from $2 million to $4 million in sales in three years with profit increasing $270,000 between the first and second years of operation at ABC University. At XYZ University, sold so many off campus meal plans the university had to impose a waiting list. Substantially increased client satisfaction.
- Achieved a profit margin of 20% while developing extraordinary client relationships at QRS College in Charlotte.

Success Stories

Don Graff

Don Graff is a consultative salesperson par excellence who has been downsized several times through no fault of his own. Fortunately, because he has great people skills and a superior track record, he has always found another comparable position. After the latest rightsizing at Heller Financial, Don worked with an outplacement firm and landed a job as Vice President, Health Care Lending with Bank United.

Will Griffeth

Will Griffeth also found himself out of a job when his latest employer had a reduction in force. While he continued to be interested in warehouse management, he was also open to other possibilities. Will changed careers to start as a Management Trainer for Jack in the Box. Because of his project management and construction experience, he was quickly tapped to supervise the remodeling and improvements of Jack in the Box kitchens in restaurants across the country.

Donald W. Graff, Jr.
610 B St. W.
Tampa, FL 33603
Res: 352-979-2425
Bus: 352-680-2000, x42
graffjr@worldnet.com

Objective:
Business Development/Sales Management Position

Personal Qualifications:
- Over twenty-five years of successful experience in business development, consulting and banking
- Comprehensive knowledge of healthcare industry
- Excellent business origination, sales presentation, negotiation and closing skills
- Progressively responsible sales and marketing positions
- Regard professionalism, integrity and reliability as critical elements of my business philosophy
- MBA, Accounting, BS Finance supplemented by continuing education in sales, negotiation skills, computer programs, and financial analysis
- Willing to travel or relocate

Related professional accomplishments:
- During the last five years, originated over 50 new business opportunities annually and closed two of Heller Healthcare's largest accounts, as well as numerous other account relationships.
- Set up over 200 meetings annually with prospects and referral sources, including equity sponsors, investment bankers and attorneys in the healthcare industry, resulting in a national contact base of hundreds of professionals.
- Annually participated in four national healthcare conventions, as well as five healthcare investment banker conferences.
- While in healthcare real estate consulting, originated ten major client relationships and fifteen prospective clients within three years. A cold-calling program to over 300 major hospitals nationwide resulted in generating client business in excess of $120 million in project costs and $3 million in fees.
- Coordinated and participated in marketing and development plan presentations for healthcare facilities in over 100 senior managers and boards within a five-year period.
- Worked with the President of VHA Development Company designing the company's marketing brochure, direct mail, lead tracking system, marketing plan and slide presentation, which resulted in significant new business and increased revenues.
- As an investment banker, originated, underwrote and closed more than $200 million in healthcare securities.

Donald W. Graff, Jr.   Page 2

Employment History:

Heller Financial, Inc.   **Tampa, FL**   **1992–Present**
Vice President, Sales and Marketing
   Contact, negotiate and sell to senior executives in the healthcare industry. Make
   presentations to referral sources including equity sponsors, investment bankers and
   attorneys.

Ameritrust Texas, N.A.   **Dallas, TX**   **1990–1991**
Vice President, Business Development
   Originated and closed public and corporate financings in the Midwest market.

VHA Development Company   **Irving, TX**   **1985–1990**
Vice President, New Business Development
   Originated and coordinated development of healthcare real estate with hospitals
   throughout the country.

Underwood, Neuhaus & Co., Inc.   **Houston, TX**   **1983–1985**
Vice President
   Developed new business and underwrote bond issues on healthcare facilities.

The Ziegler Company, Inc.   **Chicago, IL**   **1980–1983**
Vice President
   Originated, underwrote and coordinated financings on industrial revenue bonds and
   healthcare projects.

Education:

   MBA, Accounting   Loyola University   Chicago, Illinois
   BS Finance, Dean's List   University of Illinois   Champaign, Illinois

   Continuing education in Windows 95 programs

Professional:

   Healthcare Financial Management Association
   National Association for Homecare

Civic Activities:

   Board of Directors - University of Illinois Alumni Club
   Brookhaven Business Association

Personal

   Interests: Skiing, golf and travel

WILLIS E. GRIFFETH
1190 Sunshine Terrace
Raleigh, NC 76954
910-543-7780
griffeth@msn.com

Objective: Special Projects Manager for Foodmaker, Inc., owner of Jack-in-the-Box restaurants

Warehouse Management

- Managed the receipt and shipment of 200,000,000 pounds of product, raw materials, and packaging supplies in a one-shift operation.
- Extensive use of LTL, UPS, export and full truck-load shipments for U.S. and international distribution. Varied packaging from small to 55 gallon containers.
- Improved distribution information system resulting in a decrease from two shifts and four managers to one shift and one manager. Cost savings of approximately $200,000 per year.
- Redesigned warehouse layout and racking to use 5000 fewer square feet.
- Coordinated move of sales people to plant. Managed facility construction and renovation. Achieved a cost saving of approximately $275,000 per year.
- Spearheaded and managed the installation of a new security system to maximize security of the building's perimeter and interior. Reduced incidents of false alarms and resulting expenses from eight or nine per month to zero.

Environmental Management

- Helped develop a closed-drain system designed to capture all wash and rinse water from mix and hold tanks, and recycle it rather than treat it to release to the city each time.
- Developed and managed recycle programs for plastic, computer paper, and cardboard, resulting in a cost saving of approximately $5000 per year.
- Convened semi-monthly meetings with the Fork Lift Involvement Team to brainstorm ways of improving productivity and warehouse conditions. Some results included warehouse reorganization and a new temperature control system.
- Provided monthly safety meetings on procedures, symptoms of job-related illness (such as heat stroke), and first aid techniques.
- Monitored and audited packaging and labeling of products on a weekly basis to maintain quality standards.

Emergency Medical Training

- Certified to provide training in Basic First Aid, CPR, and Advanced First Aid and Emergency Preparedness. Over the last 15 years have trained between 500 to 600 people including EMT'S and corporate employees.
- 15-year member of Red Cross Disaster team which assesses the magnitude of disasters for federal relief purposes, furnishes a concession truck for emergency workers, and sets up disaster shelters for flood, tornado, and fire victims.

Willis E. Griffeth   **Page 2**

Employment
- Warehouse Manager, **Ecolab,** Durham, N.C.   1989 to Present
- Fork Lift Operator, **Ecolab,** Durham, N.C.   1979 to 1989
- Rail Tender, **Ecolab,** Durham, N.C.   1978 to 1979

Education
- In-house courses in Interactions, Interaction Management, Total Quality Management, Problem Solving/Decision Analysis.
- Outside Courses: Better Warehouse Management, Supervising Difficult People, and Professional Writing Skills

Other Facts
- Softball Umpire   12 years
- Hardball Coach for Youth   3 years
- Softball Coach for Adults   6 years
- Registered Boy Scout, Girl Scout, Eagle Scout, and Order of the Arrow Brotherhood
- Taught Sunday School for 1st and 2nd graders for Oates Drive Baptist Church

Other Good Hybrid Resumes

Candidates in a variety of careers prepared the collection of hybrid resumes that appear on pages 152–159.

Marketing

Elise D. Starrett

47 Crystal Court
Morgantown, West VA. 21234
Phone: 304-972-7660
Voice Mail: 800-696-1030, Ext. 1234
E-mail: elise_starrett@aol.com

Objective

Senior Level Management, Regional Vice President

Summary of Qualifications

- Extensive experience in management of outsourced hospitality services and commercial restaurants.
- A passion for service that compels me to constantly seek innovative, more effective means of delivering it.
- Uncommon drive for perfection and quality.
- A track record of raising standards while achieving constant growth.
- Marketing expertise in gaining and keeping market share.
- Via a recent MBA, conversant with technology's power in aiding better decision-making.

Experience

Growing Revenue and Profit

In the three following roles, my areas of responsibility exceeded sales and profit targets every year. In addition, many new accounts in other parts of the country as a result of potential client visits to my accounts.

– As a District Manager
  - ✓ Increased number of accounts from 8–17, sales from $12 million to $23 million in 4 years.
  - ✓ Progressed from one of the smallest to one of the largest districts in the country.
  - ✓ One of the first district managers to achieve profit of over $1 million.

– As an Account Director
  - ✓ Went from $2 M to $4 M in sales in 3 years, with profit increasing $270 K between the first and second years under my direction at ABC University.
  - ✓ At XYZ University, sold so many off campus meal plans the university had to impose a waiting list.
  - ✓ Achieved a profit margin of well over 20% at QRS College in Charlotte.

– As Vice President of Marketing
  - ✓ Division experienced unprecedented growth during my second tenure leading the Marketing Function.

Building Strong Client Relationships

Possess a natural talent for understanding current and potential clients' spoken and unspoken needs.

– As a Regional Vice President, District Manager and Account Director
  - ✓ Communicated regularly with client management to integrate strategic plans, discuss progress and operations, seize opportunities and prevent problems.
  - ✓ Participated in activities and influenced company relations with client regional and national professional associations, such as Central Association of College and University Business Officers, National Association of College Auxiliary Services, National Association of Student Personnel Administrators.

– As a District Manager
  ✓ Instituted yearly Client/Director Workshops.
  ✓ Easily negotiated new Win/Win contracts (some in excess of $20 M) and yearly rate changes.

– As a Regional Vice President
  ✓ Coached District Managers in building stronger, well-rounded relations with their clients.

– As Vice President of Staff Support
  ✓ Sent by President to approximately 30 accounts across the United States, which were hampered by poor relationships.
  ✓ Participated in extensive client satisfaction research across all businesses of the corporation during reengineering project.

Enhancing Customer Service
Have always believed in striking a strategic balance between Customer and Client needs. Happy Customers keep Clients happy.

– As an Account Director
  ✓ Instituted active feedback/response processes.
  ✓ Kept satisfaction survey scores on an upward trend.

– As a District Manager and Regional Vice President
  ✓ Taught and coached management on how to improve satisfaction trends.
  ✓ Instituted standards for formalized two-way communication process.

– As Regional Vice President and Vice President of Marketing
  ✓ Planned competitive shopping events with District Managers and Marketing Managers to teach them to have a customer's eye and to instill a need to incorporate the latest trends into our business.
  ✓ Used Socratic methods to teach District and Marketing Managers to evaluate their roles and operations from the perspective of customers.

Managing People
– Hired, trained and empowered hundreds of management and hourly employees of whom
  ✓ Six are now Vice Presidents.
  ✓ Six went on to become District Managers.
  ✓ One is our company's top recruiter.
  ✓ Another is a key sales executive in another division.
  ✓ And, yet another is now President of a regional competitor.

– Built and motivated teams through developing common goals and recognizing each individual's role in achieving them. At the same time, did not hesitate to remove people who were not adding value to the team.

– Successfully negotiated union contracts at four campuses. Created a positive environment where one group of employees chose to decertify their union.

– Replaced by two people when I was promoted from a District Manager.

– During a merger, successfully integrated teams and accounts from three companies into one harmonious district.

Setting Trends and Innovating Products/Services
– As a District Manager and Account Director, insisted on establishing and maintaining high operational standards while satisfying customer needs. Turned many accounts into benchmarks used by other teams, including Sales.

– As an Account Director
  ✓ Created and adapted food concepts never before seen in any resident college market place.
  ✓ Developed and implemented five new, innovative retail food concepts in one year. Initiatives included menus, recipes and employee training tools.

– As a District Manager
  ✓ Took a risk and installed the first Nationally Branded Food concept in the division.
  ✓ Operated the first convenience store on a college campus.

– As Vice President of Marketing
  ✓ Led company/vendor team that designed industry's first flexible (computer generated), graphic menu board system giving managers cost-effective control through in-unit creation of strips and item identifiers.
  ✓ Instituted a mystery shopper program that expanded from the Collegiate Division to other company businesses.
  ✓ Initiated division promotions that were adapted and used throughout the corporation. "Cool Burgers" was the first corporate wide promotion that ever sold out!

Work History	**Vice President of Marketing**	DPF Services	1995–Present
	Vice of Staff Support	DPF Services	1993–1995
	Regional Vice President, Southwestern Region	DPF Services	1992–1993
	Vice President, Field Marketing	DPF Services	1990–1992
	District Manager, Account Director, Account Manager	Lake Corporation/ DPF Services	1973–1990
Education	**Master of Business Administration** Baylor University, Waco, Texas		1998
	Bachelor of Science, Business Skidmore College, Saratoga Springs, New York 1991		

Operations

Elise D. Starrett

47 Crystal Court
Morgantown, West VA 21234

Phone: 304-972-7660
Voice mail: 800-696-1030, Ext. 1234
E-mail: elise_starrett@aol.com

Objective Vice President, Marketing

**Summary
of Qualifications**
- Twenty-five years in contract food service (18 in operations and 7 in marketing support) and twelve years in commercial restaurants.
- My passion for food leads me to constantly seek new ideas.
- Uncommon determination to identify and use resources for innovative solutions.
- A track record of bringing successful projects in, on time, no matter what.

Experience

Innovation
– Led the company/vendor team that designed a flexible, graphic menu system giving managers cost-effective control through in-unit creation of menu strips and item identifiers. This innovation was an industry first.

– Instituted a mystery shopper program that expanded from the Education Division to other divisions in the company.

– As a Food Service Director created and adapted food concepts never before seen in any contract marketplace, including a stuffed baked potato format and made-to-order burritos.

– Initiated division promotions that were adapted and used throughout MMS. "Cool Burgers" was the first promotion that ever sold out!

Speed to Market
– Developed and implemented five new, innovative retail food format concepts in three months before the school year started. Initiatives included menus, recipes and employee training tools.

– Collaborated with an outside creative agency and an architectural sign company to develop and present the "original" Crossroads project (a customer area and food identification system for resident dining) within five months. The project included:
  - Creating format names, logo designs, signage, menu board designs and software for strips and identifiers.
  - Designing and developing a brochure for use as a sales or a training piece.

– Managed a cross functional team that developed a sales building initiative and trained four hundred division people at all levels in seven months:
  - Two four-hour training sessions
  - Training modules to allow operators to segment and size campus markets and identify common market needs

- Delivered tools to meet those needs including an inexpensive mobile food sales cart, a self-contained, portable convenience store for use in resident dining operations, a meal package (marketed to parents) for non-meal plan holders during exam week.
- A program, geared to managers and hourly staff, designed to promote enviable customer service.

Understanding Market Needs

− Constantly comb new restaurants, trade journals, consumer food magazines and supermarkets to learn what is hot, what is turning into a long run trend and what is no longer popular.

− Recognize we must be using a cooking style or offering a product before it is introduced into supermarkets.

− Understand how trends move across the country. I know where to find new ideas.

− Know how to glean information from potential and current customer surveys to obtain directional guidance for promotional opportunities.

− Skilled at extracting and synthesizing accurate information from qualitative sources such as focus groups and customer intercepts.

Operations Management

− As a District Manager, increased number of units from eight to 17 and sales from twelve million dollars to over twenty three million. Progressed from one of the smallest to one of the largest districts in the country.

− As a Food Service Director:
- Went from two million to four million in sales in three years with profit increasing two hundred and seventy thousand dollars between the first and second years of operation at ABC University.
- At XYZ University, sold so many off campus meal plans the university had to impose a waiting list. Substantially increased client satisfaction.
- Achieved a profit margin of twenty percent while developing extraordinary client relationships at QRS College in Charlotte.

Work History			
Vice President of Marketing	DPF Services	1995–Present	
Vice President Value Improvement Process/Support Services	DPF Services	1993–1995	
Regional Vice President, Southwestern Region	DPF Services	1992–1993	
Vice President, Field Marketing	DPF Services	1990–1992	
District Manager, Account Director, Account Manager	Lake Corporation, DPF Services	1973–1990	

Education				
Master of Business Administration	Baylor University	Waco, Texas		1998
Bachelor of Science, Business	Skidmore College	Saratoga Springs, N.Y.	1991	

CLAUDIA DIXON

9127 Hill Place   214-387-3245
Irving, TX 75060   214-938-6276
e-mail   cdixon@worldnet.att.net

OBJECTIVE   Assistant Director at Dispute Mediation Service of Dallas, Inc.

QUALIFICATIONS

- Masters in Conflict Resolution
- BA Rice University, Houston, Texas, Phi Beta Kappa.
- Mediator Certification through DMS, 40 hours, May 1995.
- Additional 24 CEUs, East Texas State University, October 1995, Family Dynamics, Child Development, and Family Law.
- Seven years' experience in word processing and data entry.
- Fourteen years' office experience in profit and nonprofit settings.

SKILLS

Administration/Organization

- Process information accurately and organize data logically.
- Plan and organize work efficiently, good follow-through with careful attention to detail.
- Manage office-coordinating responsibilities to meet needs of all parties, ensuring smooth functioning of up to four businesses.
- Handle many duties concurrently—bookkeeping, telephone work, word processing, editing material for publication, requisition of office supplies, accounts payable and receivable, scheduling and client contact.

Oral and Written Communication

- Mediate and co-mediate a variety of disputes for DMS.
- Effectively promote and explain services of diverse businesses both in person and using excellent telephone skills.
- Create clear, concise correspondence, brochures, newsletters, reports and training materials.
- Instruct groups of up to 40 adults and adolescents in public school, social service agency and community college settings.

EMPLOYMENT HISTORY

Office Manager, Dimensions Associates, 1990 to present
            Genie Weitzman, 1986–1990
            The Heart Center, 1984–1986
Associate Director, Employment Information Service, Women's Center of Dallas, 1982–1984. Employed in this capacity after working as a volunteer in the Employment Information Service.
Teacher, Austin Independent School District, 1967–69

Whit Dreher

57 Carriage Trail
Skillman, NJ 08504
908-874-4582 Home
609-452-3877 Office
wdreher@satlink.net

CAREER FOCUS

Strategic Marketing Communications Professional

PROFILE

Marketing communications professional with eight years experience in executive level management of marketing and sales projects in Fortune 500 companies. Four years experience in marketing communications consulting with fast growth companies. Proven attributes in visionary and innovative thinking leading to practical applications in the delivery of products and services. Entrepreneurial professional adept at instilling confidence and building positive, win-win relationships. Key skills and expertise include:

- Strategic Thinking
- Marketing Mix Analysis
- Major Account Sales and Management
- Written and Oral Communication

- Knowledge of Interactive Communications, Computer-Based Training, Sales Force Automation, and Direct Marketing
- Project Management

SELECTED ACCOMPLISHMENTS

Strategic Thinking
- Conceived and developed business venture and national sponsorship program for the Future Thought Career Video Network resulting in partnership with PBS affiliate WNET New York
- Created and implemented national co-op seminar series between Multimedia Learning and MacroMedia which became the primary driver of new business in all divisions of the company seminar series
- Founded and managed a profitable marketing communications consultancy providing successful marketing and communications plans for Young Presidents' Organization, Western Fidelity Insurance, SelectPlus MLink Technologies, May & Company, and The American Business Association

Marketing Mix Analysis
- Developed a marketing program that generated the highest number of sales inquiries in SelectPlus' history via trade show promotion, national advertising in *The Wall Street Journal* and public relations initiatives - all contributing toward the sale of the company to D&B Software
- Prepared integrated marketing communications plans for multiple clients (highlighted above) based on product and service mix analysis, target customer focus groups, positioning statement testing, and market trend analysis
- Managed conceptual design and implementation of advertising campaigns, sales collateral material, public relations, national trade show marketing, and multimedia-based direct-marketing programs for clients highlighted above

Major Account Sales and Management
- Awarded "Number One Business Development Manager" internationally at SoftAd
- Generated $1.3 million in annual revenue for SoftAd

Whit Dreher   **Page 2**

- Produced 24% (the highest percentage of seven national account representatives) of total advertising revenue in *Financial Product News* magazine for Enterprise Communications
- Generated first year non-media revenue of $155,000; second year increase to $236,000 for Creative Energy
- Developed profitable accounts with American Airlines/SABRE, Citibank, Coca-Cola USA, Exxon, Fidelity Investments, Harris Semiconductor, IBM and Other Fortune 500 companies

Knowledge of Interactive Communications, Computer-Based Training, Sales Force Automation and Direct Marketing
- Consulted with Fortune 500 companies and wrote proposals for multimedia-based direct marketing and promotional projects ranging from $35,000 to over $500,000
- Directed all marketing programs for a computer-based training company providing CD-ROM, Internet, Intranet and electronic performance support solutions to Fortune 500 clients
- Consulted with Fortune 500 high tech, telecommunications, consumer packaged goods and management consulting companies and wrote proposals for the implementation of sales force automation projects valued at $500,000 to over $1 million

PROFESSIONAL CAREER HISTORY

Proscape Technologies, Inc. Princeton, NJ   March 1997–Present
Manager of Corporate Accounts

**The Whitfield Group (Formerly Creative
Energy!) New Brunswick, NJ**   1997–Present
Principal

Multimedia Learning, Inc. Morristown, NJ   1996
Director of Marketing

Creative Energy!   1992–1995
Principal

The SoftAd Group, Inc. New York, NY   1990–1992
New Business Development Manager (Southern U.S.)

Enterprise Communications, Inc. New York, NY
Northeast Regional Advertising Sales Manager   1987–1990
Southeast Regional Advertising Sales Manager   1984–1987

EDUCATION
Bachelor of Arts, Journalism/Marketing from The University of
South Carolina, 1984

COMPUTER SKILLS
Microsoft Word, Excel, Power Point, Explorer, Netscape Navigator,
Major Search Engines

"You stated on your application that you have a bizarre sense of humor . . . could you be more specific?"

8

Resumes for Consulting, Freelancing, Volunteer and Internal Company Use

Generally when people think about writing a resume, they expect to send it to a future employer. That's a common use, but certainly not the only one. Professionals also need resumes to:

☆ Include in consulting proposals.
☆ Secure freelance contracts.
☆ Apply for positions within their own firm.

☆ Provide when requested for board of director or key committee positions in profit or nonprofit organizations.

Resumes for these purposes follow no hard-and-fast rules, but nonetheless have some similarities. All concentrate on accomplishments specifically tailored to the resume recipient's requirements. Many mention names of clients, task forces and projects that their readers will recognize. Job titles and dates aren't particularly significant because the length or date of a consulting or freelance assignment has little to do with its success, and an employee's contribution to her company is more important than her longevity.

Internal Resumes

This resume was prepared by a professional who seeks to advance within his company. It illustrates the significance of his work and his eligibility for higher level positions.

Martin Mueller

Martin was an industrial truck driver (hauler) at a surface mining operation in East Texas. An ambitious young man, he decided the best way to advance his career was to earn a college degree, so he enrolled full time at the University of Texas at Tyler. Since he had a family to support, he arranged to work the graveyard shift—7 P.M. to 7 A.M. After work, he drove 60 miles to attend classes until 1 or 2 P.M. He typically slept only three or four hours before returning to work, and studied while his hauler was being loaded with coal.

Martin graduated magna cum laude in four years, earning a 3.8 GPA in Industrial Technology and Speech Communication. He structured his resume to highlight this amazing feat. Within a year of graduation, he was promoted to the position of Industrial Technician.

Martin Mueller
One Mountain Ave.
North Richland Hills, Tx 75063
Work: 413-683-5408
Home: 413-954-6583
e-mail mueller@mci.com

SUMMARY

Over 20 years' experience in heavy industrial settings, including equipment operation (trucking) and machine tool production runs. Recently graduated magna cum laude from University of Texas at Tyler with majors in Industrial Technology and Speech Communication. Excellent at maintaining high-quality work and communicating information clearly and accurately. Dedicated to achieving personal and organizational goals.

ACADEMIC HISTORY

Bachelor of Science Degree from University of Texas at Tyler conferred magna cum laude. 3.8/4.0 GPA. Degree was earned while working a full-time 12-hour rotating shift and carrying 15 semester hours. A 150-mile round-trip commute was required daily.

Academic honors include:
President's Honor Society
Dean's List
Alpha Chi National Honor and Scholarship Society
Who's Who Among Students in American Universities and Colleges

WORK EXPERIENCE

Industrial Operations
Eight years' experience in operating 100-ton hauler safely and under a variety of weather conditions. Perfect safety record. Able to monitor equipment status and report operational problems.

Owner/Operator of Trucking Business
Scheduled and supervised loading, transporting, and unloading of various materials. Scheduled and performed all maintenance, service and repairs on equipment.

Machinist
Performed all phases of production runs from setup through inspection. Machine tool experience includes numerical control, mills, lathes, grinders, planer, profile, and drills in aviation, electronic and oil field applications. Commonly held tolerances were plus or minus .001 inch. Tolerances as close as .0003 inch were maintained in some production runs. Adept at working very carefully, being exact and accurate in completing each task.

Sales/Public Relations

Developed and expanded prospect list for property sales. Conducted cold calls to provide prospects with information concerning property. Supervised a crew of men in the operation, maintenance, and upkeep of property. Skilled at public speaking and adult education. Currently using these skills in voluntary situations.

WORK HISTORY

Texas Utilities Mining Company	Hauler Operator	1982–Present
Owner/Operator Trucking Business		1979–1982
Container Machinery Incorporated	Machinist	1978–1979

OTHER HIGHLIGHTS

Hobbies: Reading, Golf, Travel

Consultant Resumes

Here are some examples of the types of resume consultants use when submitting client proposals to secure contracts on a project or retainer basis.

Henri Vezina

Henri, a human resources consultant since 1986, includes this resume in client information packages and proposals. Notice how he highlights the corporations that have used his services and the projects he has completed for them. In his case, "name-dropping" is more important than quantified accomplishments because potential clients will assume that if he was hired by Digital, Kodak and DuPont, he must know what he's doing.

Donna Moniot

Donna Moniot started and managed nonprofit arts organizations for a number of years and thoroughly enjoyed the challenge of raising funds, recruiting and managing volunteers and developing new programs. Eventually she began to feel that she'd "been there and done that."

In considering what she wanted to do next, she recognized that many of her most satisfying moments involved helping people to unlock their creative potential. So she researched training programs that focused on this issue. Donna spent about a year getting certified in these programs and developing a plan for her consulting business. Today she specializes in creativity training for municipalities, school districts and corporations.

Bill Penry

Bill Penry's resume is a great example of how a consultant can summarize his experience to give potential clients an understanding of his expertise. While most resumes wouldn't have so many functional areas, a management generalist consultant can show his versatility by highlighting his diverse assignments.

HENRI A. VEZINA
4 North Prince Street
Belle Grove, NH 03049
Res: 603-783-1495
Voice mail: 800-490-2222, Ext. 147
E-mail: Vezina@earthlink.net

EXPERIENCE
1986–Pres.   Human Resources Management Consultant

- Provide strong expertise in all areas of Human Resources; management consulting, employment, employee relations, compensation, AA/EEO, information systems and training.

Clients:
- Datasec Corporation, Wilton, NH
  Management consulting, employee relations, compensation, employment, training, administration
- Digital Equipment Corporation, Hudson, Littleton, Marlboro, MA
  Counseling, employment, training, info system, outplacement
- Du Pont Imagitex, Nashua, NH
  Employment, employee relations, policies and procedures, ADA
- Kodak's Electronic Printing Systems Group, Bedford, MA
  Vice-President's advisor, evaluation of R&D managers
- Morton International, Seabrook, NH
  Staff advisor, employee relations, union avoidance
- Stratus Computer, Inc., Marlboro, MA
  Employment, employee relations, info system, training
- VMark Software, Inc., Natick, MA
  Policies & Procedures manual, AA/EEO plan, compensation program
- White Pine Software, Inc., Amherst, NH
  Management consulting, Policies & Procedures, training.

1985–1986   CHORUS DATA SYSTEMS, INC., Merrimack, NH
                 CUNEIFORM SYSTEMS, INC., Nashua, NH
                 Human Resources Director for parent company and subsidiary.

- Reported to the Chairman of the Board; advised and supported the Presidents of both companies and their staffs.
- Responsible for establishing the Personnel functions for both companies; policy and procedure administration, recruitment, employee relations, compensation and benefits.
- When both companies closed, counseled 90+ employees and coordinated outplacement of individuals into other companies.

Henri A. Vezina   Page 2

1983–1985   APOLLO COMPUTER, INC., Chelmsford, MA
                 Human Resources Manager for Engineering Organization

- Advisor to five Engineering Vice-Presidents
- Hired and managed staff of five who provided all Personnel services—
  employee relations, compensation, employment and
  management/employee development.
- Developed and directed Apollo's recruitment program.
- Established company's computerized applicant tracking system.

1974–1983   DIGITAL EQUIPMENT CORPORATION
                 Progressed from entry level Personnel Representative to Human
                 Resources Supervisor (5 levels)

                 Commercial Engineering, Merrimack, NH, '80 to '83
                 Computer Special Systems, Nashua, NH, '77 to '80
                 Central Engineering and Manufacturing, Maynard, MA, '74 to '77

- Hired, trained and managed staff at each of the sites.
- Provided employee relations, compensation, career counseling, and
  training to management and employees.
- Designed automated employment tracking system that was adopted by
  other DEC Employment groups.
- Managed complete recruiting function for all groups.
- Strong leadership role in Corporate Compensation's effort to rewrite
  Engineering and Manufacturing job descriptions.
- Conducted compensation survey of local area hi-tech companies.

EDUCATION
- Extensive course work in Management at University of New Hampshire,
  Boston University, and National Training Labs.
- Conducted Personnel Courses and Seminars at New Hampshire Colleges

SYSTEMS
- DEC, IMB PC, Stratus, Apollo Workstations

NOTE
- Speak, read and write French.

Donna R. Moniot
26F Cherrybrook Dr.
Garland, TX 75123
Phone: 214-555-6789
FAX: 214-555-6780
E-mail: drmon@msn.com

Objective:

Project management in an entrepreneurial, people-oriented organization where initiating new programs; creative problem-solving; and organizing tasks, ideas and people are a priority.

Personal Qualifications:

- Ten years of management experience in creating, designing and marketing innovative programs
- Extensive knowledge of the nonprofit, youth, arts, and political arenas
- Culturally sensitive individual comfortable and respectful of all constituencies
- Skilled at coalition and consensus building
- Excellent verbal and public speaking abilities
- Ongoing interest and study in leadership development and training

Work Experience:

- Oversaw the completion of a three-year National Endowment for the Arts Challenge Grant awarded to Dallas in 1993 and completed in September 1996
- Chaired technology committee comprised of corporate volunteers to research, evaluate and design an arts information database
- Hired and supervised staff to collect data for a calendar and database consisting of over 10,000 artists; 350 arts organizations; venues and facilities; media contacts; local, state and federal officials and funding entities
- Directed the design and prepublication of a 300-page resource guide of arts information in the North Texas area
- Supervised creation of a weekly, bilingual phone calendar to promote the arts in North Texas
- Designed workshops to train artists to use the Internet to access arts information and design their own web sites. Created an alliance with CompUSA to provide hardware, software and training facilities
- Created an Arts Resource Center to provide equitable access to technology for all artists. Obtained donation of a computer from the IBM Corporation. Established a technology center at the Sammons Center for the Arts with e-mail and graphic design capabilities
- Managed non-profit ticket service with over $1,000,000 in annual revenues
- Analyzed and initiated plan to train ticket agents which improved customer service to client organizations and increased their patron base and donor support
- Trained ticket agents to disseminate arts information to foster the growth of the arts community and increase ticket sales

Donna R. Moniot **Page 2**

- Advised client organizations on marketing techniques, such as press releases and shared mailing lists, to ensure successful events and performances
- Negotiated a partnership with Dillard's ticketing system to computerize ticketing services
- Supervised negotiations with the Park and Recreation Department, City of Dallas to ticket facilities at Fair Park, including the Cotton Bowl and the Coliseum
- Visualized, designed and implemented a program combining arts and mentorship activities for culturally-specific children. Program currently serves over 1,500 young participants annually

Current Community Involvement:

Anita Martinez Ballet Folklorico, Advisory Board	1994–Ongoing
Dallas for Children, Dallas Nominating Chair	1994–Ongoing
Junior Players, Advisory Board	1994–Ongoing
Park South YMCA, Board Member	1994–1996
City of Dallas, Youth Advisory Committee	1994–1996
Arts District Friends	1996–Ongoing
Oak Lawn Community Services, Advisory Board	1995–Ongoing
Dallas Urban League Education Committee	1996–Ongoing

Past Community Involvement:

Dallas Coalition for the Arts, Board of Directors, Co-Chair Education Committee	1994–1995
Shakespeare Festival of Dallas	
Board of Directors, Co-Chair Nominating Committee	1994–1996
Vice President, Communications	1994–1995
ArtServ, Board of Directors Director of Board Development	1994
Leadership Dallas, Co-Chair Curriculum Committee	1994–1995
City of Dallas, Youth Violence Advisory Committee	Jan.–April 1994
Greenhill School, Board of Trustees	1988–1991
Hockaday School, Parents' Club Board	1984–1990
Circles of Concern, President	1992–1993
World of Difference, Community Coalition	1990

Education:

B. A. English	College of Mount Saint Vincent, New York City	
Kansas State University	Graduate course in Sociodrama	
Western Institute	Focus Action Therapy and Psychodrama	1996/97
Leadership Dallas	1991	
Leadership Texas	1994	
Leadership America	1997	

Interests:

Theater, Travel, Reading and Leadership Development

William *(Bill)* Penry, Jr.

50 Magazine Rd.   Salt Lake City, UT 11926   801-491-1433
                                                           bpenry@world.std.com

Summary

A producer and a team building manager. More than 26 years experience as a manager and planner. Extensive experience in business capture planning, material requirements planning, personnel management, motivation, and task planning. Additional experience in small purchase procedures, software development and implementation, budget formulation and submission.

Accomplishments

Business Development

Worked with Chief Executive Officers, Chief Operating Officers, Executive and Senior Vice Presidents, to develop capture and business plans. Also developed competition analysis, proposal development schedules, and resource requirements. ***All efforts resulted in invitations for best and final submissions.***

Worked with Account Executives in assessing client requirements, recommending intervention alternatives, and recommending resourcing strategies. Worked with the Director of Sales, Central Area in development of business plans and marketing strategies for the central area. ***Company revenues increased by 15 percent.***

Led proposal teams ranging from three to eight consultants that were responsible for the coordination of proposals encompassing multivolume components, ranging from two to fourteen volumes. Resourced and managed proposal teams, with responsibilities including budgeting, administrative support, and scheduling. ***Have successfully led more large team proposal efforts than any other consultant currently working for*** *Franklin Quest Consulting Group.*

Tendered guidance and recommendations to strengthen proposal efforts. Recipients of recommendations ranged from senior vice presidents to directors. Participated in Red Team analysis of proposal submissions. Clients included many "Fortune 50 and 500" companies. Recommended pricing strategies and prepared total proposal strategy (cost and technical) analysis. ***Have always produced results which either met or exceeded client expectations.***

Integrated Logistics Support Planning

Formulated and implemented integrated logistics support plans and procedures used during contingency operations. A principal architect in the design and subsequent implementation of a management information system to monitor all aspects of the deployment and employment of equipment and personnel (more than 16,500 personnel, and equipment inventory of more than $100 million). ***Concepts and MIS systems are still being used.***

Program Support

Resolved support issues to overseas site management. Researched and prepared final and related supporting documentation for the contract close out of various contracts. Developed plans for the disposition of property for the closeout of an operating unit. Coordinated support requirements across department lines, such as Human Resources, Finance, Contracts, and Material Control. Provided program support for field programs overseas. Specifically, assisted Contact Field Support Teams which were working with of the U.S. Army during operations Desert Shield and Desert Storm. Recommended hardware and software procurement for a Local Area Network. Developed transition plans for start-up of programs, business plans and market strategies. ***Won the reputation as a "doer."***

William (Bill) Penry, Jr.   **Page 2**

Material Requirements Planning

Developed and executed integrated logistical support plans, established production control schedules, streamlined warehouse management, instituted warehouse planning, and improved inventory distribution. Developed computer models to assist in material requirements planning and job execution. Through aggressive management redistributed more than $750,000 in excess inventory that would have otherwise been declared surplus and disposed of with no value. *Met or exceeded all established goals.*

Directed the Marine Corps formal school for supply accounting and warehouse/storage operations. Responsible for review of programs of instruction, lesson plans, scheduling and budgeting. Achieved a dramatic reduction in student attrition. *Student attrition fell from just more than 9% to less than 2%, while achieving high field satisfaction.*

Prepared and submitted budgets, performed requirements analysis, and briefed senior officers. *Always funded for operational requirements.*

Small Purchase Administration

Responsible for validation of procurement requirements, soliciting bids, and establishing audit trails. Established one of the most complete technical libraries on the base. *Recognized as one of the most efficient small purchase activities on the East Coast.*

Management Information Systems Development

Director of software programming branch. Responsible for design, development, testing and fielding of logistical management information systems. Introduced bar-code technology throughout the Marine Corps. Responsibilities included customer support, development of implementation strategies and logistics support. *Directed the fielding of four major management information systems, and executed two major system updates, an achievement unequaled by any other Director.*

Personnel Administration

Commanded two organizations with more than 500 personnel. Responsibilities included administration, training, discipline and welfare of personnel. *Used communications skills for staff coordination, motivation counseling and delegation of tasks to subordinates.*

Employment History

Franklin Quest Consulting Group *(Formerly Shipley Associates)* . . . . Salt Lake City, UT

1992 to Present

- *Business Development Consultant, Central Area*   • *Senior Consultant*   • *Consultant*

General Dynamics Services Company . . . . St. Louis, MO and Fort Worth, TX

1990 to 1992

- *Senior Program Support Specialist*   • *Proposal Analyst*

United States Marine Corps (Retired) . . . . Various Bases and Installations World Wide

1969 to 1990

- *Various assignments of increasing responsibility, concentrated in logistical support, specifically material requirements planning, warehousing, and management information system design and development.*

Professional Development

Master of Arts, *Human Resources Management (1981)* - **Pepperdine University,** Malibu, CA.

Bachelors of Business Administration, *Marketing (1969)* - **University of Houston,** Houston, TX.

Associates of Arts, *Business (1967)* - **Del Mar Junior College,** Corpus Christi, TX.

Miscellaneous

- Familiar with IBM and MacIntosh platforms, as well as many varieties of dot matrix and laser printers.

- Have extensive knowledge of *WordPerfect, MS Word, Quattro Pro, MS Excel, MacDraw II, Visio, Powerpoint, MS Project.*

- Have held a **Top Secret** clearance while assigned to Marine Barracks, Ft. Meade, Maryland (1973 to 1975).

- Member of the **Association of Proposal Management Professionals**

- Member of the **Retired Officer's Association**

Freelance Resumes

Joy Taylor

Joy Taylor is working to become a professional voiceover specialist, commercial actress or books-on-tape reader. She is affiliated with the Thorton Agency and has been chosen for several parts. Note that she has included personal data generally not appropriate in a resume. Acting is one of the few professions where height, weight, and so forth, are considered bona fide occupational qualifications (BFOQs). Therefore, casting directors would consider it strange if she didn't mention these facts.

Faith Quintavell

Faith started her career at a major metropolitan newspaper but soon decided that she preferred freelancing. Her resume spotlights both her client companies and successful projects in event planning, public relations, film production, writing, editing and desktop publishing. Her resume shows that she's the person to call if a firm needs to be promoted in print or through an event.

JOY TAYLOR

Thornton Agency
4800 Blanc Avenue   304-822-8890
Parkville, WV 26505   e-mail: joy_taylor@actors.att.net   S.S. 573-20-1993

Height: 5'9"   Hair: Brown   Dress: Petite 10
Weight: 120   Eyes: Brown

TELEVISION

Job Search Series	Performer	Warner/Amex Cable, Dallas
10 O'Clock News	Weatherperson	Channel 4/15—WPTA-TV Parkersburg, WV
Broida's Stone Thomas Department Store	Fashion Commentator	WPTA-TV, Parkersburg, WV
Fairmont Food's Children's Show	Announcer/Performer	WPTA-TV, Parkersburg, WV
Greiner's Bakery	Commercial Performer	WPTA-TV, Parkersburg, WV

INDUSTRIAL

| Live on Stage—The Drama of Accessories | Intro Announcer | Southwest Homefurnishings Association, Dallas |
| A Time to Remember | Ruth Hack/Bobbie B. | 43rd Anniversary of Founding of AA in Dallas |

STAGE

The People Next Door	Performer	NCCJ, Traveling Acting Company, Chicago
Pajama Game	Mable	West Virginia University
If Men Played Cards as Women Do	Director	West Virginia University
Death of a Salesman	Linda Loman	Carnegie Institute of Technology

TRAINING

Bachelor of Arts, Theater	West Virginia University
Theatre Major	Indiana University
Acting Major	Carnegie Institute of Technology
Presently, Vocal/Film Acting Coaching	Jeff Alexander
Commercial Acting	Kris Nicolau-Sharpley

SPECIAL SKILLS

Golf, Tennis, Swimming/Diving, Fencing, Singing, Ballroom Dancing, Piano and Body Mimicry.

FAITH QUINTAVELL
16916 Canyon Road
Denton, NC 27615
704-633-0012
Voice mail: 800-373-2000, Ext. 762
E-Mail: quintavell@aol.com

WORK EXPERIENCE

MANAGEMENT AND ORGANIZATION

- For **Philip Morris** managed five employees, coordinated and executed promotional events in nightclubs in Albuquerque, New Mexico.

- For the **New Music Seminar** prepared spreadsheets and tracked production budget.

- For **Gorilla Films** produced new sample reel including hiring new director for firm, overseeing artwork and directing edit sessions.

- Also for **Gorilla Films** was associate producer for Avon industrial shoot.

- For **various film production companies** served as a freelance production coordinator and production assistant.

- For **Lobsenz-Stevens Public Relations** garnered national magazine placements for client; was assistant event planner for press conference.

- For the **American Cancer Society** organized and publicized stop-smoking clinics and other events—won the Society's Most Innovative Public Education award, State of Connecticut, 1984.

WRITING AND EDITING

- For *B-Side Magazine* wrote article on rock group Bang Tango.

- As a **self-employed resume writer** wrote, edited and typeset clients' resumes.

- For **Aiken-Savitt Temporaries** wrote, edited and typeset word processing training manuals.

- For **Coopers & Lybrand, CPAs** wrote and edited desktop publishing manual for nationwide use.

- For **VH-1** music video channel conceived and wrote skits for video jock Jon Bauman.

- For **Lifetime Cable Television** answered fan mail.

WORD PROCESSING AND DESKTOP PUBLISHING

- For **Aiken-Savitt Temporaries** taught WordPerfect word processing.
- For **Artron Graphics** "laser set" resumes using Ventura desktop publishing.
- For **Coopers & Lybrand, CPAs** "laser set" business proposals using Mass-11 desktop publishing.

EMPLOYMENT HISTORY

Freelance Promotions Event Manager, Writer/Editor   March 1985–present
and Film & TV Production Coordinator/Assistant

Freelance Word Processor/Desktop Publisher   March 1985–present

Public Education Director   February 1984–February 1985
American Cancer Society, So. Fairfield County, CT

EDUCATION

BA with Honors in Psychology, University of North Carolina, 1983; GPA 3.45

INTERESTS

Avid rock music fan and record collector, amateur photographer and natural foods cook.

Resumes for Board or Committee Positions

People often need resumes for reasons other than paid work. For instance, before serving on a nonprofit board or committee, working in a high-profile position in a political campaign, giving a speech or applying for an award, you'll be asked to submit a resume summarizing your background and focusing on specific experience or interests relevant to the assignment in question.

If you were applying for a seat on the Park and Recreation Board of your city, you might mention that you coached softball for five years, managed the common grounds of your homeowners' association and spearheaded the effort to renovate the playground of your local elementary school. But if you were being considered for a director's position on your local United Way board, your resume would emphasize your myriad corporate contacts, ongoing volunteer work with a United Way affiliate, and knack for raising large amounts of money from companies and individuals.

In other words, a resume prepared for a volunteer assignment follows the same philosophy as one prepared for a paid position: It should be tailored for the job at hand. However, nonpaid experiences are likely to be more critical qualifications than employment histories.

Joyce O'Connor

In late 1997, Joyce O'Connor, a highly respected nonprofit executive in Pittsburgh, Pennsylvania, decided to leave her full-time position to start her own consulting business, which would allow more flexibility and a lighter schedule. During the summer of 1998, she interviewed with the Pittsburgh General Office of New York Life for the Chair position of its newly forming Women's Advisory Board. Joyce was particularly interested in this project since it was part of a national pilot program to develop such boards across the country. Because of Joyce's excellent leadership experience and contacts in the community, she was chosen for the position along with four other colleagues in Dallas, Washington, DC, Phoenix and Chicago.

C. JOYCE O'CONNOR
78 Atherton Dr.
Pittsburgh, PA 16802
412-926-7565 (voice)   E-mail: 75651@compuserve.com   412-926-7832 (fax)

QUALIFICATIONS

Twenty years' demonstrated experience in working effectively with Chief Executive Officers, senior management staff, and community leaders to create and implement new programs to solve management, marketing, and communication challenges within and among organizations. Extensive and recognized ability in the planning, creation, marketing, and delivery of conferences, fund-raising events, and audiovisual presentations for audiences of corporate senior-level management, financial, legal, and nonprofit executives.

EMPLOYMENT HISTORY

1992 to 1997, GRANTMAKERS OF WESTERN PENNSYLVANIA, Pittsburgh, Pennsylvania, a professional organization of foundations, corporations, and charitable trusts which strives to promote effective philanthropy.

  1992–1997   *Executive Director*

- Advocated, coordinated funding, and assisted in the creation of the Foundation Center Library at the Carnegie with full-time staffing to provide a resource for students and the nonprofit community.
- Initiated Meet the Donor Sessions at the Foundation Center Library so that over 1,600 grantseekers could regularly meet grantmakers on neutral territory to learn about foundation-giving guidelines and philanthropic trends.
- Introduced the concept and managed the implementation of the common grant application format in western Pennsylvania which is currently accepted by 55 grantmaking institutions.
- Introduced and executed six nonprofit seminars and four annual community luncheons featuring national speakers with between 200 and 400 community leaders at each session to initiate community dialogues on critical national and regional issues.
- By creative programming, raised interest among grantmakers about youth violence issues and worked directly with the Mayor's Office to help develop concept and funding for the Mayor's Youth Initiative, now the Mayor's Serious Violent Offenders Initiative.
- Created, planned, and implemented approximately 65 programs and meetings yearly focusing on critical community, regional and national public policy issues facing the foundation community and the Western Pennsylvania Region.

1981 to 1990, FEDERATED INVESTORS, Pittsburgh, Pennsylvania, a mutual fund management company and institutional funds wholesaler with assets currently of $120 billion under management.

  1982–1990   *Assistant Vice President, Marketing Consultant, and Director of Product Information/Marketing Communications*

- Developed and delivered how-to-market financial products/services seminars for several hundred executive officers of financial institutions, attorneys, and advertising agency personnel throughout the United States.
- Wrote marketing proposals and supervised creative implementation for institutional clients throughout the United States.

C. Joyce O'Connor   Page 2

- Created, staffed, and managed Federated's Product Information and Market Development Department, an in-house advertising agency, with 20 employees and an annual budget of $1.7 million.
- Provided total marketing support to institutional sales force and corporation including market research, product line collateral materials, direct mail campaigns, ad campaigns, corporate identity, media/public relations, multi-image, video, and three convention exhibit booths.

1981–1983   *Director of Corporate Training and Development*

- Created, hired, and managed department with 21 employees and a 15-course core curriculum.
- Developed and implemented Federated's Management Development program (38.5 hours) for senior management and middle management personnel, accredited by Pennsylvania Board of Certified Public Accountants, and a five-week Sales Training program to support expansion of national sales force.

1978 to 1981, **NORTH PENN SCHOOL DISTRICT,** *Gifted Resource Instructor,* Lansdale, Pennsylvania.

1972 to 1978, **LOWER MORELAND SCHOOL DISTRICT,** *Coordinator and Instructor, Academically Talented Program,* Huntington Valley, Pennsylvania.

1969 to 1971, **REDSTONE FEDERAL CREDIT UNION,** *Assistant Loan Administrator,* Stuttgart, Germany.

1968 to 1969, **FIRST NATIONAL BANK OF BOSTON,** *Customer Relations Administrator,* Boston, Massachusetts.

EDUCATION

Doctoral Program, University of Pennsylvania (1977–1979)
Master of Education, Lehigh University (1973)
Bachelor of Arts, Connecticut College, New London Connecticut (1968)

PROFESSIONAL AFFILIATIONS

- National Forum of RAGS, Washington, DC, former Steering Committee Member
- Council of Foundations, Washington, DC
- INDEPENDENT SECTOR, Washington, DC
- Leadership Pittsburgh (Class XI), Nonprofit Selection Committee Chair
- Ronald McDonald House Charities of Pittsburgh, Vice President, Board Member, Grants Committee
- Holy Family Institute Foundation, Board Member and Chair of Communications Committee
- Pittsburgh Vision Services, Board Member and Member of Steering Committee for Merger, Development Committee, and Chair of Person of Vision Award Dinner
- Arthritis Foundation, Western Pennsylvania Chapter, Executive Committee, Board Member

"I'm afraid we don't have anything for you just now, but I'll be glad to forward your resume to our parent company."

9

Resumes for First-Time Job Seekers and Recent College Graduates

Recent college and high-school graduates face a Catch-22 in starting their new careers. Employers typically want to hire people with experience, which first-time job seekers seldom have. Yet companies advertise entry-level positions that imply no experience is required.

What can a person with good educational credentials and little paid background do to overcome this dilemma? Actually, there are a number of viable vehicles for gaining expertise other than a full-time job.

Volunteer Work

Plenty of volunteer opportunities exist for young people to try both when school is in session and during summer and holiday vacations. A short list of examples might include:

☆   Tutoring low-income children.

☆   Desktop publishing for a church newsletter.

☆   Taping books for the blind.

☆   Coaching a softball team.

☆   Working on a political campaign.

☆   Finding resources for library customers.

☆   Organizing and conducting a fund-raising campaign to buy furniture for the local family shelter.

☆   Collecting food for an area food bank.

☆   Driving senior citizens around town or to the Senior Center.

☆   Talking and reading to children in the pediatric ward of the county hospital.

All these experiences demonstrate initiative, perseverance and the desire to be of service to others, characteristics that potential employers admire. They will also substitute for paid experience if you give them a place of honor on your resume.

A Variety of Useful Experience, Not Necessarily Paid

School Activities

Extracurricular activities get a positive nod from companies as well. If you have applied and been selected for a competitive university, you already know that recruiters weigh your time away from classes as well as your academic record. Employers hold a similar view. They know that extracurricular activities usually require leadership, responsibility, follow-through and a variety of other traits that are desirable in successful job candidates. If you have been active in any school-sponsored functions, don't hesitate to use them as experience. They look good on your resume and allow you to collect stellar references.

Hobbies

Listing hobbies on a resume is particularly effective if they relate to the job you want. For instance, if you build remote-control model cars in your spare time, and you aspire to be an automotive engineer, most employers would appreciate the connection between the two. Suppose you designed and made all your clothes. Couture firms on Seventh Avenue would find this ability extremely desirable.

If a hobby coincides with your career objective, discuss it in your Experience section. If it doesn't, put it on your resume anyway, but in a less prominent position.

Clubs

Club memberships can be useful, both because of the role you play and the organization's overall mission. Fraternities and sororities are good examples of this. They offer actives the opportunity to assume highly responsible positions quickly. Anyone who has been Chair of the Homecoming Celebration or the Alumni Fund Drive can take credit for a host of demonstrated skills, including team building, leadership, problem solving, mediation, creativity, resourcefulness, perseverance, organization and follow-through.

If your club is concerned primarily with issues similar to those of the company or organization you're pursuing, mentioning it will elicit a favorable response with hiring managers. For instance, if you have been active in the Audubon Society, and you are hoping to land a position with the EPA, your obvious interest in ecology will give you an edge over the competition.

As with school-sponsored extracurricular activities, clubs can be an important addition to your resume, even if their mission doesn't apply to your job objective. Serving as an officer or committee chair always impresses potential employers, unless they are looking for a candidate who wants a dead-end job.

Internships

Paid or unpaid internships are great ways to accumulate experience in a potential career field. Concurrent with deciding whether the career is right for you, you are compiling a list of achievements that will add sizzle to your resume. Since you're just beginning your career, interviewers can't expect you to come equipped with years of experience. But if they see that you spent a summer or a semester "trying on" your new career, they assume the odds are good that you'll be a happy, successful employee.

Even if your internship is in a different field than the one you want to work in, completing it shows that you are familiar with the world of work and able to conform to its culture and policies. Transferable skills can count for a lot when there isn't much employment history to discuss.

Part-Time Jobs

As long as the puritan work ethic is an honored philosophy in American business, part-time jobs held while in school or during vacations will be excellent selling points with employers, particularly if they relate to your chosen career. Working at McDonald's, in a clothing or grocery store, the school cafeteria or an office will count in your favor as well, especially if you mention your job helped to pay for personal or school expenses. Many of the people reading your resume had part-time jobs themselves, or are parents facing the daunting prospect of footing the bill for their children's college degree. When they read about your work-study regimen, they'll either identify with you or hope their offspring will have the good sense to be as motivated. Either way, you have made yourself a friend.

As you write about paid or unpaid experience, remember to discuss accomplishments, rather than duties, if possible. The following are some typical achievements from activities or part-time job experience:

- ☆ Revised the database for the Leadership Dallas Alumni Yearbook.
- ☆ Authored a 24-chapter manual on the use of surf boats in lifeguarding.
- ☆ Carried diverse client caseload in terms of ethnicity, age and social class.
- ☆ Wrote personal letters for President Clinton's political liaison and participated in planning and executing large mailings to up to 1,500 constituents.
- ☆ Gathered and organized tourism-related information to assist staff and guests in a newly opened, 40-room upscale bed-and-breakfast inn.
- ☆ Worked on a Homecoming committee that designed and built the Grand Prize float for Texas Tech, called "ET Phone Home."

While your achievements may not have the scope of a Nobel Prize winner (or even of your parents), anything you can do to spotlight a unique contribution will capture recruiters' attention and set you apart from the hundreds of business-as-usual candidates they hear from every week.

Education

While most resume writers emphasize experience over education, graduates with highly prized degrees from prestigious universities may want to list their educational credentials first. Before you construct your resume, check with your college placement office to find out if many employers regularly recruit and hire graduates from your school. If they do, give your degree(s) a place of honor at the top of your first page, and list your part-time jobs and activities below it. You may also want to emphasize your education if your career requires a specific credential, such as an RN (nursing), an MSW (clinical social work), or a BSEE (electrical engineering). On the other hand, if your specific degree isn't essential for the position you seek, feature your experience as your most marketable asset.

Your education section should include the same types of entries as the ones discussed in Chapter 4. Because a college degree is your most important educational credential to date, it should be listed at the top of your resume as follows:

B.S. in Psychology, University of San Francisco, 1999

You can also list your GPA and number of semesters on the Dean's List, and note that you graduated magna cum laude.

Because many employers now look for multifaceted graduates, be sure to note a strong minor or a certificate in a given subject area. This approach is especially appropriate if your major field is not in great demand.

Continuing education classes in computer skills, foreign languages or other subjects that enhance your marketability also serve a useful purpose on your resume. Don't neglect to include study-abroad programs, extensive travel and other mind-expanding experiences. Most employers view these as bona fide educational background, even if you didn't receive credit for them.

Honors and Awards

Be sure to mention if you were chosen for *Who's Who in Colleges and Universities,* Mortarboard, Phi Beta Kappa or Speechmaker of the Year, or earned other kudos based on your activities or academics.

Personal or Other Facts

Finally, at the bottom of your resume, mention hobbies that aren't related to your job objective, and any other personal data a potential employer might find useful. But don't include your age, weight, health or other personal facts that frankly are none of his business.

References

You probably have been advised about the importance of having good references to provide potential employers. To be sure, it's wise to have a list of people who'll say wonderful things about you. However, it's not wise to include them on your resume.

Unless you've volunteered or worked with a well-known, admired person, you'll just be wasting resume space by listing references' names, addresses and phone numbers. The same is true for the phrase, "References Available upon Request," since prospective employers assume you'll provide them with the names of instructors, advisers, managers, fellow volunteers and other reliable sources that they can call about your abilities.

As you work on your resume, call favorite professors and other advocates to ascertain if they'll give you a good recommendation. Be sure to double-check their addresses and phone numbers and the correct spelling of their names. Then, list them on a separate sheet to give to employers who request references.

By the way, if an employer bothers to ask for references, you're a leading candidate for the position. After giving the employer the list, alert each reference that they may receive a call and explain any issues that are likely to be mentioned. This way, your advocates will be primed to spotlight your skills, personality traits and relevant activities when the employer calls.

Before-and-After Resume

Kathleen Dolan

Each month, the *National Business Employment Weekly* publishes a feature called, "Can This Resume Be Saved?" The example on pages 188–190 is a great before-and-after example from a recent edition that shows how too much humility can be harmful to your career:

> Humility is a virtue, but too much of it can hinder a job search. I've never been comfortable selling myself and when I began job hunting after completing an MBA at an international business school, I simply added my new degree and recent activities to my old resume. This version focused on my pre-MBA experience, and because I wanted full-time work, I continued to send it to employers after I started a contract consulting position in Chicago.
>
> Although this document helped me land interviews, the jobs I was offered were more appropriate for undergraduates. Neither their responsibilities nor their compensation matched my talent and experience.
>
> After discussing my situation with friends and family, I decided that modesty—reflected in a resume that didn't portray my full range of experience—was holding back my job search.
>
> To overcome this situation, I reviewed my past and current experiences with a fellow MBA grad, then used this information to structure a new resume. I emphasized my professional accomplishments in a summary at the top of the page and added my international consulting work and my activities with the international MBA "Case Competition"—key experiences that I barely mentioned in my old resume.

The reaction to my revised resume has been phenomenal. Because its content is more descriptive and targets the fields I want to work in, I'm being invited to interview for more suitable positions at higher compensation levels. Being more comfortable touting my accomplishments is paying off. I only wish that my newfound assertiveness had come earlier.

A Success Story

Amber Frantz Blaha

Amber wrote the resume on pages 191 and 192 as a sales tool to help her land a meaty summer job that would pay better than McDonald's and offer impressive resume credentials after she graduated from Northwestern. Because she knows her alma mater has an excellent reputation in the business community, she put her education at the top. She also listed her major, minor and various certificates, which show her commitment to being a well-rounded student. Amber is deservedly proud of her high school and college grades, so she has included her GPAs as well.

Her internship with the Greater Dallas Chamber was unpaid, but she received credit from her high school for the assignment. Because this program is highly competitive, interns generally participate in meaningful projects that are impressive when listed on their resumes. As you can see, this is true in Amber's case.

The numerous activities she participated in and awards she won round out her story.

With this initial resume and some strategic networking, Amber secured summer employment at Cyrix, a fast-growing company that designs microprocessors. As a personnel generalist for two summers, she handled a variety of projects, including an employee handbook, human resources database, new-hire orientation program and an information and referral system.

During the spring of her senior year at Northwestern, Amber started seeking full-time employment. Her updated resume starts on page 193. Notice how it compares with her first version. Also note how her work at Cyrix serves as an important anchor for her credentials and experience in human resources.

A colleague at Cyrix gave Amber's resume to her husband, who was with Ernst & Young. Due to her excellent internship experience with Cyrix, outstanding college record and a personal referral, she was hired as a staff consultant in Ernst & Young's Management Consulting Practice.

After two fast-paced years in consulting, Amber got married and started her MBA at Yale. Her third (one-page) resume (page 195) is the one she now uses as she looks for her next career opportunity.

BEFORE

DOLAN, Kathleen Annette
1214 Green lane
St. Louis, MO 63146
(314) 555-0616
mary1land2@aol.com

EDUCATION

1995–1997   IESE, INTERNATIONAL GRADUATE SCHOOL OF MANAGEMENT BARCELONA, SPAIN
Bilingual Master of Business Administration (M.B.A.)
International Finance, Commercial Marketing

1988–1992   SAINT LOUIS UNIVERSITY   ST LOUIS, U.S.A.
Bachelor of Arts, Communication
Magna Cum Laude
Area of Concentration: Journalism

EXPERIENCE

Sep. 94–Jul. 95   TODAY'S TEMPORARY   ST. LOUIS, U.S.A.
Long-term assignments in the following destinations:
Boatmen's Bank of Greater St. Louis-Personal Computer/Telephone Banking Division.
Assisted customers in opening PC or TB accounts for paying bills, transferring between
accounts and general account access. Also responsible for conflict resolution when
customers had problems accessing the system.

Hermann Marketing—One of the top companies in the U.S. in the distribution of
promotional materials. Bilingual customer service representative. Also responsible for
telemarketing and checking client design fits.

Simmonds Healthcare—Administrative assistant in architectural firm. Projects
included the collection and reporting of relevant data for planning purposes in regard
to possible projects in the state of Florida (i.e., medical personnel per capita, etc.).

May 93–Aug. 91   KASCO CORPORATION   ST. LOUIS, U.S.A.
Sales/Service Representative
Duties included heavy customer relations work, order entry, sales support, Spanish to
English translation, and preparation of export papers. Responsible for developing and
implementing a system to keep track of all backorders (both products manufactured
in-house as well as bought outside) and releases to customers or salesmen as the
products became available.

LANGUAGES

English - Native Language   Spanish - Fluent

GENERAL INFORMATION

Superior background in IBM and Macintosh personal computers with emphasis in software packages such
as Windows '95 (including PowerPoint, Excel and Word), Harvard Graphics and various company-specific
systems. Director of Publicity for the 1997 International M.B.A. Case Competition. Lead reporter for the
"University News" paper, responsible for one front-page article biweekly. Third-place award for in-depth
reporting (1992) from the Missouri College Newspaper Association.

AFTER

DOLAN, Kathleen Annette

1214 Green Lane
St. Louis, MO 63146
(314) 555-0616
maryland2@aol.com

SUMMARY OF QUALIFICATIONS

- **TRAINING AND DEVELOPMENT** experience demonstrates aptitude for identifying and assessing needs: customizing and designing appropriate training methods; research; writing facilitators' scripts; developing case studies for interactive learning and initiating total organizational development program.

- Professional experience in **PERFORMANCE CONSULTING** demonstrates excellent analytical skills as well as outstanding organizational ability. Superior communication skills and adaptability to cross-cultural environments; results-driven analysis of export departments, management structures, corporate communication, customer service and financial forecasts on an international level.

- Experience is supported by various academic achievements including a **Master of Business Administration** degree from a top-10 international business program, with an emphasis on **international management** gaining hands-on experience in strategic planning, international business practices and marketing communication.

PROFESSIONAL ABILITIES

Public Relations	Project Management	Trade Development
International Media Relations	Financial Planning	Project Proposals
Corporate Sponsorship	Budget Development	Strategic Planning
Event Coordinator	Market Research	Cross-Cultural Liaison
Team Management	Corporate Communication	Public Speaking
Training Program Design	International Marketing	Organizational Development

Computer Skills: Word, Excel, PowerPoint, Lotus 1-2-3, Harvard Graphics, Pagemaker, Adobe Photoshop, Frontpage; various Internet, intranet, database and statistical analysis software.

Other Relevant Skills: Fluent in Spanish. Results-driven, interactive management style.

EXPERIENCE

Training Program Development Consultant. Moran Consulting, Chicago, IL (present). Contracted to design and script an organization-wide service excellence program with separate packages for employee, middle manager and senior executive levels. Built-in areas of program for customization according to needs and industry. Product approved and purchased.

DOLAN, Kathleen Annette   Page 2

Consultant, Opel. Barcelona, Spain (1997). Key member of three-person team which analyzed the effectiveness of the implementation of a customer loyalty program on the corporate, distributor and customer levels. Identified problematic areas and proposed solutions to senior management.

Co-Coordinator, International M.B.A. Case Competition. IESE, Barcelona, Spain (1997). Part of a two-member leadership team that coordinated all planning, execution and follow-up involved in this high-profile event. Key in soliciting corporate sponsorship and international media contacts and acting as administrative liaison. Also involved in schedule development, banquet planning and general spokesperson activities.

Consultant, Bodegas Roqueta, Manresa, Spain (1996). In-depth analysis of export department and managerial structures presented to president. Focused on performance evaluation and proposed initiatives to meet forecasted sales goals.

Temporary Contract Worker, Today's Temporary, St. Louis, MO (1994–1995)

Sales/Service Representative, KASCO Corporation, St. Louis, MO (1993–1994)

Executive English Tutor, Madrid, Spain (1993)

EDUCATION AND ACADEMIC ACHIEVEMENTS

M.B.A.	Master of Business Administration	IESE International School of Management, Barcelona, Spain
B.A.	Bachelor of Arts in Communication	Saint Louis University
Certificate	Spanish	Saint Louis University

- Magna Cum Laude, Saint Louis University (1992)
- Offered teaching assistantship in M.B.A. program, Saint Louis University (1995)
- Missouri College Newspaper Association, third-place award for In-Depth Reporting (1992)
- Offered research assistantship position at master's level, Saint Louis University (1992)
- Dean's List, Saint Louis University (1990–1992)
- Missouri "Bright Flight" Scholarship, Saint Louis University (1988–1992)
- John Danforth "I Dare You" Leadership Award, Clayton High School (1988)

Amber Frantz
7646 Mustang Drive
Farmers Branch, TX 75253
214-139-1162

Education

Sophomore, Northwestern University
Communications major with political science concentration/business
institutions and leadership certificates
GPA: 3.58

Advanced honors graduate of J.J. Pearce High School, 14 in a class of
530, 95.7 GPA.

Experience

*Intern-Leadership Development Department, Greater Dallas Chamber of
Commerce, January 1991–May 1991*

- Revised and promoted the Leadership Appointment Program that
  matches community leaders with nonprofit boards.

  - Designed a survey to get input from nonprofit organizations.

  - Developed and implemented a direct-mail campaign.

  - Reformatted system to incorporate results of the survey.

- Attended meetings of the Dallas Alliance.

- Represented the Chamber at a Texas Research League meeting for
  school finance.

- Revised database for the Leadership Dallas Alumni Yearbook.

- Confirmed speakers for Leadership Dallas and Opportunity Dallas.

Sales Associate at Jay Jacobs, July 1991–September 1991, December 1991

Interim Office Manager, Dimensions Associates, Summers of 1987–1989

- Answered phones, made weekly deposits, typed newspaper columns,
  put together newsletter bulk mail, put together seminar workbooks,
  collated data from 1,000 surveys on single lifestyle issues, scheduled
  client appointments, promoted workshops.

Familiar with WordPerfect, Microsoft Word, PFS Write and Deskmate
Plus on IBM personal computers; and Microsoft Word on the Macintosh.

Amber Frantz   **Page 2**

Activities

Northwestern University

- Shepard Dorm First Floor Representative.
- Literacy Tutor for Adults.
- Pledge Class President, Delta Zeta.

J.J. Pearce High School

- Selected as one of 12 Richardson Independent School District students to participate in a cultural exchange with students from Oyama, Japan, via live teleconference sponsored by Fujitsu America.
- Chosen to represent Pearce High School at monthly meetings with school district administrators to discuss issues such as racial tensions and school finance.
- Served as Student Council officer.
- Elected Students Against Drunk Driving president.
- Played on school volleyball team, six years.
- Other activities include Pre-law Club, Interact Service Club and the Pearce Literary Magazine.

Honors

National Merit Finalist
Who's Who at J.J. Pearce
Who's Who of American High School Students
Raider Award (leadership, citizenship, excellence in academics and athletics)
National Honor Society
Spanish Honor Society

Amber L. Frantz
717 University Place
Evanston, Illinois 60201
(708) 328-3037
E-mail: alfrantz@northwestern.edu

Education:

    Northwestern University, Evanston, Ill.

    Graduating June 1995 with a B.S. in Communications Studies, Business
        Institutions minor, Political Science concentration

    Communications Department Honors Thesis Program, Leadership
        Program   Major GPA: 4.00/4.00   Cumulative GPA: 3.80/4.00

Experience:

**Intern—Human Resources Department, Cyrix Corp., Dallas, Texas
Two summers**

- Developed several documents for employee orientation: a summary of company benefits, a revised employee handbook, a services directory, and an introduction to Cyrix Corp.
- Researched and wrote company policies regarding tuition reimbursement, smoking and drug abuse
- Acted as central coordinator for Cyrix's internship program
- Researched and selected software, and developed a human resources database to track information about company employees at six office locations in the U.S., Pacific Rim and Europe. Wrote a detailed procedure manual for department managers working with this database
- Worked extensively with both the stock and 401K loan administration software packages. Piloted both programs. Trained HR colleagues on their use

Intern, Career Dimensions, Dallas, Texas   One summer

- Conducted research for *The Wall Street Journal's National Business Employment Weekly: Cover Letters*, a book to be published by John Wiley & Sons
- Brainstormed and compiled list of marketing targets for *The Wall Street Journal's National Business Employment Weekly: Resumes*, the first in a series of career books published by John Wiley & Sons

**Intern, Independent Distributors Association, Dallas, Texas
One Summer**

- Completely rewrote 1981 employee policy manual and created an I.D.A. policies and procedures manual
- Drafted a hotel contract for the Association's 1996 annual convention

- Researched, compiled and summarized information on the past 10 Association conventions to facilitate planning future conventions. Coded and analyzed a member survey regarding aspects of the convention.
- Wrote Board of Director's candidate profiles for publication in the Association's newsletter
- Confirmed speakers and worked with Association members regarding upcoming Convention events.

Intern, Leadership Development Department, Greater Dallas Chamber of Commerce, Dallas, Texas   Six months
- Revised and promoted the leadership Appointment Program which matches 400 community leaders with nonprofit boards
- Represented the Chamber at a Texas Research League meeting for school finance reform
- Confirmed speakers for Leadership Dallas and Opportunity Dallas programs

Computer Skills:

Experienced with Microsoft Word, WordPerfect, Excel, Pagemaker, PFS Write and Deskmate. Literate on both IBM and Macintosh personal computers

Activities:

Dean's Advisory Council, Northwestern University's School of Speech
Delta Zeta International Sorority: President, 1994–1995, Academics Chairperson, 1993–1994, Homecoming Chairperson, 1993–1994
Wildcat Council: fundraising, coordinating with alumni, sponsors of New Student Week for incoming freshmen, spirit organization for students
Northwestern University tour guide
Texas Scottish Rite Hospital for Children volunteer
Adult Literacy tutor

Honors:

Department scholarship for academic excellence in Communications Studies 1993–1994
Dean's List
Zeta Phi Eta Communications Honors Society
Phi Eta Sigma Honors Society
Order of Omega Greek Honors Society
President of the Year for Northwestern Panhellenic and Delta Zeta Region 1995

Amber F. Blaha
11 Sand Beach Ave.
Derby, CT 20027
203-457-8892
Email: ablaha@yale.edu

Education

Yale School of Management *New Haven, Connecticut*
- Candidate for Master's degree in Public and Private Management (MPPM), 1999.

Northwestern University *Evanston, Illinois*
- Bachelor of Science in Communication Studies, 1995.
- Business Institutions minor, Political Science concentration.
- Leadership Program certificate.

Experience
1995–1997

Ernst & Young LLP *Dallas, Texas*
Consultant, Management Consulting
- Served on a four-member team that conducted an operational review of a benefits administration firm. Evaluated hiring, training, and performance incentives, as well as quality assurance programs and performance guarantees.
- As one of four team members, worked on a change management project for a large, multinational, Mexico-based company. Assisted with facilitation of visioning sessions for three departments, identifying their current state, desired future state, and ways to move toward the future.
- Performed benchmarking studies for call center operations, employee training, incentive systems, and stock option grants.
- Conducted a current state assessment of internal call center communications for a large telecommunications company. Co-designed a future-state communications structure.
- Co-developed and delivered a three-day training session for 25 professionals on change management, teamwork, reframing, and consulting skills.
- Assessed current employee competencies and co-designed a plan that would develop and link existing and newly identified competencies with the client's future business goals.
- Conducted one-on-one interviews with the company's Directors of Operations for divisions in the United States and Spain. Gathered information about the current state and elicited ideas for potential improvement.
- Interacted closely with clients in the health care, manufacturing, retail, telecommunications, education, and nonprofit industries. Also consulted with companies in insurance, real estate, and high technology.

Activities

- Consultant for an Outreach Management Consulting project through Yale School of Management.
- Member of the Consulting and Marketing Student Interest Groups at Yale School of Management.
- Facilitator of information sessions for prospective Yale School of Management students.

Honors

- Dean's Advisory Council, Northwestern University's School of Speech, 1994–1995.
- Outstanding Sorority President Award, Northwestern University, 1995.
- Outstanding President Award, Northern Illinois Province, Delta Zeta Sorority, 1995.

Other Good Resumes

Pages 197–200 provide some other excellent resumes from beginning professionals around the country.

Jiang Ti

Although Jiang Ti grew up in China, his ability to write a highly readable resume in English is commendable, especially for a technical person. Other "techies" take note!

Virginia Kaufman

Virginia Kaufman had been a nurse for a number of years when she decided to return to school for her degree in Drug and Alcohol Counseling. After completing her degree, she needed to find an internship in her field to accumulate hours toward her certification. To draw attention to her drug and rehab background, she put her two school internships at the top of her resume, then mentioned her industrial nursing position toward the bottom. She also tailored her plant nurse experience to highlight activities that were similar to those of a rehab counselor.

Alexandra N. Smith

After graduating from Oklahoma State, Alexandra Smith needed a resume to apply for full-time positions and to include with her law-school applications. Her completed resume combines her personal, professional and academic accomplishments into a solid package—and it paid off. She was hired as a staff member of a large state political organization and accepted by all six law schools where she applied.

Jiang Ti
1155 Dennison Dr., #52
Plano, TX 75084
(972) 555-4343
jiangti@ut.edu

OBJECTIVE   Seeking a CO-OP position related to software, test, or network engineering

EDUCATION   **UNIVERSITY OF TEXAS AT DALLAS** Richardson, TX
M.S. in Computer Science 12/98, Overall GPA: 3.86

TEXAS A&M UNIVERSITY College Station, TX
PH.D. Candidate in Physics 1/92–7/97, Overall GPA: 3.90, Completed 27 hours of computer course work. GPA for computer courses: 3.80

SICHUAN UNIVERSITY Chendu, China
B.S. in Physics 7/87, Overall GPA: 3.78

COMPUTER SKILLS
- Language: C, C++, SQL, HTML, Java, Visual Basic, FORTRAN, Pascal, Smalltalk, Objective C
- Platform: Unix, Windows 95, Windows NT, Windows 3.x
- Network: TCP/IP, Sockets, **ATM,** Internet, **SONET, SS7,** Token Ring, Ethernet, Frame Relay, X.25, **PCS**
- Excellent analytical, problem-solving, communication, and documentation skills

PROJECTS
- Telecommunication Networks Project: Implemented a Centralized Telecommunication Networks Design Tool using **C** language on **UNIX** platform. Three fast algorithms were employed for multipoint line topology, terminal assignment, and concentrator locations respectively.
- Performance of Computer System and Network Project: Simulated the performance evaluation of an open Markovian queueing network and a discrete time queueing system. Expected number in the entire system, average service time, waiting time, and response time were analyzed.
- Telecommunication Software Design Project: Developed a distributed system to simulate the communication between Base Station Control (BSC) and Mobile Station (MS) with Frequency List encoding and decoding algorithms. Processes were running as concurrent servers in multi-computer environment through network. C, TCP/IP protocols and Berkeley Sockets were used in the implementation.
- Software Engineering Project: Developed a software tool with a graphical user interface designed to calculate the cost and duration of a software development project. The tool is written in MS Visual Basic 3.0 on Windows 3.x. MS Access was also employed as the database back-end.
- Computer Network Project: Designed and implemented a client/server based remote printing utility program in a distributed environment. The utility was developed by using Berkeley Sockets and TCP/IP protocols.

JIANG TI   **PAGE 2**

- Computer Architecture Project: Designed a small computer with single-bus architecture to implement the PDP-8 instructions by using Galaxy **CAD** on **UNIX** platform. The math coprocessor of the system was implemented using assembly language.
- Relational Database Design Project: Implemented a relational banking database in Oracle environment either as interactive **SQL** or as embedded **SQL** in **C.**

EXPERIENCE   **R. WELSH INSTITUTE, TEXAS CENTRAL UNIVERSITY**
2/94–7/97   College Station, TX
                 Welch Foundation Research Assistant
- Conducted scientific simulation, numerical calculations, and data analysis with **C, FORTRAN** on **UNIX** and **VMS.** Developed and modified several software systems (**TRANSPORT, GEMINI** and **EUGENE**) to simulate complex nuclear detector systems and sophisticated nuclear reaction mechanisms. Mote carol methods were used extensively in these software systems to implement the statistical events.
- Designed and implemented a distributed computing model for executing multiple copies of **GEMINI** in a heterogeneous computer environment. The distributed model allows user to utilize several computers simultaneously in a synchronized manner. The model is implemented by using the **TCP/IP** stack (Multinet package) in the **VMS** and Open**VMS**, and **DEC** Ultrix systems.

1/92–1/94   **PHYSICS DEPARTMENT, TEXAS CENTRAL UNIVERSITY**
                 College Station, TX
                 Teaching Assistant
- Participated in research activities in the Welsh Institute of the university. Conducted several scientific simulation with statistical models and data analysis. Most programming tasks were performed on **VAX** and **DEC Ultrix** using **C** and **FORTRAN.**
- Taught physics laboratory classes.

8/87–1/91   **LEE ELECTRICAL OPTICAL INC.**
                 Beijing, China
                 Associate Engineer
- Contributed to the establishment of the first PC laboratory of the corporation. Participated in the planning and purchasing of software and hardware for the lab.
- Developed a program written in Turbo Pascal to investigate energy efficiency of different industrial light sources. Parameters determined by the program were tested in light source prototype.

HONORS   - Robert Welch Foundation Fellowship Award, Texas Central
& AWARDS   University: Summer 1992 & 1993, February 1994–August 1995.

AVAILABILITY September 1998

Virginia Kaufman
P.O. Box 4973
Oklahoma City, OK 73860
405-123-9876
E-mail: v.kaufman@worldstd.com

Objective:

Internship in a chemical dependency rehabilitation facility.

Experience:

Internship   Oklahoma Regional Rehabilitation Center   1998

- Facilitated five therapy groups dealing with chemical dependency and emotional issues, observed by supervisor. Patients included primarily teen and young adult abusers.
- Counseled with four patients on an individual basis, observed by supervisor.
- Wrote and discussed summaries on group and individual sessions with supervisor.
- Presented lectures to patients on: Loss and Grief; Progression and Recovery of the Alcoholic; Adult Children's Life Scripts; Steps to Maturity; Stress, What Is It?; The Recovery Tree; Anger, Guilt and Shame.
- Counseled with families to help them understand what is happening with their hospitalized member, being careful to maintain confidentiality as needed.
- Admitted patients by obtaining their verbal histories and filling out the required paperwork.
- Represented patients in dealing with health and Medicare insurance companies to obtain treatment approval.

Internship   Dallas VA Hospital   1998

- Facilitated patient group therapy, including Vietnam veterans with cocaine and barbiturate abuse, without supervision. Discussed patient emotions and progress with two supervisors.
- Attended Board meetings with hospital executives to discuss patient cases and determine appropriate courses of action.

Industrial Nurse   Dennison Electric Corporation   1987–1997

- Facilitated preemployment and random drug testing to include documentation of results.
- Followed up for Employee Assistance Program through TRRC exit interviews upon completion of counseling before returning to work.
- Completed paperwork required to enroll new employees. Counseled employees regarding rights and standard procedures for proper utilization of insurance plan. Responsible for all computer data associated with employee insurance records.
- Prepared charts from physicians' orders and documented in-house follow-up treatment.
- Facilitated all referrals by physician to outside sources and documented treatment.
- Taught over fifty classes on health and safety issues.
- Handled health emergencies for the plant in first and second shifts. Documented appropriate paperwork.

Licensed Practical Nurse   Bristol Memorial Hospital   1979–1987

- Assignments included Surgery, Emergency Room, Obstetrics, Cardiac Care Units, to include IV therapy, Oral and IM medication and CPR. Read and worked up orders for physicians.
- Trained staff on HIV symptoms and safeguards.
- Instructed patients on proper use of medication, exercise therapy, diet, hygiene, insulin and respiratory therapies.

Education:

Associate Degree, Drug & Alcohol Counseling
Grayson County Junior College, Denison, Texas   1998
Diploma, Licensed Practical Nursing
Drumright Vocational Technical School, Drumright, Oklahoma   1974
Passed Licensed Practical Nursing exam with reciprocity

ALEXANDRA N. SMITH

Current Address
1621 Oakwood Drive #2B
Oklahoma City, OK 87741
(220) 721-2680

Permanent Address
934 Winding Creek Road
Prairie, OK 84411
(780) 980-1234

PERSONAL PROFILE:

Talented and dedicated professional with a strong record of academic and hands-on work performance. Combines creativity and resourcefulness with excellent research, analytical and organizational qualifications. Outstanding interpersonal communications skills. PC proficient with leading word processing, spreadsheet, database and Internet applications.

EDUCATION:

B.A. in Political Science   OKLAHOMA STATE UNIVERSITY   May 1998
Honors College; Theodore Roosevelt Presidential Scholarship; 3.86 GPA

Leadership Activities & Memberships:
Representative, Senate for Presidency Leadership Conference, 1998
Philanthropy Chair, Phi Delta Theta Sorority, 1996
Member, Pi Sigma Alpha Political Science Honor Society, 1994 to 1998
Member, Gamma Beta Phi Honor Society, 1994 to 1998

Advanced Honors Graduate   PRAIRIE HIGH SCHOOL   1994
Three-Year Graduate; Top 10% of Class

Graduate   DALE CARNEGIE   1993
Graduate of Effective Speaking & Communications course; Won several speaking awards

PROFESSIONAL EXPERIENCE:

Financial Assistant/Intern   REPUBLICAN PARTY OF OKLAHOMA   1998 to Present
Manage financial affairs in conjunction with numerous special projects and fund-raising campaigns for political figures throughout the state of Arkansas. Research, track and analyze contributions and expenses, prepare reports and coordinate distribution of funds. As an intern, collected constituent data, coordinated promotional efforts and conducted opposition research.

Research Assistant   JAMES PHILLIPS III, PHD   1997 to Present
Selected to assist in multimedia research of the social, economic and political environment in Angola, Africa. Collected, disseminated and presented information to professor of political science. Research provided basis for article published in *The Washington Times*, and will subsequently be used for publication of a book on Angola.

Legal Assistant   WALTER D. SMITH, ATTORNEY AT LAW   1994 to 1995
Multifaceted administrative position in this private law practice specializing in criminal defense, child custody and civil law. Scope of responsibility included scheduling of docket calendar. Worked in cooperation with office personnel to manage all scheduling, correspondence, filing and client management functions. Gained broad business and legal practice management experience.

COMMUNITY ACTIVITIES:

Volunteer, Boys & Girls Club of Oklahoma
Volunteer, Brentwood Homeless Shelter (Most Dedicated Volunteer, 1992)

"Try not to be discouraged . . . not everyone can write their
complete autobiography on a single sheet of paper."

10

Resumes for Women Returning to the Paid Workforce

One of the most important concepts for women returning to the workforce to remember is that their years of experience count for something in the paid work world. Such activities include the following:

☆ Doing volunteer work.
☆ Juggling schedules.
☆ Counseling friends and family members.
☆ Giving birthday and dinner parties.
☆ Averting and resolving crises.

☆   Making important buying decisions.

☆   Mediating disputes.

☆   Planning family vacations.

☆   Advocating and supporting causes.

☆   Developing and stretching budgets.

☆   Solving problems creatively.

☆   Redecorating houses.

☆   Coordinating thousand-mile relocations.

☆   Running an information and referral network.

☆   Challenging, shaping and nurturing young minds.

☆   Maintaining a sense of humor when everyone else is preaching doom and gloom.

While such women may not be as marketable as professionals who haven't interrupted their careers to focus on family responsibilities, they certainly have more to offer than someone right out of school. Life experience alone gives these women a host of opportunities to deal with situations not yet encountered by career neophytes.

Unfortunately, in determining their worth to the business world, reentry women may be their own greatest detractors. Unless a homemaker believes she should be compensated for her work, it will be hard to convince her that anyone else will pay her for it. After all, no one has offered her any money for her efforts to date. How can she logically assume she's now a valuable commodity just because she decided to return to the workforce? Changing this mind-set represents at least 50 percent of the process of transforming a homemaker into a paid professional. If she recognizes her worth, other people will, too. If she continues to think work is its own reward, or that she has few skills an employer would need or want, others will tend to agree with her. Her assumption becomes her reality!

If you are a homemaker having difficulty believing you have marketable achievements, go back to Chapter 2 and rate yourself against the skills inventory. This exercise is designed to help job seekers use both their paid and nonpaid experiences as raw material for their resumes. As noted in both Chapters 2 and 9, experience is valuable regardless of whether it commands a fee. You may be surprised by the number and variety of things you have done that require an abundance of transferable skills. People in other settings get paid for using those skills. Why shouldn't you?

To facilitate the transformation of nonpaid accomplishments into an effective resume, let's look at some typical areas of your life where applicable achievements abound.

Volunteer Experience

Through Renee Raglan's community involvement as a volunteer on numerous boards and committees, she developed a reputation as someone you could count on to get the job done. After she and her husband divorced, Renee decided to enter the paid workforce.

Just as she was ready to launch her own event-planning business, she received a frantic call from a friend who was on the city's World Cup Welcoming Committee. The World Cup was coming to town in six months and the volunteer troops needed an interim executive director to pull things together quickly. True to her history of service, Renee agreed to temporarily put aside her business and step into the breach.

After the World Cup was over, Renee got another invitation to join the staff of an independent nonprofit group charged with planning and advocating a thirty-year vision for the city. She's still there today.

Why did the World Cup Committee choose Renee for their highly visible PR and management position? Why was she selected over many other qualified people to play a pivotal role in charting a city's long-range future? Her outstanding volunteer work and its resulting contacts.

Patti Clapp is vice president of education and governmental affairs for her city's Chamber of Commerce. Before joining the chamber, Patti hadn't held a paid job for a number of years. What convinced a group of high-profile business leaders to hire her instead of one of the many other qualified candidates who applied? Her volunteer leadership in her children's school district and with various other nonprofit organizations that seek to enhance opportunities for women and children in the community.

While your volunteer background may not qualify you to be a VP, it can be an excellent source of relevant experience for your resume. The following are a few examples of volunteer achievements that are transferable to many paid positions:

☆ Serving as an officer or committee chair for your local PTA.

☆ Chairing the social or governmental affairs committee of your homeowners' association.

☆ Coordinating the fund-raising bazaar for your church.

☆ Being a Big Sister to a troubled or disadvantaged youth.

☆ Teaching an adult to read.

☆ Organizing a local campaign to put a park in your neighborhood or a stoplight at a busy intersection.

☆ Designing and producing your club newsletter.

☆ Working with the senior class to plan an all-night event after graduation.

☆ Planning the monthly programs for your sorority alumnae club.

☆ Writing and gathering names for a petition to start a high school softball program for girls.

☆ Working on a political campaign.

☆ Doing crisis counseling for a mental-health hot line.

☆ Serving on a task force to fulfill site-based management requirements
for your child's school.

The list of possibilities is endless. The point is that you deserve credit for
the bona fide work you have done for your child's school, community, favorite social service agency, church, fraternal or social organization, volunteer league or
alumni association.

Hobbies

Hobbies are another source of experience to include on your resume, especially if
they are related to your job objective. For instance, if you have become a semi-
professional flower arranger, mention this when you apply for a job in a flower
shop. If you love to give dinner parties and help friends plan their children's
weddings or graduation celebrations, you could be a very valuable addition to a
catering or event-planning firm.

Hobbies increase your knowledge of a specific subject. They give you on-the-
job training and a level of expertise in areas that relatively few people may possess. Consider Debbie Fields of Mrs. Field's cookies. She turned her recipe for
chocolate chip cookies into a multimillion-dollar enterprise.

Just as you did with your volunteer experience, examine your hobbies carefully to extract the skills that apply to your new profession. Whether you have
been paid to use them isn't nearly as important as how well you sell them on
paper and in person.

Hobbies are incredibly diverse, but here's a short list of activities that many
homemakers have turned into paid careers:

☆ Cooking.

☆ Interior design.

☆ Party planning.

- ☆ Organizing closets, work spaces or kitchen cabinets.
- ☆ Making clothes for adults, children and even pets.
- ☆ Planning vacations.
- ☆ Reading.
- ☆ Collecting cookbooks, antiques, depression glass, etc.
- ☆ Exercising.
- ☆ Gardening.
- ☆ Writing articles, stories or books.
- ☆ Breeding purebred animals.

Do some brainstorming about how your hobbies might relate to your work. You may be surprised at some of the correlations.

Previous Paid Experience

Think about paid work you may have done before you decided to become a full-time homemaker. Teaching is a good example of a career in which the basic skills haven't changed substantially over the years. While you may want to take a few courses to brush up on some new learning techniques, the process of imparting knowledge to young minds isn't radically different than it was 10 years ago. If you were a good teacher then, you're likely to be a good teacher now.

To give yourself maximum credit for skills that continue to be relevant after a number of years, use a functional resume format instead of a chronological one. Attaching dates to job titles automatically prioritizes them because it's assumed that recent experience is more important than more dated credentials. The assumption that expertise decreases with time makes sense if you are dealing with such highly technical subjects as computer programming, electrical engineering or heart surgery. But it doesn't hold true with all careers. For instance, customer service skills haven't changed much either. No doubt the follow-up techniques you used 15 years ago will work just as well today, except you will probably rely on a computer instead of a *Day-Timer* to generate your tickler file. Hence, you should list your relevant skills without attaching dates to them.

After experience, education will probably be the next most important resume category. Use the Education section in Chapter 4 as your guide. If you have taken some catchup courses or boast a newly minted degree that's relevant to your job objective, give your academic background a prominent place on your resume. Fresh credentials are always a powerful selling point.

Success Stories

Pages 209–212 contain two excellent examples of resumes submitted by women who successfully returned to the paid workforce.

Linda Reed Chennell

After caring for an Alzheimer patient for several years, Linda decided to pursue a career where she could travel around the world and still have time for her estate liquidating business. Notice how she used past paid and unpaid experience in her resume to highlight activities similar to those of a flight attendant.

Today she is a flight attendant for American Trans Air, a well-established vacation charter airline. She also continues to run a thriving business in estate liquidation.

Paige Louise Minsky

Paige Minsky was the consummate professional volunteer, holding several leadership roles in community organizations. Of all the projects she spearheaded, she particularly enjoyed those that involved the welfare of children. As her own children grew older, she decided to seek a paid position that would use her expertise and contacts developed during 12 years of nonprofit service.

One of the organizations she applied to was the Anti-Defamation League. When it realized that a professional with an extensive background in diversity issues was available, it quickly hired Paige to manage a new "A World of Difference" program, which teaches children the intrinsic benefits of our country's blend of cultures.

Now Paige is ready to take her message on diversity to corporations. She is using the following resume to sell herself to business executives. Notice how she combines her paid and unpaid experience to illustrate the depth of her expertise.

Other Good Resumes

Several good resumes have been reproduced on pages 213–215.

Linda Reed Chennell
1224 Princeton Lane
Westchester, PA 19065
610-324-5776
E-mail: lchennell@arols.com

Objective
A flight attendant for a fun or charter airline.

Applicable Experience

Part-time positions held simultaneously:

Linda Reed Chennell, Estate Liquidator   Philadelphia, PA   1993–Present

Own and operate an estate liquidation business that requires:

- Walking a fine line between client and buyer interests to get the most satisfaction and a fair price for both parties.
- Being sensitive in dealing with family heirlooms and memorabilia.
- Projecting a positive and congenial manner with individuals who may be argumentative and unreasonable.
- Flexibility in meeting deadlines established by realtor and family needs.

Caregiver for Alzheimer Patient   Wayne, PA   1994–1996

- Developed a trusting relationship with an initially paranoid and angry patient.
- Gradually assumed a variety of tasks as the caregiver including conversing with a non-lucid woman, bathing her, cooking meals, mending clothes and running errands.

Funeral Reception Coordinator   Philadelphia, PA   1995–1996
Our Redeemer Lutheran Church

Coordinate luncheons for families of deceased church members.

- Collaborate with family members to schedule the event, determine the number attending and the type of food required.
- Supervise volunteers in buying, preparing and serving the meal.

Registrar Northeast Swap Meet   The Meadowlands   1995–1996

Handle pre and post registration, sales and assignment of 4,000 + parking spaces with overall sales of $100K+. Customer satisfaction is the ultimate objective.

Linda Reed Chennell   Page 2

Full-time positions:

Started as an operator and moved through the ranks, over the course of 23 years, to eventually become a Specialist in Data Management/Contract Administration with Southwestern Bell and AT&T.

Provided excellent customer service that met or exceeded Public Utility Commission requirements. Emphasized high work standards, safety, attendance, communication, and strong interpersonal skills.

Education

60+ credits in college courses at the University of Alabama, Dallas Baptist University, and the University of Arkansas accumulated over many years of night classes.

Community Work

Boards of Endowment and Evangelism at Our Redeemer Lutheran Church

Member of Board of Directors and Christmas party chairman for the Horseless Carriage Club of America.

Executive Board of Directors, Historian, Photographer, and Yearbook Editor for the Telephone Pioneers.

Under the auspices of the Telephone Pioneers, served with the following organizations:
  Fund Raising for:
    Scottish Rite Hospital, Love for Kids
  Warehouse, inventory and shipping medical supplies to other countries through Medisend.
  Field trips, parties, special events for:
    Special Olympics, Texas Sports Jamboree, Love for Kids
  Race registration, Susan G. Komen Foundation
  Collect and distribute items donated for the Asian community through the East Dallas Store Front.

PAIGE LOUISE MINSKY
17181 Park Hill Drive
San Antonio, TX 78239
512-702-3774
E-mail: plminsky@msn.net

OBJECTIVE

Seeking a challenging and responsible position in Community Relations/Diversity Management in the public or private sector.

PERSONAL QUALIFICATIONS

- Fifteen years of increasing responsibility in nonprofit management in areas of diversity, community education and awareness.
- Expert in volunteer management and recruitment.
- Heavy background in public relations for the public sector.
- Experience in planning and coordinating special events.
- Extensive work in public schools as an educator in special program areas.
- A change agent, comfortable in developing new programs.
- Strong problem-solving skills particularly in identifying options and resources.
- Skilled in communicating with people in a variety of roles from corporate CEOs to teachers and their students.

EMPLOYMENT

Assistant Regional Director   Anti-Defamation League   1995–present

Community Relations Programming

- Staff "A World of Difference" and relate its message to corporate and public sector. This program has been presented to over 2,000 teachers in the metroplex.
- Effectively communicate with the media on a wide range of issues.
- Serve as liaison including meeting with and speaking to community groups such as schools and civic organizations, religious institutions and area businesses.
- Initiate and mentor young leadership group and plan ongoing programs.
- Staff committees including fund-raising, legal affairs and program.
- Develop and maintain relations with volunteer board to promote ADL program.

Fund-raising:

- Organize direct solicitations including planning and executing fund-raising events that gross $400,000 per year.

Paige Louise Minsky   Page Two

Problem Solving
- Troubleshoot for individuals regarding diversity issues.
- Manage information and referral activities.
- Investigate discrimination complaints.

Writing/Editing
- Create and edit newsletters, press releases, speeches, promotional and thank-you letters.
- Write reports documenting organization activities.

SIGNIFICANT COMMUNITY EXPERIENCE

- Vice President for volunteers, Hamilton Park Elementary School (the only magnet school in the Richardson School District)
- Program Co-Chair, Community Board Institute
- Board of Directors, Temple Emanu-El
- Chairman, Celebrations Committee, Temple Emanu-El
- Volunteer Teacher, National Council of Jewish Women, "Hello Israel"
- Recording Secretary, National Council of Jewish Women

EDUCATION

University of Texas at Austin
Bachelor of Arts with double major in Political Science and History

Rebekah A. Taylorson
14 Sawgrass Boulevard
Ponte Vedra, FL 33138
Phone: 305-250-8887
Fax: 305-250-8814
rebekah@mailbag.com

OBJECTIVE   Position in public or community relations, especially in event and/or program planning where project management, volunteer coordination, development and knowledge of community resources would be useful.

APPLICABLE EXPERIENCE

Chaired the March of Dimes campaign for the City of Ponte Vedra, 1992–93. Coordinated neighborhood and local volunteer organizations. Contributions increased 29% over previous year.

Served on the Highland Park United Methodist Church solicitations committee for 1998 Wesley-Rankin Community Center auction. Asked for donations and filled tables. Raised $47,000. (Wesley-Rankin Center does community outreach in Ponte Vedra. It teaches women to be self-sufficient, provides day care, scouting, and sports activities for low-income families.)

Coordinated volunteer efforts as President of the Ponte Vedra County Alumnae Panhellenic to interest young women in attending college and joining a sorority. Planned a fund-raiser that brought in 500% of 1996's proceeds. Organized the annual tea and high school visits to recruit young women and their mothers. Invited to attend many key civic functions in the Ponte Vedra area as a result of this position.

Worked on development activities for the Ronald McDonald House in St. Petersburg, including the Fantasy Forest (an annual holiday train exhibit), yearly fashion shows and a Mardi Gras party.

Active member of First United Methodist Church in Ponte Vedra for the past 10 years, serving in these capacities:

> 1999 Membership Chair. Coordinate volunteers who recruit new members by visitation, marketing and planned church activities. Keep track of current membership data.

Rebekah A. Taylorson   **page 2**

1994–1997 President, Rachel Group (United Methodist Women). Planned and scheduled monthly meetings and served as liaison between the group, UMW and the Church board.

1998 Member, Worship Committee. Coordinated all greeters for weekly services.

1996–1998 Member, Pastor-Parish Relations Committee. Took an active role in this human resources committee, which evaluates and recommends salaries, ministerial placement, congregation/staff relations etc.

OTHER COMMITTEE INVOLVEMENT

Chair, Neighborhood Crime Watch
Delivery Committee, Meals on Wheels
Ponte Vedra County Friends of the Library
Presbyterian Hospital of Ponte Vedra Auxiliary
Ponte Vedra P.T.A.

EMPLOYMENT

Bookkeeper in husband's dental practice for past 10 years.
Loan Processor, Fox and Jacobs Credit Union
Financial Planner, Fox and Jacobs
Senior Payroll Clerk, Enserch Corporation
Teller, St. Petersburg National Bank

EDUCATION

BBA Florida Tech University, 1978

Continuing Education:

Marketing and Practice Management Seminars, with my husband and staff in Banff, Canada; Hilton Head, SC; Phoenix, AZ; and Dallas, TX. These seminars focus on marketing and management skills, self-motivation, financial planning and income analysis. I am very involved in the overall decision making of my husband's dental practice.

Nicole Dorsey

3321 Redbird   Dallas, Texas 75205   214-238-7355
                                                                        nicole_dorsey@city-net.com

OBJECTIVE   Entry-level position in computer programming that provides an opportunity to
                       use my skills and experience and offers a challenging and stimulating
                       environment.

PERSONAL   • Capacity to learn quickly and use newfound knowledge concisely and
QUALIFICATIONS   accurately.
                       • Broad-based understanding of basic business principles and applications.
                       • Facility for talking with people at all organizational levels.
                       • High commitment to getting the job done right.
                       • Delight in new techniques and concepts.

EDUCATION   BS in Math, Computer Science Option, UTA, GPA: 3.57   1998

APPLICABLE   • Created programs to set up and maintain files for database management.
COURSEWORK   • Wrote programs to access various types of sequential and linked list files.
                       • Designed a program to implement a two-pass assembler and direct linking
                         loader.
                       • Developed an interactive program to play "move the mouse through the
                         maze."
                       • Utilized programs to analyze and predict outcomes of statistical models.
                       • Used FORTRAN, PL/I, SAS, Data General Nova, and Assembly languages
                         in conjunction with the IBM 4341, Tektronix, DEC 20, and PDP-11
                         hardware.
                       • Have six credits in general accounting techniques and practices.

EXPERIENCE   Tutor, for high school students in programming, geometry, and algebra,
                          1984 to present
                       Junior League of Dallas, 1988 to present
                          • In charge of inventory, ledgers, sales, money, setting up, dismantling,
                            and redistribution of goods at Senior Citizens' Craft Fair.
                          • Helped design and sew costumes for the annual fund raising ball.

                       General American Oil, 1981–1982
                          Promoted to production clerk.
                          • Maintained oil production ledgers for company's entire output of over
                            200 wells.
                          • Developed graphic reports of production capabilities for designated
                            wells.
                          • Managed records for production reports on both wholly and consortium
                            owned properties.

                       Office "Jack of All Trades" including PBX and telex operator.

PERSONAL   Hobbies include tennis, sewing, and reading.

11

Resumes for Career Changers

While it may seem paradoxical, career changers and homemakers share similar concerns about their marketability. Both worry about their ability to compete with other candidates in their newly chosen fields. Both are afraid they'll have to start at the bottom, as though they were novice job seekers. And both tend to belittle their overall experience while magnifying their lack of knowledge of a particular subject. In assessing their worth to prospective employers, they often give their transferable skills cursory consideration. Even if they award themselves credit for functional skills, they often assume their accomplishments are so unrelated that they can't be used as viable selling points.

Career changers often brood about forsaking their expertise. They contemplate their years of education and experience and feel guilty about wasting the valuable knowledge they have accrued. They worry about their income plunging—

never to regain its previous level. They fret about their identities. And even though they desperately want to, they have difficulty believing family and friends, who say the power, prestige and compensation they derived from their former positions aren't important.

If you're having these feelings, it may comfort you to know that other career changers are experiencing them, too. Unfortunately, knowing that you aren't alone doesn't help you to write a resume.

Points to Ponder

To start a new career, you must decide that tomorrow holds the promise of a fresh and exciting future. You'll need to put aside your former career's persona and concentrate on the skills and achievements from your paid and unpaid experience that relate to your new occupation.

A few years ago, Darryl Canterberry, a professor of anthropology, decided to move from academia to "the real world." To make the transition, he sought help from a career planner, who guided him through a series of exercises to identify his ideal career. After talking to a number of people and conducting library research, Darryl decided he would make an excellent sales or customer service representative for a company expanding into Latin America. He was confident about his decision because he spoke both Spanish and Portuguese, had many contacts in Central and South America, and possessed excellent interpersonal and research skills.

To prepare himself for job interviews, Darryl worked with the career planner to construct a resume that highlighted his salient experiences in international business, banking, and relief efforts and his uncommon understanding of cultural and business mores in Latin America. After much effort, he finally finished the resume.

But when Darryl reviewed it, he felt panicky. The person the resume described was a stranger! When his counselor saw the expression on his face, she asked what was wrong. He told her he couldn't use the resume because it described someone else. The counselor smiled and systematically pointed to each achievement saying, "Did you do this? And this? And this? And this?" Sure enough, Darryl answered yes to every one of them.

A few minutes later, he had a revelation. He realized that he wasn't only an academic, he was also an international business executive. All his volunteer and paid experience working with the World Bank, arranging for archaeological expeditions with Latin American officials and helping governments to coordinate resources for hurricane and earthquake relief efforts gave him a tremendous edge that few other people in his city possessed for doing business south of the border.

Armed with the conviction that he had something substantive to offer, Darryl concentrated his job-search efforts on companies selling heavy equipment products and services internationally. After a few months, he landed a customer service position at Jet Fleet, a firm that leases and maintains corporate jets. During his first year there, he doubled its service contracts.

Before Darryl could discuss his value to potential employers, he had to convince himself he was marketable. If you are grappling with this issue, use the transferable skills inventory from Chapter 2 (just like he did) to summarize the activities and functional skills that are most adaptable to your new career.

While our business culture places a priority on specialties, functional skills are actually more salable because they are useful in a variety of contexts. High-level positions demand more transferable skills than entry-level ones: The farther you progress in an organization, the more of a generalist you must become. When IBM's board of directors chose Louis Gertsner as their CEO, they selected an executive from an entirely different industry. They were more interested in his ability to "reengineer" a company than in his knowledge of computers. They made a wise choice.

If you investigate the requirements of any position, then match them with related activities from your skills summary, you will have a better-than-average chance of eliciting an interview. Since so few people take the time to tailor their experience to their job objective, your resume will stand out from the others. And even if your background isn't as relevant as the competition's, customizing your resume will make you seem more qualified, especially if other applicants mail generic resumes.

Employers want colleagues who can solve problems or bring new options to the table. If you have discovered an organization's most pressing opportunity or problem and have ideas about how to resolve it, a hiring manager should be eager to discuss how your skills and experience can benefit his company. If you do a credible job of addressing a manager's needs on paper, he'll give you the chance to discuss the details in person.

As a career changer, you must be careful to choose a resume format that showcases your experience effectively. A chronological format can do more harm than good because it focuses on experiences you want to minimize. If you spent the bulk of your career in banking, and want to switch to nonprofit management, listing your experience by job title will only accentuate your banking background. On the other hand, if you categorize your background by function, you can reduce the emphasis on your old career and direct readers' attention to what you can do for them. If you decide on this approach, a hybrid or functional format will probably serve you better than a chronological one.

Although a functional format works well for career changers, you may choose to play devil's advocate and consider the potential benefits of using a chronological approach. Suppose you have spent several years supervising the continuing education department of your local community college, but you would like to be a training and development manager for a corporation. While most professionals would call this a career change, the two positions have some strong parallels. Because your old and new job responsibilities are similar, a chronological format may be to your advantage because a human resources recruiter is more comfortable with it and:

☆ Your current position obviously gave you significant experience in managing an educational function for adults.

☆ Many corporations use college or university continuing education courses for their employees.

☆ A recruiter will know that you're familiar with assessing training needs, developing programs to fit specifications, convincing students to take courses and evaluating and revamping curriculum as needed.

☆ A potential employer knows your management position requires you to generate annual budgets, hire and supervise staff, interact with other department managers about common issues and advocate strategies with high-level managers.

If you state how your achievements in your current position might be beneficial in your new job, a potential employer should get the point.

As in any resume, your education section should relate your academic credentials to your job objective. If your major isn't compatible, delete it, stating only your degree level and institution. If you want to switch from accounting to a more people-oriented profession, use "BSBA, University of California at Berkeley" rather than "BSBA, Accounting, University of California at Berkeley."

It's also wise to discard specialized continuing education courses that are pertinent only to your former career or company. But include training in generic skills, such as MSWord or Lotus, that are always in demand.

Also omit irrelevant professional organizations. If you're a teacher who plans to change careers, leave out your membership in the National Education Association because very few businesspeople belong to it. On the other hand, if you are a state or national officer of the NEA and widely known as an advocate for collaborative programs between education and the private sector, be sure to mention it.

Example Resumes

Sue Carpenter

Sue Carpenter is a world traveler with a successful track record in both profit and nonprofit organizations. Having recently spent several lucrative but unhappy years in financial services, she decided to return to the public sector. In her networking to identify potential career opportunities, she found two that particularly interested her: account executive with the business and professional institute of the local community college district, and branch director for the YWCA. She has written two completely different resumes for these openings, one hybrid and the other chronological. Why do you think she did this?

Sue decided to use a chronological resume for the community college position for three reasons:

- ☆ Her last job was a marketing rep for a service provider, so it has many similarities to her new objective.

- ☆ Because she'll be selling to business professionals, she wants to emphasize her recent experience in that role.

- ☆ All of her other positions were with educational institutions. The one in Yokohama had cache and her instructor role with another community college district indicates her familiarity with that environment.

Every one of her former jobs reinforces why Sue would make a good account executive for a community college.

This resume is a hybrid format because:

- ☆ Sue's two most recent jobs had little to do with managing a YWCA. Using a chronological style would have buried her most relevant experiences on the second page of her resume.

- ☆ By listing her achievements by function, Sue emphasizes the specialized knowledge from her profit, nonprofit and volunteer experience, which mirror the responsibilities of a YWCA branch manager. These include everything from water sports to crisis counseling, folk singing, home economics, public speaking and cultural diversity.

- ☆ Sue has a good deal of management experience from her various careers. Under decision making skills, she mentions her background in supervising staff, marketing programs, budgeting and administering funds, raising money, designing facilities, and evaluating and recommending options. Combining all skills into a concise format would have been much more difficult using a chronological model.

Chronological Resume

SUE E. CARPENTER
702 Sabrina
Lakewood, MA 02332
(617) 419-7818
sue_carpenter@world.std.com

OBJECTIVE   Account Executive with the Business and Professional Institute of the Monmouth County Community College District.

EMPLOYMENT

Marketing Representative (1993–present)
Baldwin Financial Group
Boston, MA

— Sold insurance, mutual funds, and real estate limited partnerships to businesses and individuals.

— Developed a marketing plan to reach desirable prospects.

— Cold called 40 prospects a day either by phone or in the field.

— Completed a 5-week training program in sales techniques.

Pension/Profit Sharing Specialist (1988–1993)
RepublicBank, Dallas
Dallas, Texas

— Provided support to one Trust Officer. As a team we were responsible for 150 accounts totaling $164 million in assets.

— Evaluated investment needs of clients and implemented investment options.

— Directed assets to proper accounts through wire transfers, direct trade confirmation or written instruction to the Accounting Department.

— Supervised an average of three allocations per week.

— Calculated 25 termination benefits per week.

— Responded to 30–40 telephone contacts per day.

Athletic Director, Physical Education and Home Economics Instructor (1983–1988)
Yokohama International School
Yokohama, Japan

— Developed and implemented curriculum in two subjects for 300 students grades 1–12.

— Evaluated student performance; lectured to groups; advised individuals; fostered a stimulating learning environment; developed rapport and trust with students.

— Coordinated athletic activities; mediated between headmaster and coaches; prepared budget.

SUE E. CARPENTER—2

Instructor of Consumer Education (1982–1983)
Rancho Santiago Community College District
Santa Ana, California

— Directed and taught consumer education programs to low-income adults.

— Developed curriculum that was adaptable to a diverse audience using visual communications to illustrate principles.

EDUCATION

1993	Completion of NASD exams, Series 63 and 22
1989	Certificate of Employee Benefits Specialist (CEBS) courses: Pension Plans and Asset Management
1982	MA Home Economics with Family Finance emphasis California State University, Long Beach
1981	BS Recreation Administration California State University, Hayward
1982–88	Extensive travel in Far East, Australia, Nepal, and Europe

ACTIVITIES

Member, Downtowners Toastmasters, Dallas
Member, International Folkdance Coop
Member Downtown YMCA Squash League
Avid Sailor and retired marathoner

REFERENCES

Available on request

Hybrid Resume

SUE E. CARPENTER
702 Sabrina
Lakewood, MA 02332
617-419-7818
sue_carpenter@world.std.com

OBJECTIVE   A director's position with the YMCA using my decision making, communication and people skills.

EXPERIENCE

Decision-Making Skills

—Coordinated 12 athletic programs involving 300 participants at the interschool, intramural and extracurricular levels.

—Marketed a water exercise package to 10 municipal recreation departments, YMCAs, and private clubs throughout California. The package provided a water exercise program, instructor, publicity assistance and all administrative and financial bookkeeping.

—Administrated 150 retirement plans totaling $164 million as a team with one Trust Officer.

—Evaluated financial investment needs of clients and implemented investment options.

—Designed and supervised construction of a home economics classroom.

—Prepared budget for physical education department.

—Raised $7,500 for gymnasium project by running a full marathon and collecting on pledges.

Communication Skills

—Developed curriculum adaptable to a diverse audience using visual communications to illustrate principles.

—Planned two workshops for employee benefits staff.

—Conducted evaluation workshop for public speaking club members.

—Hired and trained 10 water exercise instructors.

—Mediated between headmaster and coaches.

—Coached three intermural sports during the school year.

—Sold insurance and mutual funds to businesses and individuals by cold calling 40 prospects a day by phone or in the field.

—Competed in four regional speech contests.

—Performed in a folk-singing group.

SUE E. CARPENTER—2

People Skills

—Taught consumer education to Spanish-speaking adults, adapting course content to suit particular needs.

—Taught water exercise in classes of 12–30 adults.

—Counseled individuals in a family financial crisis clinic who felt they were on the verge of bankruptcy.

—Fostered a stimulating learning environment.

—Developed rapport and trust with students.

—Taught two diverse subjects to 300 international students grades 1–12.

—Volunteered in free health clinic assessing patient need and assisting medical staff.

EMPLOYMENT CHRONOLOGY

1993–present	Marketing Representative Baldwin Financial Group, Boston, MA.
1988–93	Pension/Profit Sharing Specialist RepublicBank, Dallas, Texas
1983–88	Athletic Director, Physical Education & Home Economics Instructor Yokohama International School, Yokohama, Japan
1982–83	Instructor of Consumer Education Rancho Santiago Community College District, Santa Ana, California
1977–82	Area Director, Instructor Aquathenics, Long Beach, California

EDUCATION

1982	MA Home Economics with Family Finance emphasis California State University, Long Beach
1981	BS Recreation Administration California State University, Hayward
1982–88	Extensive travel in Far East, Australia, Nepal, and Europe

ACTIVITIES

Member, Downtowners Toastmasters, Dallas
Member, International Folkdance Coop
Member, Downtown YMCA
Member, American Society for Training and Development
Avid sailor and retired marathoner

Marc Bloomfield

After a successful career in the military and nonprofit, Marc Bloomfield decided it was time to have a more balanced life and a higher income. Note how his resume's functional titles reflect those often seen in business and his quantified accomplishments fit nicely with the bottom-line results corporations covet.

Julie Moore

If you met Julie Moore, you would immediately assume she's in sales, not accounting. A misplaced, but highly capable professional, Julie longs to concentrate less on numbers and more on people. Her resume paints a picture of a fast-moving, can-do individual whose most important asset is her ability to interact effectively with both internal and external colleagues.

Military Resumes

Professionals leaving the military represent a large group of careers changers who have a host of marketable skills and relatively little information about how to promote themselves to civilian employers. On pages 231–233 are two resumes written by former officers who are pursuing very different careers. One is interested in administrative management; the other wants a position in high-tech sales or marketing support. Both have chosen a functional approach to highlight their achievements and de-emphasize their military backgrounds. However, they've listed courses obviously provided by the armed forces which relate to their new careers.

Marc C. Bloomfield

600 Gravel Rd., Apt. 505   (972) 555-3232
McKinney, TX 75069   email: mcbloomfield@aol.com

OBJECTIVE: A leadership position in a for-profit organization requiring special skill and attention to developing and maintaining relationships both with employees and customers, while at the same time providing oversight and direction to operations within a department or territory.

QUALIFICATIONS

- Coordinator and catalyst for developing events/programs that both educate and bring people together for a common goal.
- Expert in prioritizing the important from the urgent.
- Adept at promoting courses of action to decision makers and implementors.
- Experienced at working with diverse groups of people and personalities.

EXPERIENCE HIGHLIGHTS

Business Development

- Designed and managed a pilot campaign which grew income 2.5 times the goal and became the model in most of the 271 locations throughout the United States.
  —Listened to volunteer ideas and incorporated them into the plan.
  —Created a presentation format which included critical information, plus an immediate "close."
  —Convinced staff leadership to try the new program.
  —Recruited and trained volunteer presenters to solicit contributors from individual units.
  —Promoted, scheduled and coordinated all presentations (60–70) over a three-month period.
  —Achieved a 75% "prospects solicited" ratio versus the 40% industry standard.
- Developed a radically different and very successful approach to recruiting which increased membership 40% and became the standard model within the local organization.
  —Sold the plan to council management, both volunteers and professional staff.
  —Put together volunteer teams to recruit members throughout the district instead of relying on overworked unit leaders.
  —Coordinated all of the teams and their paraphernalia.

Project Management/Event Planning

- Managed numerous annual projects, events and training courses (consistently under budget):
  —Quarterly leader trainings averaging 100–125 participants
  —Canned food drive produced nearly one-third of local food banks' yearly inventory.
  —Recognition banquet experienced 30% increase in attendance over previous five-year average
  —Numerous spring and fall "camporees" involving 600–1000 participants
  —Ad hoc "Special Events" cooperating with other United Way agencies to promote programs
  —Week-long Day Camps averaging 100–150 participants
- Created a 47-page annual "Program Preview" packet for unit leaders which includes a yearly calendar of events, plus registration fliers and deadline information.

Marc C. Bloomfield   Page 2

Public Relations/Customer Service

- Improved and solidified both the organization's public image and internal rapport after a turbulent merger.
  —Spoke extensively to service clubs (Rotary, Kiwanis, etc.) and civic groups (VFW, church councils etc.)
  —Networked with unit leaders to focus everyone's attention on moving forward.
- Defused a delicate situation with a high profile volunteer and two supervisors, which prevented a public relations disaster.
- Successfully mediated dispute between volunteer factions using techniques learned in conflict resolution training, as well as old fashioned common sense.

Organizational Development

- Persuaded volunteer leaders to adopt an industry standard organizational structure after six predecessors were unable to do so.
- In two different states, rebuilt a volunteer staff of 20 plus people committed to customer service.

WORK HISTORY

Young Leaders of America
- District Director, Long Horn Council, Ft. Worth, TX 1997–present
- Sr. District Executive, Long Horn Council, Ft. Worth, TX 1994–1997
- District Executive, Long Horn Council, Ft. Worth, TX 1991–1994

United States Army Reserve
- 1st Lieutenant, Air Defense Artillery, Honorable Discharge 1998
- 2nd Lieutenant, Air Defense Artillery, 1st Battalion, 6th Brigade (ADA), Ft. Bliss, TX 1989–1990, Battery Executive Officer, 1990

EDUCATION

- B.A. Texas A&M, 1989
- Honor Graduate, U.S. Army Officer Basic Course, Ft. Bliss, TX 1990
- Young Leaders of America People Management Training, 1996
- Young Leaders of America National Executive Institute I, II, III, 1991–1994
- Covey Leadership Center: "Principle Centered Leadership" and "First Things First"

COMPUTER SKILLS

Microsoft Word, Excel, Publisher and Works

AWARDS RECEIVED

- Eagle Scout
- Annual Chief Executive's "Winner Circle" every eligible year
- YLA Southern Region "Silver Award" for new unit sales growth
- U.S. Army Commendation for duties performed as Battery Executive Officer

JULIE L. MOORE

3100 Laguna Ave.   Oakland, CA 94116   415-239-8712   juliemoore@pacbell.com

Analytical . . . Team Player . . . Assertive . . .
Versatile . . . Telecommunications Experience

Extensive experience in dealing with people. Key strengths include problem solving, high energy, interpersonal skills, and customer service. Area of expertise is accuracy and organization skills. Major emphasis on product knowledge.

PROFESSIONAL EXPERIENCE:

1994–PRESENT   Pacific Bell Mobile Systems, Inc.   Palo Alto, CA
Tax Manager

- Produce returns recognized **as "highest quality returns"** in the history of the company, resulting in 50% reduction in penalties.
- Received **highest (10%) performance bonus** each year.
- **Liaison** to both in-house and outside counsel. Responsible for communicating issues to legal group and coordinating litigation and tax-related lobbying efforts.
- Established **strong relationships with personnel** at market-area locations, increasing exchange of information and ideas.
- **Created quality team** by recruiting, hiring, and retaining talented personnel resulting in reduced overtime and **increased productivity.**
- **Manage** team of up to 5 professionals.
- Ensure timely filing of hundreds of tax payments exceeding $25 million annually to over 20 states.
- Manage income tax budget in excess of $100 million.
- Demonstrated ability to produce large volume of work with limited staff and remain "big picture" oriented.
- Presented and executed planning ideas with annual savings in excess of $1 million.

1991–1994   Energy Resources   San Francisco, CA
Senior Tax Accountant

- **Promoted** to senior tax accountant after one year.
- Consistently received **"outstanding"** rating.
- Recognized for **superior verbal and written communication** skills. Requested to draft official legal protests as a senior tax accountant.
- Implemented new calendar system to track payments and insure that deadlines are met and costly penalties avoided.

Julie L. Moore   Page 2

1989–1991   **Price Waterhouse**   San Mateo, CA
                       Tax Consultant
                       • Recognized for **service-oriented** attitude.
                       • **Negotiated favorable tax settlements** with Departments of Revenue
                         officials resulting in savings of hundreds of thousands of dollars to clients.
                       • Spearheaded research for million dollar cable industry project.

1987–1989   **Arthur Andersen & Co.**   San Francisco, CA
                       Tax Associate
                       • Developed idea for state tax newsletter for distribution to clients which was
                         used as a marketing tool; team member of contributing authors.
                       • Prepared tax returns, including corporate, individual, and partnership.

EDUCATION:

1987   **University of California—Berkeley**   Berkeley, CA
                       Master of Tax Accounting
                       G.P.A. 3.3/4.0

1986   **San Francisco State University**   San Francisco, CA
                       Bachelor of Professional Accountancy
                       Graduated Cum Laude
                       Member Beta Alpha Psi, accounting honorary fraternity
                       G.P.A. 3.4/4.0

LICENSES: **Certified Public Accountant,** State of California

**ADDITIONAL
INFORMATION:**   Member of The 500 Inc.; Volunteer for Suicide and Crisis Center

REFERENCES: Available upon request.

Military Resume

Davis Fisher
27 Coral Cove
New Haven, CT 06515
203-461-1718 (phone)
203-461-1711 (fax)
d_fisher@world.std.com

OBJECTIVE
Administration management position.

BACKGROUND
Twenty years of problem solving, decision making, upward movement and increasing responsibility. Extensive hands-on experience administering, planning and managing operations in the following functional areas: facilities management, purchasing, personnel/staff development, financial management, management information, program management, logistics, maintenance, transportation and telecommunications.

PROFESSIONAL EXPERIENCE

Facilities Management
— Planned, coordinated with principals and successfully completed a physical relocation of 75 people and equipment resulting in minimal disruption to service and measurable improvements to work flow.
— Managed eight-person staff responsible for administrative support services and helped facilitate rapid expansion; growing the organization from 250 to 800 people with no increase in staff and 95% customer satisfaction.
— Orchestrated consolidation of supplies and equipment in storage resulting in a 19% reduction in space requirement and $63,000 cost savings, in the first year.
— Directed a project to identify, prepare, occupy and close out administrative offices, living and dining facilities for 200 people; completing the project on time and 10% under budget.

Purchasing
— Identified requirements for supplies and equipment, sources of supply/vendors, and negotiated to select responsive/responsible bidder resulting in materials available on time at the best cost.
— Developed procedures to expedite acquisition of low dollar supplies and equipment resulting in a material receipt time reduction from five days to one.
— Implemented just-in-time motor vehicle repair parts same-day purchase procedures, resulting in vehicle down-time reduction from three days to one.

Personnel and Staff Development
— Assessed work load, identified critical skills, recruited, and hired qualified candidates.
— Managed organizational realignment and 100% turnover in key management positions resulting in virtually no disruption in timeliness or quality of service to customers.
— Resolved sensitive personnel problems achieving consensus with employees, unions and management.
— Developed personnel requirements, schedules, scope, content and travel plans resulting in 99% of the inspections completed on-time, within budget and to the satisfaction of senior management.

Davis Fisher   Page 2

Management Information
— Led automation improvement initiative, saving three man years in labor and $70,000.
— Instituted cutting edge bar code inventory system technology resulting in a $100,000 cost savings, the first year.

Financial Management
— Actively managed budget development, allocation and expenditures resulting in significant cost saving.
— Prepared budgets, allocated resources, monitored execution, reallocated funds and established internal controls to comply with existing policy, guidelines and constraints.

CHRONOLOGICAL EXPERIENCE

Congressional Fellowship   **1995–Present**
Legislative Assistant to a U.S. Senator. Analyze data, develop sophisticated positions, summarize issues, recommend key votes, create opportunity for member to achieve goals, prepare oral/written floor/committee statements and testimony, negotiate/coordinate with colleagues/congressional committees, develop bills/amendments and resolve constituent problems.

Manager of Inspections   **1991–95**
Directed 30-person organization responsible for conducting complex systemic inspections of personnel, administration, budget, financial management, logistics, maintenance, transportation/travel functions for a 150,000 employee worldwide organization. Determined personnel, space, equipment and supply requirements. Developed, allocated, executed and redistributed organizational budgets.

Senior Executive for Program Management   **1988–91**
Developed budgets, overseeing allocation, execution and follow-up. Researched and analyzed complex programs. Determined and fulfilled management information requirements.

Director of Logistics   **1986–88**
Directed a diverse organization of 300 administrative, purchasing, budget, supply, maintenance, transportation and quality assurance people providing support to a community of 15,000. Determined personnel requirements, managed facilities, operated office supply facility, purchased supplies and office equipment. Developed, allocated and monitored expenditures.

EDUCATION
° Bachelor of Arts, Education, Whittier College, California, 1974
° Armed Forces Staff College
° Defense Systems Management College, Program Managers Course
° U.S. Army Logistics Executive Development Program
° Specialized training: Basic Contracting Course; Graduate Level Business Accounting

MISCELLANEOUS
° Top Secret Security Clearance
° Certified Army Acquisition Manager
° Hands-on experience with IBM PC, Apple, Macintosh, WordPerfect and Microsoft Works

Military Resume

James L. Ferris
2831 Northwest Hwy.
Washington, DC 81496
202-814-9332
Voice: 800-998-5500, Ext. 285
42579@compuserve.com

Objective   A sales or marketing support position with a high-tech firm.

Personal Qualifications
▶ Excellent at networking and building client rapport.
▶ Proven record in developing and conducting training programs for sophisticated systems.
▶ A quick learner who particularly enjoys involvement with cutting-edge technology.
▶ Always looking for professional growth and new challenges.
▶ Enjoy domestic and international travel.

Experience Highlights
▶ In the past year, have introduced a new product with a start-up company, a T-shirt that changes color with heat, to the Southwest. Currently serving approximately 40 accounts. This quarter sales revenues at $200,000.
▶ Responsible for technical support and repair to in-flight radars and computer systems on board a U.S. Navy P-3 Orion Radar aircraft.
▶ Provided technical support and assisted in developing a new product for Microspec, a Texas-based software firm.
▶ Developed a more effective system for tracking, monitoring and destroying classified naval materials.
▶ Taught courses in scuba diving at San Jose State University, Moffet Field Navy Base and other locations for more than 200 students.
▶ Spearheaded a turnaround of the struggling scuba program at Moffet Field Navy Base resulting in a 70% increase in attendance.
  ▶ Negotiated with the Navy to cosponsor the classes.
  ▶ Encouraged local media to promote the program.
  ▶ Developed an advertising strategy to reach all base personnel.

Education
▶ Interdisciplinary studies degree in business and law. GPA:3.1.
▶ Navy Avionics A1, electricity and electronics schools.
▶ Vector marketing: sales training course.
▶ Leadership and computer language courses through the Navy and University of Texas at Dallas.

Personal Data/Interests
▶ Honorably discharged from U.S. Navy, member inactive Navy Reserves.
▶ Clearance secret.
▶ Enjoy physical fitness, golf, scuba diving/instructing.

12

Resumes for Seasoned Professionals

Points to Ponder

If you ask a veteran careerist how his job search is going, quite often he'll say, "People keep telling me I'm overqualified. But what they really mean is I'm too old." If you ask him what types of jobs he's pursuing, he's likely to mention positions that are obviously beneath his expertise.

In effect, he's propelling himself into a nasty downward spiral of rejection and despair because he's afraid to go after hard-to-find, higher level positions that he's better suited for. If this negative spiral continues for several months or longer, he may wonder if he's capable of performing even rudimentary jobs, let alone the ones appropriate to his level. Unless he raises his sights and develops a good support system, he's likely to succumb to the "Black Hole Syndrome," a serious psychological condition that sucks energy and hope from its job-seeker victims.

If it's just as hard to find a good job as a bad one, why not apply only for positions that will take advantage of your expertise and allow you to grow? Employers expect to see gray hair and a few wrinkles on candidates for highly responsible positions. In fact, in consulting situations, the distinguished look may be a definite plus.

There'll always be companies that offer "low-ball" salaries, recruit young turks and work their employees like dogs, but you wouldn't want to work for them anyway. And some firms discriminate against older workers to avoid paying higher benefit costs. As a general rule, organizations want to hire people who will be productive. For every manager who thinks young people work harder, you'll find another who maintains that wisdom is more valuable than a strong back. Your mission is to find the ones in the second category.

Resume research can help you do this. Investigating a company by talking to current employees and reading its annual report and trade journals will reveal important clues about its culture. For instance, if executive officers pictured in the annual report look like a fraternity composite, you can probably assume the corporation doesn't hire many recruits over age 35. But if the firm is expanding, it's likely to need an infusion of seasoned experts who can hit the ground running. If it's moving into territories where current managers have little experience, chances are it needs to hire some pros to guide the new venture.

Seasoned professionals who are seeking salaried positions should be especially careful not to write resumes that overwhelm potential employers with their many years of experience, high compensation packages or lifetime employment with one company. While none of these background facts are intrinsically bad, they may bother recruiters sufficiently to deny you interviews. To skirt these issues, use the following techniques:

☆ Avoid any mention of salary. If an ad asks you to provide a salary history, state that you're flexible or ignore the request. The recruiter will be able to tell from your experience whether your expected compensation is in the ballpark.

☆ List no more than 20 years of experience. Positions that you held early in your career usually have little to do with the job you want now, so delete them. You aren't lying if you don't mention your entire work history. Most recruiters don't care what you did when you were 25.

While the previous statement is generally true, some executive recruiters and human resources professionals want to know about every position you've ever had and will assume you're hiding something if you don't supply a complete work history. In some circumstances, you'll have to make a judgment call on whether it's riskier to list every job or stick with your experience of the last 20 years or less. Resume writing is part art and part science. You're entitled to bend or break any of the rules if you have a good reason.

☆ If you have spent a number of years at one company, attach dates to each of your job titles to show your upward progression. Some potential employers might worry that you're deadwood—someone who stayed with one organization too long because he lacked the courage or initiative to try something more challenging. If you prove you took advantage of the opportunities available in your own company, you'll easily dispel this concern.

At this juncture of your life, you may decide to do some consulting to earn income while you look for a full-time position. This option will remove you from the pool of older workers and put you into the ranks of the ageless self-employed. There's practically no age discrimination for consultants. Your biggest problem will be competing for assignments against more seasoned advisors. Suddenly you'll be the new kid on the block. Ironic, isn't it?

You might also want to start a company that accommodates a more flexible work week. Perhaps you'll select a business in an entirely different field from your former career, or investigate franchising. In either case, your age isn't critical to your success.

Whatever direction you choose, you'll need to prepare a resume that sells you to an employer, investor or client. If you choose the small business or consulting route, reread Chapter 8, which includes resumes for people in those professions. If you decide to stay in your current field, it's likely that Chapter 5, (chronological resumes) will serve you best. But if you're seizing the opportunity to make a career change, review the advice on functional and hybrid resume formats in Chapters 6 and 7.

Success Stories

Marvin B. Sutton

Marvin "Bucky" Sutton was a 52-year-old technical professional in the textile industry when he was laid off. He sent out 40 resumes, had 10 formal interviews and received five job offers. His resume on pages 239–240 is a major reason his job-search campaign was so successful.

Bucky offers some tips for other seasoned job hunters. While they represent a simple, commonsense approach to job hunting, their impact can be profound. Put this list in a convenient spot where you'll see it often.

Bucky's List

Be enthusiastic! Be honest with the employer and yourself. Know what you want. Be assertive. Maintain your sense of humor. Be dedicated to the search but be reasonable—it can't be done eight hours a day. Reward yourself when you have a successful interview.

Step 1	Network, network, network.
Step 2	Seek professional help.
Step 3	Get leads from networking, help-wanted ads and headhunters.
Step 4	Know the company before contacting it.
Step 5	Find out what the employer wants.
Step 6	Write a resume that fits the employer's needs.
Step 7	Send out resumes and follow up.
Step 8	Follow up with headhunters.
Step 9	Practice the interview.
Step 10	Control the interview.
Step 11	Perform a self-evaluation.
Step 12	Reward yourself for a successful interview.

Bonnie Gabriel

Bonnie's "before and after" resumes are taken from the *NBEW's* "Can This Resume Be Saved?" column and are great examples of how a seasoned professional can make her resume more appealing to potential employers.

In the "before" resume, Bonnie squeezed 30 years of experience on only one page, thereby damning herself with faint praise. By concentrating on duties instead of accomplishments, she made it very difficult for employers to see what she had achieved in each of her jobs. Her work history section takes up a great deal of space and covers a lot more years than necessary.

Her "after" resume has a great key-word summary that both recruiters and computers enjoy reading. She does an excellent job of explaining the unique contribution she made in each of her positions. And she extends her experience back to 1980, which is plenty of chronological information for a potential employer. She also deleted her college dates. How important is it for a recruiter to know her degree is from 1965?

Chronological Resume

MARVIN B. SUTTON
917 Crestlodge View
Rocky Mount, SC 29210
803-433-9991 (res)
803-736-2377 (bus)
mbsutton@wiscassett.com

OBJECTIVE   Product/Market Development Manager

SUMMARY   My varied background includes product development, process development, market development, plant engineering and customer interface in the textiles business. I am recognized for my creativity and ability to develop products and create markets by using technical, marketing and communication skills.

EXPERIENCE   **WISCASSETT MILLS**—Major high performance yarn manufacturer for industrial and apparel applications.

Development Manager, Albemarle, NC (1991–Present)
Responsible for product and market development.

-Expanded business 25% by developing products for industrial and apparel end uses.
-Managed programs resulting in 50%–300% improvement in margins implemented into innovative niche businesses.
-Introduced two new high-performance fibers from product specifications through customer support and acceptance.

HOECHST CELANESE—$25 billion multinational manufacturer of fibers, plastics, chemicals and pharmaceuticals.

Senior Development Engineer, Charlotte, NC (1987–1991)
Responsible for new end-use product development for innovative applications of PBI fiber.

-Managed development resources for new thermally protective industrial products that doubled the number of marketed end uses.
-Introduced PBI into the industrial laminated fabric area including laminated PTFE, aluminized and neoprene coated fabrics.
-Engineered test equipment evaluating end-use product performance thereby strengthening the company's competitive advantage.
-Used communication skills as technical spokesman at seminars, authored technical papers and marketing bulletins, and earned a solid reputation of technical competence and integrity for the company.

Senior Plant Engineer, Rock Hill, SC (1981–1987)

-Managed plant engineering services for a $32 million new fiber plant start-up that was completed on time and within budget. Resin and fiber processes include polymerization, dope preparation, spinning and drawing.
-Supervised in-house and contractor support to implement design, fabrication, installation and commissioning of $4.5 million in equipment improvements.
-Engineered the control strategy, software development, installation and commissioning of a plantwide computer system that manages all major process functions.

Project Engineer, Greenville, SC (1978–1981)

-Pioneered a sitewide quality control computer system that accelerated the quality control decision-making process by automating data collection.
-Innovated microprocessor-based textured yarn monitor equipment resulting in fewer customer complaints.

EDUCATION   BS, Chemical Engineering, North Carolina State University, Raleigh, NC.

PROFESSIONAL   National Fire Protection Association (NFPA)
American Institute of Chemical Engineers
ASTM
S.A.F.E.R. & F.I.E.R.O. (fire service organizations)

INTERESTS   Golf, competitive speaking, director of NAIC, Toastmasters International.

BEFORE

Bonnie Gilstrap Gabriel
130 North Sandler Court
Chicago, Illinois 60102
630.555.1212
gilgabriel@mci.2000.com

JOB TARGET
Controller, Business Manager, Consultant

ACCOMPLISHMENTS
- A controller and/or consultant for 20 years with multi-line domestic and foreign dealerships
- Experience with all major automobile computer programs-R&R, ADP and specializing in UCS
- Design, build, maintain and reconcile all computer schedules, docs and functions specific to each department needs
- Implement and develop inventory and expense controls

CAPABILITIES
- Cultivate professional and long-lasting relationships with financial institutions, factories, insurance companies, unions and support agencies
- Hire, train, supervise and motivate accounting personnel and support staff to work to their optimum potential and accuracy
- Forecast, prepare and implement budgets and expense controls to increase profitability
- Execute and supervise efficient, accurate and timely paper flow reports and financial statements
- Maintain constant dialogue with all department managers to work together for maximum profitability
- Prepare, analyze and interpret financial and changing business trends in all departments and implement positive action for adjustment

WORK HISTORY
1996–1997	Consultant/Controller
	West Chicago Car Co.: West Chicago, Illinois
1995–1996	Consultant
	Torco Auto Group: Dundee, Illinois
1982–1995	Controller
	Gateway Chevrolet, Geo, Oldsmobile, Inc.: Chicago, Illinois
1980–1982	Office Manager
	Superior Toyota, AMC, Jeep Inc.: Aurora, Illinois
1977–1980	Assistant Office Manager
	LaGrange Chrysler Plymouth Inc.: LaGrange, Illinois
1974–1976	Owner
	White Hart Inn: Savannah, Georgia
1965–1973	Comptroller
	Superior/Rogers Graphics Inc.: Chicago, Illinois

EDUCATION
1963–1965	University of Miami: Coral Gables, Florida
	B.A.-Accounting, Business Education
1961–1963	Stephens College: Columbia, Missouri

AFTER

BONNIE J. GILSTRAP GABRIEL
130 North Sandler Court
Chicago, Illinois 60102
(630) 555-1212
gilgabriel@mci.2000.com

Results-oriented accounting and financial management professional with progressive experience in high-volume, metro-area dealership environments.

Background encompasses establishing and implementing internal procedures in both start-up and established environments, resulting in maximum profitability and return on investment.

Comprehensive knowledge of multiple industry-specific computer programs to support all business functions; experienced in installing new systems, managing transition to new automated environments and training staff in all pertinent accounting functions.

An aggressive problem-solver and decision maker with the ability to set realistic priorities and initiate viable courses of action to attain objectives.

AREAS OF EXPERTISE

FINANCIAL/ASSET MANAGEMENT	*BUSINESS ANALYSIS*	*GENERAL ACCOUNTING*
REPORTING/ DOCUMENTATION	*CONSULTING*	*STAFF MANAGEMENT*
POLICY/ PROCEDURE	*MULTI-FRANCHISE•DOMESTIC/ IMPORTS*	*COST CONTAINMENT*
BUDGET ADMINISTRATION	*NEW/USED•SECONDARY FINANCE*	*INVENTORY MANAGEMENT*

EXPERIENCE AND ACCOMPLISHMENTS

West Chicago Car Co. - West Chicago, Illinois   1996–Present
Controller/Consultant
Oversee and control all general accounting and financial management functions of this high-volume, metro-area dealership. Manage a staff of 15 in all day-to-day functions to ensure attainment of financial and business objectives. Compile data, prepare financial statements, analyze business trends, expenditures and revenues and provide the Dealer Principal with all pertinent information and recommendations. Hire, train and supervise administrative and professional support staff.
• Assumed management responsibilities, revamped and introduced improved accounting procedures.

Bonnie J. Gilstrap Gabriel   **Page two**

- Implemented corrective measures and enhanced internal controls for the Secondary Finance Department which has resulted in substantial increases in revenues.
- Applied extensive knowledge of the automotive industry and solid computer literacy to build and utilize internal systems and staff to fullest potential.

Torco Auto Group - Dundee, Illinois   1995–1996
Consultant
Fulfilled a short-term consulting assignment for this multi-franchise/multi-site organization with domestic and import lines. Established and implemented procedures in compliance with IRS regulations and provided input and guidance regarding daily general accounting procedures. Communicated regularly with the Controller and the Dealer Principal on relevant business and financial issues. Administered systems for all internal departments.
- Reviewed and restructured job descriptions and paper flow for all sites resulting in increased productivity, efficiency and reporting accuracy.

Gateway Chevrolet, GEO, Oldsmobile Inc. - Chicago, Illinois   1982–1995
Controller
Fulfilled relevant duties including budget administration, financial/asset management, analysis, merger and acquisition expenditures, payroll, documentation, taxes, reporting and staffing. Hired, supervised and motivated subordinate staff and established effective lines of communication throughout the dealership to ensure superior service and productivity.
- Developed and implemented highly effective procedures to improve expense and inventory controls, documentation and cash-flow management and profit-building.
- Identified existing or potential problem areas and defined effective start-up and turnaround procedures to facilitate business launch and growth.

Superior Toyota, AMC, Jeep Inc. - Aurora, Illinois   1980–1982
Office Manager
Hired, trained and managed all accounting staff at this start-up dealership. Performed all general accounting, including financial statement preparation/analysis and personnel-related functions.
- Created and implemented internal procedures and policies, developed inventory and expense controls and streamlined documentation guidelines to achieve maximum efficiency.

EDUCATION
University of Miami - Coral Gables, Florida • Bachelor of Arts in Accounting and Business Education
- Completed additional training through UCS, Reynolds & Reynolds and General Motors Accounting and Business Management courses.
- Computer proficiency includes: Reynolds & Reynolds, UCS, EDS, DCS, ADP and Quick Books programs

Lawrence George

Larry's case is similar to those of thousands of highly productive professionals who assume they have implicit contracts with their organizations until retirement, then are suddenly terminated due to a corporate downsizing, merger or hostile takeover. Fortunately, since so many "Larrys" are looking for jobs, it's no longer a stigma to be unemployed.

This former CFO took a two-pronged approach to his job search. He investigated the viability of starting his own consulting business and interviewed for CFO positions at medium-size firms that have good growth potential and may go public in the near future. He worked on his search at an outplacement facility four days a week and considered his job search his job. But, like the Larry mentioned in Chapter 1, he spent more time with his family, played golf often and completed special projects he had put off for years.

Larry prepared an excellent resume, starting with a clear objective. He quantified and emphasized his accomplishments, used action verbs, and minimized his "one company" career. However, his resume doesn't follow all the usual guidelines. He listed his education before his experience and showed all the jobs he's held in his career. Even though he knows the rules, he consciously chose not to follow some of them because he thinks the combination of his business and high-tech degrees is important enough to warrant prime space and because he doesn't trust people who delete portions of their backgrounds. He exercised his prerogative to break rules that disagree with his personal philosophy. If mentioning more than 20 years of experience disqualified him for consideration, that was OK with him because he values his integrity.

After networking with many people and interviewing for several CFO positions which didn't pique his interest, Larry decided to start a consulting firm to help small, established businesses write business plans and find funding for their next stage of development. As he refined his mission over the course of a few months, Larry put together a new resume, or fact sheet, about his business and himself to give to prospective clients. It's on page 247.

LAWRENCE GEORGE
2392 Northwood Lane
Boise, Idaho 83703
Off: 208-881-1301
Res: 208-142-7964
E-mail law_george@well.com

OBJECTIVE **CHIEF FINANCIAL and ADMINISTRATIVE OFFICER** where my strengths in administration, analysis and presentation will improve staff efficiency and management effectiveness.

QUALIFIED BY Over 20 years of broad-ranging experience, including two periods of rapid growth and numerous acquisitions. Particularly adept at straightforward communication, capturing the essence of complex subjects and getting the job done right the first time. Skilled in financial analysis, administration, investor relations and human resources in addition to traditional CFO responsibilities.

EDUCATION MBA, Management, Pennsylvania State University
BS, Aerospace Engineering, Pennsylvania State University

Professional Accomplishments at Saffron Energy

Saffron Energy is a diversified energy company with $500 million in sales operating through six autonomous divisions. It went public in 1996 with 17% of its stock in a $90 million offering led by Merrill Lynch and Salomon Bros.

- Directed the efforts of Saffron staff and coordinated the activities of investment bankers and operating divisions in the "due diligence." Prepared the prospectus and the road show presentation and was one of the four road show participants in 14 cities in the United States and Europe.
- Built a quality investor relations program from scratch and later hired a top-notch investor relations VP recruited from a giant competitor. Designed charts and gave presentations to groups of analysts and one-on-one to key investors around the country. Increased coverage from 2 analysts to 10 and "retail" ownership from 5% to 25%.
- Designed management information and public reporting systems including detailed monthly spreadsheets and variance explanations, annual budget/forecast spreadsheets and presentation charts, quarterly reports and the annual report to stockholders.
- Prepared extensive board requests for over 100 acquisitions and asset purchases ranging in size from $1 million to $100 million during 1979–1985 and 1990–1993.
- Designed annual and long-term incentive programs, linking awards to specific financial objectives unique to each operating division.
- Presided over the closing of our 60-person Boise corporate office. Designed the severance policy, hired an outplacement firm and set up program to explain termination schedule and benefit plan options to employees.

Professional Experience

Saffron Energy Corporation, Boise, Idaho

<u>**Senior Vice President and Chief Financial and Administrative Officer.**</u>
Responsible for Investor Relations, Human Resources, Economics and Legal functions in addition to Accounting, Tax, Treasury and Financial Planning. Directly managed staff of 60 people with annual overhead budget of $10 million. Set policy and example for several hundred financial employees in six divisions. Served as Chief of Staff to Saffron Energy President (and effective CEO) in all aspects of strategic planning and operations. (1990–1997)

<u>**Vice President Financial Planning.**</u> Managed annual and long-range planning, prepared all capital expenditure requests, acquisition analyses, competitor studies, management reporting and analysis. Managed 6–10 MBA financial analysts in addition to MIS, Word Processing and Reproduction departments. (1982–1989)

<u>**Manager Financial Planning.**</u> Supervised financial analysts and assisted in managing MIS, Word Processing and Reproduction departments. Designed 1001 column spreadsheets for each of 10 divisions for monthly reporting of key industry data and Saffron Energy financial results. (1979–1981)

Recreational Vehicles Division, W.R. Love & Co., Los Angeles, California

<u>**Manager Financial Planning and Analysis.**</u> Prepared budgets, capital expenditure requests, operating variance analyses, competitor studies and cash flow projections. Two companies, Shasta and Fan Coach, produced travel trailers and motor homes in 10 U.S. plants. (1978)

Footwear Group, W.R. Love & Co., New York, New York

<u>**Controller.**</u> Reviewed budgets and capital requests. Performed consolidations, summaries and divestment analyses, and prepared board charts. Performed "what-if" calculations on an acquisition "kicker" formula. Analyzed operating results for the group executive and participated in monthly meetings with the chairman. Business included three shoe importers, a domestic manufacturer and a 34-store retail shoe chain. (1976–1977)

Other Relevant Experience:

<u>**Senior Financial Analyst,**</u> Corporate Office, W.R. Love & Co., New York, New York (1974–1976)

<u>**Financial Analyst,**</u> Corporate Office, General Dynamics Corp., New York, New York (1973–1974)

LAWRENCE GEORGE

2392 Northwood Lane
Boise, Idaho 83703

Home Office: (208) 881-1301
Voice Mail: (208) 142-7964
E-mail: law_george@well.com

Services Provided and Benefits to Entrepreneurs

- Prepare a detailed *business and financial plan* to explain your business to potential investors and to interest them in providing equity or debt capital
- Sharpen the *focus* of your objectives, define what you do best
- Design *presentation charts* that summarize the most important features of the business to quickly attract the attention of investors
- Counsel you on how to make an *effective presentation* either to individual investors one-on-one or in a group setting
- *Evaluate* various investor proposals
- Help *negotiate* the most attractive deal
- Show you how to *communicate* ongoing results to investors or bankers after the money has been raised
- Analyze your financial performance and tell you how to *improve profits* and accelerate cash flow

Ideal Clients

- Established businesses, 1 to 3 years old
- Those seeking first outside financing after exhausting savings and credit cards
- Typical size: $1–5 million revenue, any industry
- Current clients include computer sales & leasing, securities brokerage and consumer goods manufacturing

Accomplishments

- Wrote business plans for dozens of companies in service industries and in manufacturing
- Designed business plan charts for presentations to top management and boards of directors
- Coached CEOs on how best to present their business plans to management and investors
- Prepared text and spreadsheets justifying more than 100 new businesses acquired by my employer from 1979–1997
- Gave presentations to hundreds of brokers, securities analysts, and investment and commercial bankers

Qualifications

- MBA, with a BS in engineering
- Former Chief Financial and Administrative Officer of a large, diversified, public energy company
- Also experienced in the footwear, recreational vehicle, chemical and aerospace industries
- For seven years managed investor relations, human resources and legal functions plus traditional CFO duties of accounting, tax, treasury and financial planning
- Started consulting business in 1997

"I don't care if you *can* break into our mainframe computer . . . we're not hiring any programming engineers right now!"

13

Scannable Resumes

I f you want to be the first candidate employers and recruiters think of when trying to fill openings, you'd better get cracking on a second version of your resume—one that can be scanned by computer. That's because resume scanning will soon be "the way companies screen applicants in the future."

When you look at the numbers, you can understand why. A local high tech company's database of scanned resumes has grown to nearly 200,000 from 12,000 in 1994. About 12,000 new applicants are added monthly, while all but the most qualified technical candidates are purged yearly and the non-technical ones every six months to hold the volume down. Without a sophisticated automated tracking, there's no way the company could locate qualified applicants from among such a voluminous database and match them to available positions.

What Is Resume Scanning?

Electronic applicant tracking systems scan your resume into computers so it can be retrieved later. The document may be stored exactly as you submitted it, in ASCII (a computer language), as an extracted summary which uses predetermined "key words" to capture your most critical skills and experience or as a combination of these formats. Here's how it works, according to Resumix literature: "Your resume is scanned into the computer as an image. Then OCR (optical character recognition) software looks at the image to distinguish every letter and number (character) and creates a text file (ASCII). Then artificial intelligence 'reads' the text and extracts important information about you such as your name, address, phone number, work history, years of experience, education and skills."

Since companies are just now getting up to speed with electronic resume storage systems, expect employers to use the process with varying levels of sophistication. While EDS can probably scan just about any resume, including those that include italic and underlined type, another employer's software might not be able to handle anything more complicated than plain text.

Key words or nouns describing skills and qualifications are used to identify qualified candidates whose resumes are stored in the systems. While Raytheon Systems may have built into its software thousands of key words and synonyms for sorting candidates, XYZ company may have just a few. Given these different capabilities, recognize that when applying to a company that scans resumes, you're taking a risk unless the format and content of your document is totally scanner-friendly.

Who Uses Resume Scanning and Why

Corporations and Government

Corporations and large government agencies use electronic sorting systems to store resumes from internal and external candidates. They secure these resumes from want ads, unsolicited direct mail, computer home-page inquiries, succession planning concerns and internal job postings. If you prefer high touch to high tech, having your resume read and categorized by a computer might be heretical. However, companies and public sector agencies use scanning systems for several reasons:

☆ They save time and money. Large corporations and governments have cut work forces to bare-bones levels, swamping the job market with millions of employees. This means that HR departments that once had 10 people handling recruiting may now have only three or four. Without electronic help, there's no way this skeletal staff could handle the daily resume deluge.

☆ Companies and government agencies can keep a huge database of applicants current, instead of more-or-less counting on recent mail and ad responses to ensure an active file of candidates. Recruiters feel this longer resume "shelf-life" gives employers and applicants a better chance of making a good match. For instance, instead of your resume being discarded after three months, it has as good a chance of being selected for an opening through a key-word sort as one that arrived two days ago.

☆ Electronic tracking programs allow companies to communicate more effectively with job seekers. For example, Motorola Inc.'s Land Mobile Products sector uses its system to regularly send letters to promising candidates, including college interns nearing graduation and engineers with specialties the company values. Having critical information readily available about such candidates give Motorola an edge over other high-tech competitors. There's always a source of superior candidates for future openings as the company needs them.

☆ How about all those times you've replied to a help-wanted ad but never heard back from the company? Automation allows employers to reply to thousands of applicants who would otherwise be left waiting and wondering. Once your resume is scanned, the computer will automatically kick out a letter to you. Admittedly you might prefer a personal note from an HR recruiter, but a computer-generated response is better than none at all.

Of course, these systems aren't perfect from a corporate perspective:

☆ They can be hard to integrate with other MIS programs.
☆ They're rarely used for all levels of positions.
☆ Many line managers with access to them either don't know how to use them or don't have the time or inclination to learn how they work.

Executive Search Firms

Executive search firms use resume tracking systems in much the same way as companies. They store and retrieve credentials on thousands of solicited and unsolicited resumes while conducting searches for clients. Of course, third-party recruiters rely primarily on networking to find qualified candidates, but having a database of eligible possibilities can speed the process tremendously.

Online Employment Service Providers

To find employees, large and small companies alike increasingly are turning to online career centers operated by third parties. These centers are operated through commercial online services, such as America Online, or can be accessed via the Internet. By posting descriptions of available openings, they can attract responses from thousands of computer users nationwide.

While subscribing to one of these service providers isn't cheap, it's less expensive for employers than hiring an executive search firm and less of a hassle than slogging through hundreds of responses to one classified ad. As one of the advisory board members of CareerWeb, an online career center, says, "It costs me more to fill one engineering position through an ad or search firm than to buy an entire year's membership with CareerWeb." Subscribing to an online employment service provider is also less expensive than buying and continuously updating the software needed to build an in-house system.

Smaller firms particularly appreciate using Internet service providers because they gain exposure to so many more candidates than would otherwise notice them, which levels the recruiting playing field between them and larger corporations. For Gary Cook, president of Themis Instructional Services, using an online service is extremely cost-effective. While Themis can reach thousands of technical trainers nationwide with one online listing, it couldn't afford to buy the same exposure through newspaper and trade journal ads, Mr. Cook says.

Many online career sites also feature electronic resume banks where individual job seekers can post resumes as well. For the service providers, it's just as easy to match corporate clients with candidates located via a posted resume as with those uncovered through a posted job listing. (See Chapter 8 in the *NBEW's Cover Letters* for information about the most popular career sites.)

The Good News about Resume Scanning

You may have an initial aversion to being chosen or rejected by a machine. However, consider the advantages of sending your resume to an employer with an automated tracking system:

☆ With continual downsizing and the advent of "the executive with port-folio," it's important to keep your credentials in circulation. Resume databases can help you to do this.

☆ If you contact your key databases every six months to a year, you'll automatically update your resume and be ready to respond to new opportunities.

☆ Just as online service providers can connect employers with qualified applicants worldwide, they can open doors to thousands of opportunities you couldn't learn about otherwise.

☆ Using a resume database service is more time- and cost-effective than conducting a direct-mail campaign.

☆ It can be difficult to move to another department within your company or government agency—especially if your manager blocks you or you don't know people in other areas. Fortunately, internal tracking systems accept resumes from people throughout the organization. If your credentials match an available position, there's a good chance you'll be called.

And the Bad News . . .

Computers aren't nearly as smart as people, nor are they as discerning when it comes to identifying the human factors or personality traits that distinguish candidates who *can* do a job from those who *will* and *want to*. Even the most sophisticated sorting programs have a long way to go before they'll possess the insight and finesse of a skilled recruiter.

Because they rely heavily on key-word searches to match applicants with required skills, computer systems will knock most career changers out of the running. Consider a retiring military officer who wants to enter the civilian workforce. He's seeking a management position, but even if he was a top-ranked leader of an elite corps of paratroopers, his resume isn't likely to include the specific key words that cause it to be pulled for such a managerial role. Yet this individual might make an exceptional manager in any number of situations where he could apply his seasoned leadership skills while quickly learning the business.

While employers supposedly are seeking professionals with good communication skills who can wear many hats, computers programmed to extract only the resumes that include certain key words haven't been given this message. As far as they're concerned, generalists need not apply.

The same is true for recent college graduates with liberal arts degrees. These articulate, broadly-educated first-time job seekers are often brilliant, quick learners, but if their resumes don't include an internship or two, they may be rejected for lack of technical expertise.

And Yet, There's Hope!

Remember, sending a resume isn't the most effective way to land an interview. Most interviews result from networking contacts. Fortunately, generalists, career changers and liberal arts graduates are pretty good at developing rapport with other people. And it's people who make hiring decisions. If your experience isn't suited to a key-word search, make a habit of personally seeking out managers who can say yes. Computers can't get in your way if you make an end run around them.

Do's and Don'ts for Writing Scannable Resumes

When writing a resume that will be read by a computer, keep in mind two main concerns: format and key-word content.

Tips on Scanner-Friendly Formatting

Format deals with how a resume looks. It involves decisions concerning white space, font styles and size, paper selection, bold or underlined titles and other elements that will make a resume pleasing to the eye and easy to read. Unfortunately, what's most attractive to human screeners can drive computers crazy, slow down the scanning process and ultimately produce a bunch of stored gibberish. To avoid becoming a tracking system statistic, use these tips when formatting your resume:

- ☆ Use a printable grade of white or other light-colored paper. Print your resume only on one side of 8½-by-11-inch sheets. Unusual colors and paper sizes are indigestible to computer scanners.

- ☆ Use either a laser or high quality ink-jet printer. Dot matrix print confuses resume scanners because the text isn't sharp enough for them to delineate one letter from another. For instance, e's can be misread as c's, and i's as l's, resulting in the words being garbled and stored incorrectly.

- ☆ The printed message on outdated computer key-punch cards—"don't fold, staple or mutilate"—applies to electronic resumes unless you want to sabotage the system and abandon all hope of getting a job with ABC company.

- ☆ Use a standard typeface and a 10- to 12-point font size. To most computer scanners, sans serif typefaces are the most readable. (This is a sans serif typeface.) However, most computers can also recognize type-faces like the one used in this book (Times Roman, 12-point type).

☆ Always put the most important data—your name, address, e-mail address, phone and fax numbers—on separate lines at the top of your re-sume. Otherwise a scanner will likely merge the words in nonsensical ways. Here's how to do it:

Larry Abercrombie
222 Alsace Boulevard, Richardson, Texas 75080
Phone: 214-233-9900
Fax: 214-233-8989
E-mail: LA10101@aol.com

☆ Put your name at the top left corner of every subsequent page. This can save confusion should a page accidentally be orphaned during the screening process.

☆ Allow plenty of white space to help the scanner separate important elements of your resume. Use a second and even a third page instead of cramming all your information into one or two pages. Humans can deal with a shoe-horned resume, even if they don't like it. Computers can't. The trade-off is that computers read faster than people. They don't care if your resume takes three pages as long as it's scannable.

☆ Confine yourself to ALL CAPS or **boldface type** when delineating major section headings from less important items because the majority of scanners can read both of these. Don't use italicized or underlined words, though, because all but the most sophisticated systems will mis-interpret them.

☆ Keep your format simple. Boxes, shading, graphics, hollow bullets and other intriguing elements might delight humans but they'll only serve to confuse computers. For instance, a scanner will read a hollow bullet as an "o," not as a marker for a new phrase. Regular bullets are scannable, though.

☆ Because it's so difficult for scanners to read degraded (faxed or copied) text, always make sure that the company receives a hard copy original of your resume if possible. For instance, should a company advertising a position suggest that you fax or e-mail your response, by all means, do so. However, be sure to send via "snail mail" (regular mail) originals of both your cover letter and resume.

☆ Always include a cover letter with your resume. The computer will give it little attention, except to record it as a text image. But if you make the initial screening cut, the hiring manager may ask to see actual hard-copy versions of your letter and resume to get a better feel for your style and personality.

☆ If you are replying to an ad on the Internet, send your resume in an ASCII format, rather than as typical text. ASCII is the language that computers use to speak to each other. If you supply the appropriate language, computers anywhere on the Internet will understand. If you don't use ASCII, funny things may happen when you e-mail your resume. It may reach its destination as an assortment of hieroglyphics instead of your brilliant prose.

Two resumes provided by Wendy Enelow, president of Enelow Enterprises International, an executive resume and professional employment center in Lynchburg, Virginia, illustrate the difference between traditional and scannable resume formats and wording. Humans would prefer to receive the version shown on pages 257–258. The computer-friendly version is on pages 259–260. While the second resume may seem like boring, plain vanilla stuff to us, it's cookies and cream to a computer.

Of the two resumes, it's easy to understand why the first is more pleasing to a human recruiter. The graphical features, variety of type sizes and boldface and italic type give it tremendous eye appeal. But to computers, this version is fraught with problems. The italicized words are hard for scanners to read. The double lines identifying the different resume sections might merge with the headings during the scanning process and prevent the computer from translating the words correctly. There's also too little white space for easy scanning.

By taking out the italicized words and horizontal lines and increasing the white space, Olivia has done the computer and herself a great favor. Removing the boldface treatment probably wasn't necessary, but some companies are still using outmoded scanners that just can't read it. With thousands of resumes arriving each year, companies don't worry about the ones that don't scan properly. If you have any doubts about how well your resume will scan, change it. It's better to be safe than sorry.

OLIVIA ONLINE
119 Old Stable Road
Lynchburg, Virginia 24503

Phone (804) 384-4600   E-mail oonline@aol.com

SENIOR MARKETING EXECUTIVE
Banking, Financial and Leasing Services

Dynamic and high-impact Marketing Strategist with proven results in leading consumer-driven and business-to-business marketing organizations. Successful in creating powerful, "call to action" campaigns that have consistently delivered revenue and profit within highly competitive markets. Strong management and leadership talents combined with creativity and innovation. Executive MBA.

PROFESSIONAL QUALIFICATIONS:

- Strategic Market Planning
- Tactical Field Implementation
- Advertising Agency Management
- Market Research & Intelligence
- New Product Launch & Positioning
- Inbound & Outbound Telemarketing

- Print & Broadcast Advertising
- Public Relations & Promotions
- Corporate Communications
- Direct Mail & Direct Response
- Corporate Identity Campaigns
- Special Events Management

PRODUCT PORTFOLIO:

- Consumer & Commercial Deposit & Loan Products
- Commercial & Residential Mortgages
- Capital Equipment Financing & Lease Transactions
- Personal & Corporate Investment Products & Services
- Personal & Commercial Lines Insurance
- Trust Services
- Credit & Debit Cards

CAREER HISTORY:

1994 to Present   **Senior Marketing Consultant—Finance & Banking Industries**
ONLINE ASSOCIATES, Garden City, New York

- Designed and implemented comprehensive business/marketing plan to promote sales of investment mortgage, insurance and other financial products by newly affiliated companies. Resulting new business booked far exceeded expectations.
- Spearheaded a series of community-based public relations campaigns to introduce expanded loan programs. Delivered 6% increase over previous year.
- Created multi-faceted marketing communications program for regional operating division of national organization. Delivered 14% growth through effective database marketing, targeted communications, promotional events and media/publicity placement.
- Designed corporate communications campaign that generated 300 qualified sales leads within one month for a diversified financial services corporation.

OLIVIA ONLINE *Page Two*

1990 to 1994	**Chief Marketing Officer / Director of Development**
	MERCY MEDICAL CENTER, Rockville Centre, New York

- Drove forward the strategic marketing planning process, wrote first annual sales and marketing plan, and created new corporate identity program.
- Designed and launched marketing campaign that added $2+ million in new revenues.
- Created corporate development and capital campaign that collected $7.5 million in funds.
- Developed grassroots public relations campaign to influence public perceptions, and won support of local community leaders and politicians.

1987 to 1989	**Senior Vice President of Marketing**
	EUROPEAN AMERICAN BANK, Uniondale, New York

- Restructured Marketing Department, realigned staff responsibilities, repositioned business development focus, and delivered 15% increase in productivity at no additional cost.
- Created integrated marketing campaign for new CD program that generated a 12% increase in business volume within 10 days.
- Orchestrated fully-integrated marketing campaigns for two new product launches that produced $3 million in revenues.
- Revitalized print and broadcast advertising program, expanded into new markets, and achieved an 8%+ improvement in response rate and product sales.

1982 to 1986	**Vice President / Director of Marketing & Public Relations**
	LONG ISLAND TRUST COMPANY, Garden City, New York

- Created multi-channel campaign to introduce home equity program that grew into $10.5 million portfolio within first year.
- Launched a series of high-profile promotional tie-ins to increase regional visibility (e.g., U.S. Open Golf Championship).
- Designed campaigns for credit card customer acquisition, resulting in 30% growth.

1977 to 1981	**Director of Marketing Services**
	CIT FINANCIAL CORPORATION, New York, New York

- Achieved strongest volume growth in the 150-year history of the company.
- Originated auto loan marketing program which increased volume 30% within first year.
- Recruited and developed a team of top-flight national marketing directors.
- Promoted from Advertising & Sales Promotion Manager to Director of Marketing Services for CIT's three largest operating subsidiaries.

EDUCATION:

Executive MBA Degree / Management Major, 1981
BS Degree / Marketing Concentration, 1980
PACE UNIVERSITY, New York, New York

PROFESSIONAL AFFILIATIONS:

American Marketing Association	Bank Marketing Association
Direct Mail Marketing Association	Int'l Association of Business Communicators

OLIVIA ONLINE
119 Old Stable Road
Lynchburg, Virginia 24503

(804) 384-4600   E-mail   oonline@aol.com

SENIOR MARKETING EXECUTIVE
BANKING, FINANCIAL AND LEASING SERVICES

Dynamic and high-impact Marketing Strategist with proven results in leading consumer-driven and business-to-business marketing organizations. Successful in creating powerful, "call to action" campaigns that have consistently delivered revenue and profit within highly competitive markets. Strong management and leadership talents combined with creativity and innovation. Executive MBA.

PROFESSIONAL QUALIFICATIONS:

- Strategic Market Planning
- Tactical Field Implementation
- Advertising Agency Management
- Market Research & Intelligence
- New Product Launch & Positioning
- Inbound & Outbound Telemarketing

- Print & Broadcast Advertising
- Public Relations & Promotions
- Corporate Communications
- Direct Mail & Direct Response
- Corporate Identity Campaigns
- Special Events Management

PRODUCT PORTFOLIO:

- Consumer & Commercial Deposit & Loan Products
- Commercial & Residential Mortgages
- Capital Equipment Financing & Lease Transactions
- Personal & Corporate Investment Products & Services
- Personal & Commercial Lines Insurance
- Trust Services
- Credit & Debit Cards

CAREER HISTORY:

1994 to Present   Senior Marketing Consultant—Finance & Banking Industries
                                   ONLINE ASSOCIATES, Garden City, New York

- Designed and implemented comprehensive business/marketing plan to promote sales of investment mortgage, insurance and other financial products by newly affiliated companies. Resulting new business booked far exceeded expectations.
- Spearheaded a series of community-based public relations campaigns to introduce expanded loan programs. Delivered 6% increase over previous year.
- Created multi-faceted marketing communications program for regional operating division of national organization. Delivered 14% growth through effective database marketing, targeted communications, promotional events and media/publicity placement.
- Designed corporate communications campaign that generated 300 qualified sales leads within one month for a diversified financial services corporation.

1990 to 1994   Chief Marketing Officer / Director of Development
                                   MERCY MEDICAL CENTER, Rockville Centre, New York

- Drove forward the strategic marketing planning process, wrote first annual sales and marketing plan, and created new corporate identity program.
- Designed and launched marketing campaign that added $2+ million in new revenues.

OLIVIA ONLINE   Page Two

- Created corporate development and capital campaign that collected $7.5 million in funds.
- Developed grassroots public relations campaign to influence public perceptions, and won support of local community leaders and politicians.

1987 to 1989   Senior Vice President of Marketing
                                EUROPEAN AMERICAN BANK, Uniondale, New York

- Restructured Marketing Department, realigned staff responsibilities, repositioned business development focus, and delivered 15% increase in productivity at no additional cost.
- Created integrated marketing campaign for new CD program that generated a 12% increase in business volume within 10 days.
- Orchestrated fully-integrated marketing campaigns for two new product launches that produced $3 million in revenues.
- Revitalized print and broadcast advertising program, expanded into new markets, and achieved an 8%+ improvement in response rate and product sales.

1982 to 1986   Vice President / Director of Marketing & Public Relations
                                LONG ISLAND TRUST COMPANY, Garden City, New York

- Created multi-channel campaign to introduce home equity program that grew into $10.5 million portfolio within first year.
- Launched a series of high-profile promotional tie-ins to increase regional visibility (e.g., U.S. Open Golf Championship).
- Designed campaigns for credit card customer acquisition, resulting in 30% growth.

1977 to 1981   Director of Marketing Services
                                CIT FINANCIAL CORPORATION, New York, New York

- Achieved strongest volume growth in the 150-year history of the company.
- Originated auto loan marketing program which increased volume 30% within first year.
- Recruited and developed a team of top-flight national marketing directors.
- Promoted from Advertising & Sales Promotion Manager to Director of Marketing Services for CIT's three largest operating subsidiaries.

EDUCATION:

Executive MBA Degree / Management Major, 1981
BS Degree / Marketing Concentration, 1980
PACE UNIVERSITY, New York, New York

PROFESSIONAL AFFILIATIONS:

American Marketing Association   Direct Mail Marketing Association
Bank Marketing Association   Int'l Association of Business Communicators

Tips on Scanner-Friendly Content

Once your resume makes it through image scanning, it's translated into ASCII language and searched for predesignated key words. A key word is a noun or noun phrase identifying particular types of experience, education, certificates and licenses earned, memberships in professional organizations or number of years in a certain role. Typical key words for a human resources professional might include: salary and benefits administration, training and development, affirmative action, executive compensation, union liaison, recruiting, salary survey, EAP program, downsizing, reengineering, health-care cost containment and government reports. These words or phrases describe specialized human resources areas. Transferable skills, such as planning, organizing, creating and listening, rarely are designated as key words, even though they might be equally important factors for success in an HR position.

For a computer to select you as a likely candidate for an opening, your resume must make liberal use of the key words commonly linked with the position you seek. You're actually playing a numbers game where winning the selection lottery depends on how many times you hit on the key words describing skills a potential employer believes are critical, useful or nice to have in a qualified applicant. The people with the most "hits" will win a chance to talk to a real person. Those who make no effort to tailor their resumes won't.

Talk about *tailor or die.* Computers will eliminate you without a second thought unless you play by their rules. They can't be finessed or cajoled. They're just machines.

Whether you like dealing with them or not, resume scanners are becoming an increasingly important part of the internal team that matches candidates to jobs. They're like a pesky colleague whom you must grudgingly tolerate because his specialized skills help keep you in the game.

These tips can help you to enhance your relationship with your new team member:

☆ Most of the guidelines that apply to regular resumes also pertain to scanner-friendly ones. Some recruiters still like to see a specific objective at the beginning of the document. It not only provides your first key words, it also gives human recruiters a clear idea of the job you want.

☆ The next section after your objective should be the key word summary. This resembles a Professional Qualifications Brief because it highlights the most important assets you have to offer an employer. But instead of stating your experience, personality traits and philosophy, use specific nouns or noun phrases to describe your areas of expertise.

Olivia Online's Professional Qualifications and Product Portfolio section are excellent examples of key-word summaries.

Some experts argue that job seekers don't need to insert a key-word summary at the beginning of their electronic resumes because computers are perfectly capable of finding key words elsewhere in the documents. However, from a computer's perspective, key words are the more important facts in your resume, after your name, address, e-mail address, phone and fax numbers. If you agree with this premise, you'll put the key-word summary at the beginning. If you don't buy into it, you'll be happy to see examples at the end of this chapter of good scannable resumes that don't begin with specific key-word summaries, including one that resulted in a job interview at EDS.

☆ Stress accomplishments and results rather than duties and responsibilities. The more specific you are, the more likely you'll include more critical key words which, in turn, will generate more hits.

☆ Use the same sections and headings as you would in any resume. The key-word summary is the only exception to this rule.

☆ As with any employment document you create, be truthful and concise. However, you can change buzz words to match industries and careers. For instance, a teacher hoping to move into corporate training can substitute the word "training" for "teaching" and "program design" for "lesson plans." This tactic might create enough key words for her resume to make the interview stack. Whether she can convince an HR recruiter who wants only trainers with corporate experience that she deserves the position may be another story.

☆ Deciding whether to outline your entire work history or just mention the past 10 to 15 years is just as controversial when creating a scanned resume as it is when preparing those sent to individuals. The computer doesn't care one way or another as long as you provide employment dates in numerals, not words. Otherwise, delete dates altogether. Example: Use 1997–1999, not "three years" to describe the time you performed a position or activity. Don't have gaps in employment, even if you are unemployed.

☆ Use key words in your experience or employment section, too. Here are three experience statements chock full of key words. (The italicization of key words is mine.) As we say in Texas, reading the following would send a computer to hog heaven!

Conducted *performance testing* of *Parallel Fortran* on *CD4000* and of *C* and *Vector Fortran* on *Cyber systems. Analyzed results for conformance* with *design requirements.* Used *Excel* to generate results of *spreadsheets.* Prompt reporting enabled developers to rapidly pinpoint *areas of degradation.*

Designed, developed and implemented a *succession process* to focus on *executive management replacement* and *development.*

Provided leadership and support to a task force of *senior line managers* that resulted in a new *companywide performance management process.*

☆ Use synonyms if a credential or process might be described in more than one way. For instance, a "company performance management process" could also be called a performance appraisal system. "Executive management replacement and development" is also known as succession planning. If you don't know the specific key words to use for a skill or activity, try describing it in several different ways.

☆ Be careful of acronyms and abbreviations, unless you're confident everyone knows and uses the ones you've chosen. When in doubt, spell them out.

☆ Specific degrees, universities, leadership programs, professional licenses, certifications, trade organizations and honors are often used as key words to retrieve resumes for further consideration. By including them on your resume, you may score added hits at certain employers.

☆ Personality traits are hard to sell to any but the most sophisticated automated scanners, but human resources professionals like to see them anyway. Include these qualifications when it seems appropriate, but remember that they'll rarely be acknowledged in the initial sort.

☆ Send only one resume to a company with an automated tracking system. Since every resume is scanned into the same computer database, candidates with more than one in the system will seem desperate, sneaky or forgetful. If you send your resume directly to the hiring manager, mention in your cover letter that you already sent a copy to the HR department, but thought she might like one as well.

Once you know your resume is in the system, don't call again. Multiple calls annoy HR people, who may flag you as a nuisance. And once you become a designated nudge, it doesn't matter whether your electronic resume includes a cornucopia of terrific key words. You'll never be chosen for an interview.

Scannable Resumes That Work

The following resumes appeal to both people and computers. Some have obvious keyword summaries, while others include their keywords within the text of each function or position.

Ruth Kimbell

Having gone through one downsizing too many, Ruth decided to start her own consulting firm. With the advice of Russ Yaquinto, a vice president and senior consultant with Right Management Consultants, she designed her resume to focus on how her background would benefit her potential clients. Her keyword summary spotlights her areas of expertise, while the accomplishments section gives her accumulated greatest achievements a prominent place on the first page. She was sure to put her most recent and highest level position on the front page as well.

This resume is very scanner friendly, except for the few underlined job titles, which could easily be fixed by simply removing the underlines and keeping the bold type.

Harry Lu

Harry Lu's resume is a computer scanner's dream. You might say Harry knows how to speak its language.

RUTH KIMBELL

58 Sapphire Ave.
Wichita, KS 28097

Res: 316-555-8989
Ofc: 316-427-8000
E-mail: kimbell@aol.com

OBJECTIVE

A Business Management position where proven skills in leadership, planning, decision making and communication will be utilized to assure strong company performance.

BACKGROUND SUMMARY

Diversified experience in Human Resources, Operations and Administration, with a unique blend of technical and interpersonal skills. Track record of success and bottom-line contribution in challenging environments. A straight-forward communicator, negotiator and resource. Able to identify problems and develop solutions in a multi-task work environment through teamwork, goal setting and follow-through. Major strengths in:

- Administrative/Facilities Services
- Strategic Planning
- Compensation and Benefits
- Executive Compensation
- Training and Development

- ADA, FMLA, EEOC
- Employee Relations
- Staffing
- Workers' Compensation and Safety
- Acquisition Planning

ACCOMPLISHMENTS

- Set the strategy, direction and implementation for staffing a start-up national sales force of 70.
- Initiated and developed a profit sharing program to improve productivity and revenue.
- Developed and implemented a Workplace Violence Program to assure a safe work environment and minimize liability.
- Streamlined data management by implementing a human resource and payroll database. Reduced time and staffing required for data gathering and improved critical reporting capability.
- Implemented programs to reduce telephone costs saving $100,000 the first year.
- Gained Board of Director approval and successfully implemented a company-wide Proactive Employment Related Legal Exposure Program.
- Reduced Workers' Compensation claims by implementing a Safety and Ergonomic Awareness Program decreasing premiums for five consecutive years.
- Redesigned copy program which reduced costs by $200,000 while improving service.
- Successfully managed a $2 million budget.

PROFESSIONAL EXPERIENCE

ORTHOFIX INC. (formerly American Medical Electronics, Inc.)

Vice President Human Resources/Administrative Services
Designed and implemented all Human Resource programs and policies throughout this international medical device organization. Directed staff of five. (1988–1997)

- Developed, as a member of the Executive Management Team, the business strategy for the organization.
- Delivered Board of Director presentations including Executive Compensation/Benefits and Acquisition Planning.
- Directed compensation, benefits, recruitment, training, EEO/AAP, safety, administrative services, employee relations and business insurance.

Ruth Kimbell
Page Two

SELF EMPLOYED

Human Resources Consultant
Delivered a broad range of human resource services on a direct contract basis to client companies which included Pitney Bowes, Digital Equipment Corporation and BancA. (1987–1988)

TELINQ SYSTEMS INCORPORATED (currently ADC Telecommunications, Inc.)

Manager, Human Resources
Directed all Human Resource activities for this venture capital funded telecommunications company. These included staffing, stock option programs, employee relations, training, procedure development, and salary administration. (1986–1987)

ITEC LABORATORIES, INC.

Personnel Manager
Provided all staffing, employee relations, purchasing and facilities management for this start-up telecommunications Research and Development facility. (1984–1986)

UCCEL (acquired by Computer Associates)

Director, Employee Relations
Managed all recruiting, salary administration, counseling, policy interpretation, turnover analysis, EEO compliance and personnel programs design for the three software divisions of the company. Directed staff of 11 in three locations. (1982–1984)

BOOZ, ALLEN & HAMILTON, INC.

Staff Selection Representative
Recruited highly classified technical candidates to meet the professional staffing needs of the partners. Created the college recruitment program for the Government Sector. (1980–1982)

UNITED INFORMATION SYSTEMS (a subsidiary of United Telecommunications)

Employment Manager
Directed all recruitment efforts for Corporate Headquarters. Provided benefit and EEO/AAP administration for the entire organization. Directed staff of three. (1973–1980)

EDUCATION

MBA Program, University of Kansas
BA, Psychology/Sociology, Northwest Missouri State University, Maryville, Mlssouri
Graduated Cum Laude

PROFESSIONAL DEVELOPMENT

Gallup Profile Process, Targeted Selection (DDI), Crosby Quality College
Attended numerous management, leadership and personal development courses

PROFESSIONAL ASSOCIATIONS

Society for Human Resource Management Association
Wichita Human Resource Management Association
SMU Human Resource Roundtable
Northeast Wichita Personnel Association

Harry S. Lu
2700 Mission Circle * San Diego * CA 95180 * 619-441-1275
e-mail: harry-lu@well.com

CAREER INTEREST

• Design, development, implementation and maintenance of software.

PROFESSIONAL EXPERIENCE

DTM   5/96 to present
San Diego, California
Senior Software Engineer II

• Currently modifying and testing a Message Switching System (MSS) for Year 2000
  compliance on HP-UX and SCO UNIX platforms. MSS is a UNIX based communications
  system supporting TCP/IP, X.25 and other network services.
• Currently developing a communications system based on the IBM MQSeries
  middleware. Lightweight Directory Access Protocol (LDAP) is used to provide
  directory services between MQSeries Queue Managers on different nodes.
• Ported a Network Management System (NMS) from HP-UX to SCO UNIX. NMS is built
  on top of the HP Open View Network Node Manager and is used to monitor different
  subsystems on the network.
• Provided enhancement to DHL's WWW-based package tracking system. The system contains a Web Query Engine written in Perl that provides track and trace capability for packages. Conducted testing on commercially available Web browsers.

Systems and Software used: HP-UX, SCO UNIX, Solaris, C, C++, Perl, HTTP, HTML, CGI, HP
Open View, TCP/IP, Netscape Directory Server, LDAP, MQSeries, Curses, Continuus/CM.

Hughes Space Information Systems   1994 to 1996
Houston, Texas
Engineering Systems Analyst

• Responsible for developing test tools for shuttle software on the IBM PC and the
  RS/6000 workstation using C++ and Rogue Wave Foundation Classes. Performed object-
  oriented design using Paradigm Plus (CASE tool). Created automated test drivers and
  tested code on both OS/2 and AIX platforms.
• Developed software to support system and application logging. Provided X
  Windows/Motif graphical user interface (GUI) for delogging. This is a client/server
  application that supports both local and remote logging/delogging requests.
• Developed software to handle inter-node and interprocess communications (IPC) on
  the DEC Alpha workstation and IBM ES/9000 mainframe. Utilized sockets, message
  queues, semaphores and shared memory.
• Served as configuration management (CM) administrator for development and
  maintenance organizations. Received award for developing procedures and shell scripts
  to streamline the CM process.

Systems and Software used: Digital UNIX, AIX, OS/2, C, C++, X/Motif, Rogue Wave
Tools.h++ Class Library, Paradigm Plus, Teamwork, C Shell, Sed & Awk.

Harry Lu
Page 2

ETG Corporation   1989 to 1994
Federal Systems Company, Houston, Texas
Senior Associate Programmer
- Developed POSIX compliant system application program interface (API) for C Language Real-time Extension and Ada Binding.
- Designed and developed tools to check out data retrieval software on workstations. Provided X Windows GUI for user input and data display.
- Developed real-time data acquisition software to track and display space shuttle positions.

Systems and software used: Ultrix, Real-time UNIX, MVS/ESA, OpenMVS, TSO, ISPF, C, Ada, X Windows.

Taylor Manufacturing Company   1985 to 1986
Harlingen, Texas
Design Engineer
- Designed conveying systems for industrial and agricultural applications.

ETG Corporation   1985
Entry Systems Division, Austin, Texas
Programmer (co-op)
- Responsible for the testing of vendor logo software on various IBM PC configurations. Conducted usability, performance and stress testing.
- Documented test procedures, prepared test reports and made recommendation on product appearance.

Systems and software used: DOS, R:base, R:base Extended Report Writer

---

EDUCATION

Master of Computer Science, Texas A&M University, May 1989 (GPA: 3.84/4.0)
M.S. Mechanical Engineering, Texas A&M University, May 1983
B.S. Mechanical Engineering, Texas A&M University, May 1980

MISCELLANEOUS

Member, Upsilon Pi Epsilon (Computer Sciences Honorary)
Member, Tau Beta Pi (Engineering Honorary)
Member, Phi Kappa Phi (General Scholastic Honorary)

Other Resume Examples

The following examples were taken from other chapters in this book. While they may not have been specifically designed for resume scanners, they're still computer-friendly, with the few noted exceptions.

While Dale Martinson's resume doesn't have a keyword summary, a computer can easily find the appropriate buzzwords within the text describing his various positions. Scan through it yourself to see how many keywords you can find.

The only thing Dale may want to change to make his resume more computer friendly is a couple of lines of italicized words. Otherwise it's ready to roll.

Benetta Rusk's and Will Griffeth's resumes were designed with people in mind, yet they will communicate with computers just as easily.

Dale Martinson   555 Main Street, Anytown, US 55222 555-555-5222
                                            dmartinson@citynet.com

Material Planning & Logistics professional with a strong track record of devising systems and leading teams to ensure efficient, effective support to the manufacturing operation. A proven performer ready for a new challenge.

Strengths
- Comprehension of all facets of materials management and how it impacts the overall manufacturing operation.
- Knowledge of production processes and purchasing functions.
- People skills: Leading self-motivated, cooperative work teams to high levels of performance; collaborating with all functions throughout the organization; maintaining positive customer relationships.
- Analysis and planning abilities: Designing efficient systems; selecting cost-effective vendors; developing and applying sound business strategies to all functional and management assignments.

Professional Experience

MAJOR AUTO COMPANY, City, State   1978–November 1997
Manufacturer of Transmissions and Service Parts for Major Auto Motor Vehicles

Material Planning & Logistics

- **Superintendent** (1990–1999)

Held primary responsibility for all plant receiving and shipping activity; acquisition of required production materials; purchasing and monitoring of general stores; movement of production and non-production material throughout the plant; delivery/distribution of finished parts to locations in the U.S., Mexico and Europe.

Worked collaboratively with Production and Engineering departments to determine materials needs and ensure a smooth materials flow to and from the plant. Resolved scheduling and delivery problems; expedited parts for unexpected needs; served as primary customer liaison.

- Managed transfer and overlap of 2 production lines; simultaneously handled production requirements for both lines for 2 years.
- Analyzed logistics and materials plans for new production line; revised operation to achieve a more efficient system (e.g., reducing by a factor of 3 the number of times a part was handled).
- Achieved $500K annual savings by analyzing freight charges and selecting a more cost-effective carrier.
- On at least 3 occasions, prevented temporary plant shut-down due to part shortages through initiative, resourcefulness and knowledge of materials distribution systems.
- Successfully maintained shipping schedule, without increasing manpower, while handling 80% increase in service parts shipment.
- Instrumental in plant's successful ISO 9000 audit for the past 2 years.
- Managed entire Material Planning & Logistics Department on an interim basis on numerous short-term occasions and once for 4 months.

Dale Martinson

Supervised, directed, and motivated staff of 6 salaried and 72 hourly employees working 3 shifts.

- Upon promotion to Superintendent, took over supervision of 3 shifts and all responsibilities previously handled by 1 Superintendent and 2 General Foremen.
- Motivated and led staff to high levels of performance; team's cooperation and positive attitude recognized by plant management.
- Eliminated staff redundancies and reorganized job functions to create more efficient work processes. Resulted in staff reduction by 19% and a more highly motivated and satisfied work force.

Oversaw removal of waste and scrap materials from plant (aluminum chips, production scrap, cast iron borings, aluminum turnings, used production equipment).

- Analyzed a 75% increase in removal costs and discovered equipment removal tied to new production system was being charged back to the wrong cost center. Presented findings to division level and succeeded in removing $48K monthly from plant's operating expenses.
- Conducted detailed price and service comparisons of waste removal contractors; findings used to justify switch to new contractor.

- **Unit Supervisor** (1986–1990)

Supervised 6 salaried employees with responsibility for analyzing cycle reports and overseeing records integrity, thereby ensuring adequate parts supply throughout the manufacturing operation.

Managed delivery of transmissions to domestic and international customers.

- Consistently No. 1 of 6 plants in on-time customer delivery.
- Performance in distribution to assembly plants rated "10" on a 1–10 scale.

- **Senior Analyst** (1980–1986)

Promoted to more senior position based on successful job performance and initiative in learning and assisting in all areas of the department.
Assumed additional responsibilities as service parts distributor to domestic and international locations. Served as liaison/coordinator for shipping of experimental parts to Major Auto R&D/Engineering.

- **Analyst** (1978–1980)

Met the challenge of ensuring adequate production parts for daily plant operations. Analyzed part and line counts from daily cycle checkers to monitor material supply. Handled rejected and returned material.

Education
WASHINGTON STATE COLLEGE, Washington, New Jersey
BA in Spanish Civilization; Minor in Psychology.
SPRINGFIELD INSTITUTE, Springfield, Illinois
Graduate credits toward MA in Spanish Literature and Modern Psychology.

Additional Information
Proficient in a variety of computer applications including MS Office.
Fluent in Spanish.
Perfect attendance in 19 years with Major Auto Company.

BENETTA L. RUSK, CCIM
222 Redbird Ave.
Tulsa, OK 45454
(h) 918-387-2567
(w) 918-392-4000
blrusk@mailbag.com

Experienced real estate professional with a diverse background in acquisition, disposition and finance of retail, industrial and office properties.

PROFESSIONAL EXPERIENCE

INTERSHOP REAL ESTATE SERVICES, Dallas, Texas   1994 to 1999
  Manager Acquisitions/Dispositions
  • Involved in disposition of entire U.S. operation of Intershop Real Estate Services, totaling 5.1 million square feet of commercial real estate assets.

Acquisitions
  • Prior to the divestiture, was directly responsible for or assisted with purchasing more than $100 million in over 1.3 million square feet of shopping centers and institutional quality single tenant properties for Intershop and third-party clients.
  • Evaluated new deals and developed packages involving power retail centers and single tenant triple net properties for review by Intershop investment committee in Zurich, Switzerland; screened unsolicited offers to determine if they met Intershop's investment criteria; worked broker network; marketed the firm by networking with members of ICSC, CCIM, CREW; researched, analyzed, and evaluated targeted markets; monitored investment rates; performed detailed analysis of projects under consideration using ARGUS; coordinated and managed due diligence process and closing.

Dispositions
  • In addition, was responsible for disposing of portions of non-strategic assets, selling 35 properties with an aggregate value of $65 million.
  • Negotiated purchase and sale agreements, letters of intent, listing agreements; responded to broker and principal inquiries on properties for sale; evaluated offers based upon company objectives, then recommended the best deals; developed flyers and sales packages for direct dispositions; researched and selected brokerage firms for properties throughout the U.S.; managed broker marketing material to assure it met seller's standards; set up and monitored marketing process internally and with each broker; coordinated and managed the information necessary for purchaser's due diligence.

AETNA INVESTMENT GROUP, Dallas, Texas   1991 to 1994
  Assistant to Managing Director in charge of sales
  • Managed sales by coordinating principals, brokers, attorneys, asset and property managers, surveyors, and title companies to perform disposition activities for a commercial real estate portfolio of approximately 90 properties worth over $370 million.
  • Managed 60 property closings for the Southwest Region totaling 7.5 million square feet.
  • Disposed of assets using the same process detailed under Intershop.

TRAMMELL CROW COMPANY, Dallas, Texas   1988 to 1991
  Assistant Asset Manager/Analyst
  • Planned, coordinated and reviewed initial PRO-JECT modeling for approximately 200 properties in the $500 million Equitable Refinance Transaction.

BENNETTA L. RUSK Page 2

- Managed property information for a combined $800 million portfolio.
- Interacted with field partners to analyze problem areas for strategic planning purposes.
- Performed individual project and portfolio analysis for management action.
- Developed operating performance reports for use in portfolio analysis.

Audit Senior
- Managed and coordinated financial and property management audits.
- Presented audit reports to all levels of management, including partners and controllers.
- Recommended improvements in operating efficiency/effectiveness for divisional administration.

TEXAS SAVINGS AND LOAN DEPARTMENT, Austin, Texas   1984 to 1988
Examiner
- Planned, coordinated, and set scope for audit examinations.
- Reviewed and analyzed overall condition and lending procedures.
- Reviewed and analyzed appraisal assumptions and conclusions.
- Performed credit analysis.
- Prepared examination reports for supervisory action.
- Performed special investigations.

W.M. MURRAY & ASSOCIATES, INC., Austin, Texas   1981 to 1984
Gross Sales Auditor
- Conducted gross sales audits of tenants on percentage rent leases.
- Reviewed and generated reports of audit field work.

COMPUTER SKILLS
ARGUS; PRO-JECT; Microsoft; Excel, Word

EDUCATION/CERTIFICATION
Certified Commercial Investment Member (CCIM) - #6489
(Educational equivalent of 240 hours of graduate-level curriculum in real estate
finance and investment plus documentation of actual market experience.)
The University of Texas at Austin
Bachelor of Business Administration in Finance, 1981
Texas Real Estate Broker License No. 0338326

Federal Home Loan Bank Board
- Finance 1 and Senior Finance Schools
- Real Estate Appraisal Schools I and II, incorporates SREA Course 101 and 201

PROFESSIONAL & CIVIC AFFILIATIONS
North Texas CCIM Chapter
Commercial Real Estate Women (CREW)
International Council of Shopping Centers (ICSC)
Susan G. Komen Foundation, Dallas Chapter Treasurer
Dallas Ninety-Nines (International Women's Pilot Organization)
Dallas Junior League volunteer

PERSONAL ACHIEVEMENTS
Two Year Letterman, University of Texas Cross Country & Track Team
Private Pilot License ~ Instrument and Multi-Engine Rated
United States Parachute Association ~ C (Advanced) Licensed

WILLIS E. GRIFFETH
1190 Sunshine Terrace
Raleigh, NC 76954
910-543-7780
griffeth@msn.com

Objective: Distribution/Warehouse Management Position

Warehouse Management

- Managed the receipt and shipment of 200,000,000 pounds of product, raw materials, and packaging supplies in a one-shift operation.

- Extensive use of LTL, UPS, export and full truck-load shipments for U.S. and international distribution. Varied packaging from small to 55 gallon containers.

- Improved distribution information system resulting in a decrease from two shifts and four managers to one shift and one manager. Cost savings of approximately $200,000 per year.

- Redesigned warehouse layout and racking to use 5000 fewer square feet.

- Coordinated move of sales people to plant. Managed facility construction and renovation. Achieved a cost saving of approximately $275,000 per year.

- Spearheaded and managed the installation of a new security system to maximize security of the building's perimeter and interior. Reduced incidents of false alarms and resulting expenses from eight or nine per month to zero.

Environmental Management

- Helped develop a closed-drain system designed to capture all wash and rinse water from mix and hold tanks, and recycle it rather than treat it to release to the city each time.

- Developed and managed recycle programs for plastic, computer paper, and cardboard, resulting in a cost saving of approximately $5000 per year.

- Convened semi-monthly meetings with the Fork Lift Involvement Team to brainstorm ways of improving productivity and warehouse conditions. Some results included warehouse reorganization and a new temperature control system.

- Provided monthly safety meetings on procedures, symptoms of job related illness (such as heat stroke), and first aid techniques.

- Monitored and audited packaging and labeling of products on a weekly basis to maintain quality standards.

Emergency Medical Training

- Certified to provide training in Basic First Aid, CPR, and Advanced First Aid and Emergency Preparedness. Over the last 15 years have trained between 500 to 600 people including EMT's and corporate employees.

- 15-year member of Red Cross Disaster team which assesses the magnitude of disasters for federal relief purposes, furnishes a concession truck for emergency workers, and sets up disaster shelters for flood, tornado, and fire victims.

WILLIS E. GRIFFETH

Employment

- Warehouse Manager, **Ecolab,** Garland, Texas   1989 to Present
- Fork Lift Operator, **Ecolab,** Garland, Texas   1979 to 1989
- Rail Tender, **Ecolab,** Garland, Texas   1978 to 1979

Education

- In-house courses in Interactions, Interaction Management, Total Quality Management, Problem Solving/Decision Analysis.
- Outside Courses: Better Warehouse Management, Supervising Difficult People, and Professional Writing Skills.

Other Facts

- Softball Umpire   12 years
- Hardball Coach for Youth   3 years
- Softball Coach for Adults   6 years
- Registered Boy Scout, Girl Scout, Eagle Scout, and Order of the Arrow Brotherhood
- Taught Sunday School for 1st and 2nd graders for Oates Drive Baptist Church

The reason many resumes are never returned.

14

Resume Follow-Up

Once you've gathered and organized your job-search supplies and accoutrements, you'll need to set up a flexible schedule that allows you sufficient time for the activities required to find a new position. Blocking out one to three hours per task on a daily or weekly basis is important for several reasons:

☆ It provides a structure to replace your normal daily work routine. If you're still employed, establishing a schedule isn't an issue. But if you're getting up in the morning and wondering, "Where do I go from here?" knowing you have a plan for your day can be comforting.

☆ It's a good time-management technique. Scheduling activities in advance not only forces you to perform tasks you would rather avoid, it also assures that you won't let important follow-up activities inadvertently fall through the cracks.

☆ Job seekers have so little control over their lives they sometimes feel like balls in a pinball machine, careening around at the whim of some unknown player. If you develop and stick to a plan, you may not be calling all the shots, but at least you'll gain some control over the direction and momentum of your search.

When setting up your schedule, think about how long it will take to complete the following activities each week: scanning and answering ads, making initial and follow-up phone calls, conducting information interviews, writing resumes, cover letters and thank-you notes, visiting the library, brainstorming ideas, lunching with friends, attending job club meetings and reading magazines and newspapers. Don't forget to budget time to have exercise or enjoy some other activity that rewards you and takes the pressure out of the grind of searching. Then set aside the appropriate amounts of time on your calendar. If you can't stick to a self-imposed schedule, make a commitment to a friend that you'll adhere to this plan unless something really important requires you to change it.

The Components of a Tracking System

Combining all the forms in this book into a simple tracking system will save you time and frustration. Whether you use a computer, an indexed notebook or a set of manila or hanging folders to keep track of your contacts doesn't really matter. Your main objective is to organize your notes and correspondence into a simple, easy-to-use file that's readily accessible, reminds you when something needs to be done and stores valuable information you might otherwise forget. It should include the components described in the following sections.

A Prospect Log

Your prospect log is the glue that holds your job search together. It consists of one or more pages organized to include space for each contact's name, title, address and phone number, your communication to date and any required follow-up activity. Note important details and reminders in your log, then consult with it when transferring important "to do" items to your calendar.

Examine the sample prospect log in progress shown in this chapter. The first three columns contain the contact's name, title, company, phone number and address. Whenever you hear about new contacts with whom you want to network, add their names to the log to automatically remind yourself to call or write them. Also note the names of people or companies you sent resumes to in response to an ad, as part of a direct mail campaign or at the suggestion of a mutual acquaintance.

After putting an individual on your list, use columns 4–9 to track the results of your conversations and any plan you have for following up via meetings, phone calls or the mailing of a resume. Column 4 (Info Source) designates how and when you first learned about this person: through an ad, a headhunter, library research, or from a networking contact. Column 5 (Resume Sent) shows the date you mailed a resume. Column 6 (Follow-Up) shows when any type of follow-up activity was completed, including when you called to confirm receipt of resumes or to inquire about a pending job opening, conducted library research prior to an interview, or performed any other activity to promote yourself to a potential employer. Column 7 (Job Interview) notes the dates of any scheduled employment interviews. Column 8 (Thank You Note) shows when you sent a thank-you note for a networking appointment or employment interview. And Column 9 (Comments) states the specific follow-up needed for each contact with your potential job source.

Let's use the Bill Parker entry as an example. If you sent a resume to him on September 25 and you planned to follow up with a call on October 1, you would write in the comments section "10/1 Call to follow-up on resume." After calling him, you would write "10/1" in the follow-up column. If your call resulted in an interview invitation, mark the interview date in the column labeled "Job Interview" and mention the need for some library research prior to your meeting under "Comments." If you visited the library October 5, place "10/5" in the follow-up column. Finally, after your interview on October 7, send a thank-you note, writing the date you sent it, "10/9," in the thank-you note column.

Review the candidate's progress with Lon Chalmers, Betty Blevins and John Tice. Since this form is the basis for tracking your progress, it's important to understand it.

However, if this approach doesn't work for you, create one that does. The only thing that matters is that you develop a system that meets your needs.

Company Files

Create a filing system for keeping track of resumes and cover letters, thank-you and other follow-up letters, research and phone-call notes, interview evaluations, ads, proposals for a new position or consulting assignment, and other correspondence with each company or contact. An easy way to organize your filing system is simply by designating separate folders for each person or corporation and arranging them alphabetically. Then everything you accumulate about an employer will be located in one convenient spot. If you like the format for the forms in this book, refresh your memory of them by referring to Chapter 2. (The exception is the phone-call log mentioned later in this chapter.)

Prospect Log

A—ad
H—Headhunter
LR—Library Research
NP—Networking/Phone
NI-Networking/Interview

Contact Name and Title	Company Phone #	Address	Info Source	Resume Sent	Follow-Up	Job Interview	Thank You Note	Comments
Bill Parker President	Landor Group 905/239 1478	2222 Mill Road Parker, TX 75036	9/21- LR	9/25	10/1 10/5	10/7	10/9	10/1 Follow-up call on resume. Flesh out ideas on dinnerware line before 10/7. Send Thank-You note.
Lon Chalmers VP Of Marketing	Tyler Corp. 140/369 7775	6217 Belknap Blvd Phoenix, AZ 26283	9/22- NP	9/26	10/1			10/1 Follow-up call on resume. Call on 11/1 to check on job opening status.
Betty Blevins Recruiter	Chambers Co. 480/936 7223	1302 Grason Drive Flushing, MS 20322	9/23- A	9/25	10/1	10/10		10/1 Follow-up call on resume.
John Tice CEO	Tice Enterprises 214/984 7676	1962 Southpoint Drive Dallas, TX 75236	9/24- NI					No point in pursuing this.

Other Useful Folders

"To Do This Week"   This file might include a to-do list developed from your calendar and prospect log, plus any ancillary material necessary to complete your to-do tasks. For instance, if you are planning to follow up on a resume you mailed by making a phone call in the next week, place a copy of the resume in your folder as a reminder and as a reference when making your call. If you are preparing for an interview, you might want to put your research notes on the company into this file for easy access.

As you may have surmised, this folder serves as a "tickler" file, reminding you when tasks need to be completed. By dealing with each item as it comes up, you'll feel more productive and satisfied about your efforts. This, in turn, can raise your self-esteem. There's nothing more gratifying than finishing a to-do list or disposing of a stack of documents. As you face the slings and arrows of a typical job search, you'll really appreciate a sense of genuine accomplishment.

"To Do Whenever I Have the Time and Inclination"   This folder is a good place to include an ongoing list of ideas gained from brainstorming, articles about companies that you might want to contact and other informational tidbits that intrigue you but aren't urgent.

"Job-Search Information"   If you read the *National Business Employment Weekly*, a daily newspaper, business journals or other publications that deal with economic or self-help issues, you'll undoubtedly encounter articles about industry forecasts, job-search techniques, tips for mending a bruised ego and helpful books that you want to save for later reference. If you're a truly ardent clipper, you may want to label various folders within the master file for the different types of information you're collecting.

Do You Want a Computerized or a Manual System?

Record-Keeping on Your Computer

For those who love computers, the process of tracking job-search contacts can be both convenient and fun. The computer's directory system is naturally suited for developing a tickler file, company folders, databases, and so forth. With word-processing, database and contact programs, such as ACT or Goldmine, you can produce contact lists, write correspondence and enter information from various sources, while simultaneously creating a permanent record of them. Certain software programs also provide automatic daily and weekly reminders for your to-do list.

Although the computer is excellent at keeping track of what you're doing, it can't incorporate ads, correspondence from companies and articles into your automated records (unless you have a scanner). You'll have to create a parallel manual filing system for storing them. However, the computer's flexibility and ease of use may compensate for this minor inconvenience.

The Job-Search Notebook

Keeping all your job search information in a large indexed three-ring binder or notebook works well for those who don't own or like computers. Start with the prospect log, followed by the weekly to-do folder, indexed pockets or tabs for each company, and the brainstorming and general information sections. You can then store important information about your job search in one easy-to-transport container. An accordion sorter is another portable, space-saving method for hassle-free record-keeping.

Temporary and Permanent File Folders

Those with sufficient space in their desks or offices may prefer a manila or hanging file folder system. Most executives had such systems at their previous jobs, so the system is convenient and familiar to them. Hanging and manila folders can be stored in desk drawers, file cabinets or in inexpensive cardboard or plastic holders that can be disassembled after a search. A file-folder system is probably easiest because it doesn't require the parallel record-keeping needed for a computer system or hole-punching of important documents, as for some notebooks. However, it takes up space and isn't portable.

Follow-Up Calls and Letters

Phone calls and letters are the two primary techniques for following up on resumes and interviews. Since you can build rapport faster over the phone than in a letter, call whenever possible to see if your resume was received. However, if you don't know the name of the company or an ad has specifically requested no calls, seek confirmation that your resume has arrived in writing.

Follow up after interviews by writing a thank-you note that states your interest in the position, reiterates your qualifications and mentions that you'll be calling to determine the status of the opening if you don't hear from the company. If further contact is required, switch to making phone calls because they generate urgency and promote rapport.

Resume Follow-Up Calls

When you call to check whether your resume arrived and if you'll be invited to interview, ask for the person to whom you sent the cover letter. Say, "This is

Hillary Smith. May I please speak with Bill Parker." By using a resume recipient's first and last name, and not just Mr. Parker, you imply you are on his level and deserve attention.

If a mutual contact suggested that you send the resume, be sure to mention this person's name at the beginning of the conversation. This referral automatically boosts your credibility and reminds contacts that you're a person of consequence.

After introducing yourself, confirm that your resume arrived and ask if there are any questions you can answer. If your contact seems interested in interviewing you (and the feeling is mutual!), schedule an appointment, mention that you're looking forward to finding out more about the position and the company, and repeat the time and date of your meeting. It's often helpful to use a phone-call form, as shown in this chapter, for taking notes about future activities you should pursue.

DATE _____

PHONE CALL

☐ **INITIAL CONTACT**   ☐ **FOLLOW-UP**

NAME _____   **ADDRESS** _____

TITLE _____

COMPANY _____   **PHONE #** _____

NOTES

_____

_____

_____

_____

_____

_____

_____

_____

_____

_____

You may need to call several times before you get through to your contact. Don't be discouraged or assume she doesn't want to talk to you. Chances are she's juggling numerous projects and hiring a new employee isn't a top priority. Leave messages each time you call. Phone every other day for a week or two until you talk with her or become convinced she has no interest in you.

Resume Follow-Up Letters

If you can't call because you answered an ad with a box number or that requested "no phone calls," write a letter to confirm the receipt of your resume. It should be short and succinct, stating:

☆ You are writing to follow up on your resume.

☆ You remain interested in the position for *A, B, C* reasons.

☆ You have *X, Y* and *Z* experiences and skills that are a good match for what the job requires.

☆ You look forward to a meeting where you can discuss how your background and the position are complementary. (The sample follow-up letter in this chapter shows a typical format.)

You may also want to include a self-addressed, stamped postcard for recruiters to return showing their interest in you as a candidate and where you stand in the search process. Human resources people often are bombarded by hundreds of resumes weekly and don't have the time or resources to reply to every one of them. If you make it really easy to respond, they will comply.

Here's what to put on your postcard:

Please check the statement(s) that applies to my resume:

_____ We received your resume.

_____ We will be calling you for an interview.

_____ We have nothing for you at this time, but we will keep your resume on file for other openings.

_____ Your background is not a good fit for any of our employment needs.

This approach almost always guarantees a response. While it may not be the one you are hoping for, a specific answer is easier to live with than a pending "maybe."

1864 Camilee Drive
Montfort, California 92506
November 12, 1999

Personnel Department
Mariah Systems
2212 Britannia Way
Short Hills, New Jersey 07078

Good Morning:

I am writing to you to confirm receipt of my resume for the position of Systems Analyst. I continue to be interested in your company because of its outstanding work in developing cutting edge software for biomedical applications, especially involving nonintrusive diagnostic techniques.

In the past six years, I have been conducting research at the University of California, where my contribution in designing state-of-the-art software for MRIs has been documented in *The Journal for Biomedical Research*. As both of our organizations are running on parallel tracks, it seems my experience would be an asset to your company. Given Mariah's reputation for innovative products, I know I would enjoy the excitement of working with your team while it continues to stretch the envelope in software applications for the medical community.

I look forward to talking with you about how your company and I might form a mutually beneficial relationship. Please contact me at the address above or call 513-388-2121 to schedule an interview.

Sincerely yours,

Lawrence Topkins, PhD

Index

A

Accomplishments:
  experience section, 72–73
  in functional format, 115
  history of, 21–23
  importance of, 3
  objective and, 68
  priority of, 12
  quantifying, 21, 74
Acknowledgment, of receipt, 16
Acquisitions, 15, 81
Action verbs, 73–74
Advertisements, as information source,
  36–39
Advice, dealing with, 2–3
Analyzing skills, inventory of, 33–34
Anger, handling, 61
Annual reports, as resource, 12, 40, 236
Answering machines, 66

Appearance, importance of, 20, 57
Applicant tracking computer systems,
  251
Artistic skills, inventory of, 31–32
ASCII, 250
Awards, 79, 185

B

"Black Hole Syndrome," 236
Blaha, Amber Frantz, 187, 191–195
Bloomfield, Marc, 226, 227–228
Board positions, resumes for, 177–179
Bona fide occupational qualifications
  (BFOQ), 79
Brainstorming, 21, 207
Browne, T. C., 116–117
Bullets, use of, 58–59
Business journals, as resource, 40

C

Calendar, time-management and, 20
Canterberry, Darryl, 218–219
Career changers:
  achievements, 220
  career choices, 52–53
  chronological format and, 88, 218–219
  decisions of, 218
  education section, 220
  emotions of, 218
  functional format, 219–220
  functional skills, 115, 217
  hybrid format, 131, 219
  marketability of, 217
  professional associations, 220
  sample resumes, 221–233
  transferable skills, 219
Career counselors, role of, 3, 84–85
Carpenter, Sue, 221–225
Chennell, Linda Reed, 208, 209–210
Chronological format:
  benefits of, 87–88
  career changers, 89, 219
  dates in, 87–88
  defined, 16
  examples of, 88–111, 137–138, 222–223
  functional vs., 115
  preference for, 76, 132
  problems with, 88–89
  tradition of, 87–88
Club membership, 183
Committee positions, resumes for, 177
Communication skills, inventory of, 25–26
Company files, 279
Competition, 4, 237
Components, generally:
  awards, 79
  education, 77–78

experience, 72–77
name, address, and phone number, 65–66
objective, 66–70
organizations, 78–79
personal data, 79
professional qualifications brief, 70–72
reason for leaving, 81, 83
references, 83
salary history, 80–81
Computers:
  applicant tracking systems, 251
  recordkeeping on, 281–282
  resume scanning, 250
  value of, 19–20
Conciseness, 55–56
Consultants:
  resumes for, 165–172
  role of, 4, 236
Continuing education, 184–185
Corporate philosophy, 38
Cover letter:
  contact names, 17
  mail-merged, 4
  openings of, 12, 17
  resources for, 39–40
  scannable resumes, 255, 262
  tailored, 41
Credentialing, 78, 184–185
Credibility, 4–5
Customizing resumes. See Tailoring resumes

D

Databases. See Scannable resumes
Dates:
  in chronological format, 88
  in experience section, 76–77

in functional format, 114–115
in hybrid format, 132
Demographics, research and, 39
Desktop publishing, 19–20. *See also*
    Computers; Scannable resumes
Detail skills, inventory of, 34–35
Direct mail campaigns:
    checklist for, 41
    information gathering, 36–39
    launching, 12
    objectives and, 69
    response rate, 39, 41
    targeting for, 39
    use of, 3
Dixon, Claudia, 155
Dolan, Kathleen, 186, 187–190
Dorsey, Nicole, 215
Downsizing, 81, 244
Dreher, Whit, 158–159

E

Ebsco, 39
Education:
    importance of, 39
    lack of, 2
Education section:
    career changers, 219–220
    degrees, 78, 184–185
    first-time job seekers, 78, 184–185
Employers:
    needs of, 3–4, 14, 38, 51–54
    prospective (*see* Prospective employers)
    screening process by, 3, 115
Enelow, Wendy, 256
Evaluation skills, inventory of, 33–34
Executive office service, role of, 19
Executive search firms:
    objectives and, 69
    resume information, 49

role of, 15
use of, 3, 39
Executive suites, role of, 66
Experience section:
    accomplishments, 72–73
    action verbs, 73–74
    dates of, 76–77
    jargon, 75
    by job title, 77
    omissions from, 76
    placement of, 78
    pronouns, 74
    quantifying, 74
    unpaid work, 75–76
    volunteer work, 75–76
Extracurricular activities, 21, 182

F

Ferris, James L., 233
File-folder tracking system, 282
First impression, 58, 66
First-time job seekers:
    experience section:
        club membership, 183
        hobbies, 182–183
        internships, 183
        part-time employment, 183–184
        school activities, 182
        volunteer work, 181–182
Fisher, Davis, 231–232
Follow-through skills, inventory of,
    34–35
Follow-up:
    importance of, 11–12, 16
    letters, 284–285
    schedule for, 277–278
    telephone calls, 282–284
    tracking system:
        company files, 279

Follow-up *(Continued)*
    computerized, 281–282
    job search notebook, 282
    permanent folders, 282
    prospect log, 278–279
    temporary folders, 282
    useful folders, 281
Fonts, 20, 254–255. *See also* Typefaces
Format:
    readability and, 58–59
    types of (*see* Chronological format;
        Functional format; Hybrid
        format)
Freelance resumes, 173–176
Functional format:
    career changers and, 219–220
    categories for, 116
    chronological format vs., 115
    cons of, 115–116
    dates in, 115
    defined, 16
    examples of, 116–128
    experience section:
        by functional area, 113–114
        by job objective, 114–115
        seasoned professionals, 77
    pros of, 115
Functional skills:
    career changers, 219
    inventory of (*see* Functional and
        transferable skill inventory)
Functional and transferable skills
    inventory, 24, 25–36

G

Gabriel, Bonnie, 240–243
Gaps, in employment, 115
George, Lawrence, 244–247
Gill, Lisa Brady, 118, 122–123

Graff, Donald W., 145, 147–148
Griffeth, Willis E., 146, 149–150,
    274–275
Guidelines:
    appearance, 57
    applicant needs, 61–62
    emotions, controlling, 61
    employer needs, 51–54
    humor, 55
    length, 55–56
    prioritizing, 57–58
    readability, 58–60
    writing, 56
Guiding skills, inventory of, 26

H

Headhunters:
    research on, 12
    role of, 15
Helping skills, inventory of, 26–28
Hobbies, 21, 76, 182–183, 206–207
Homemakers, return to paid workforce.
    See Reentry women
Honors, 185
Hostile takeovers, 15, 81, 244
Human relations skills, inventory of,
    26–28
Humor, 55, 240
Hybrid resumes:
    career changers and, 220
    cons of, 132
    dates in, 132
    defined, 131
    examples of, 135, 139–140, 152–159,
        224–225
    experience section, 132
    functions, 141–145
    objectives, 131–140
    pros of, 131–132

I

"I," use of, 74
Influencing skills, inventory of,
    28–29
Information gathering:
    advertisements, 36–39
    direct mail campaign, 39–41
    sample form for, 42–43
Information Interview Evaluation Form,
    48
Information interviews, 41–47
    networking, 44
    scheduling, 45–47
Initiating skills, inventory of, 29–30
Innovating skills, inventory of, 30–31
Instructing skills, inventory of, 26
Internal resumes, 162–164
Internships, 183
Interview goals, 4
Intuitional skills, inventory of,
    30–31
Investigating skills, inventory of,
    33–34

J

Jargon, 12, 74
Job description, ideal, 54
Job-hopping, 115
Job requirements, 36
Job search, generally:
    illustrations of, 10–13
    recordkeeping, 282
    scheduling for, 278
    self-confidence and, 15
Job search notebook, 282
Job titles:
    in Experience section, 74
    in functional format, 115

K

Kaufman, Virginia, 196, 199–200
Keywords, electronic resumes, 250,
    262–263
Kimbell, Ruth, 264, 265–266
KISS principle, 59

L

Layoffs, 81
Legal liability, of references, 83
Length, guidelines for, 55–56
Letterhead, 20
Letters, follow-up, 284–285
Library, as research source, 12, 39
Life experiences, 21, 78, 115, 185,
    204
Line spacing, 58
Lu, Harry, 264, 267–268

M

Main headings:
    order of, 59
    spacing between, 58
Management skills, inventory of, 30
Margins, 58
Martinson, Dale, 270–271
Mathematical skills, inventory of, 34
Mentoring skills, inventory of, 26
Mergers, 15, 244
Michalak, William C., 110–111
Military resumes, samples, 231–233
Million Dollar Directory, The, 40
Minsky, Paige Louise, 208, 211–212
Misconceptions, 5
Moniot, Donna, 165, 168–169
Moody's Complete Corporate Index, 40

Moore, Julie, 226, 229–230
Mueller, Martin, 162, 163–164
Myers, Kenneth, 103, 105–106

N

Name, address, and phone number,
    65–66
Name-dropping, 21, 75
Needs:
    applicant's, 61–62
    employer's, 14, 38, 51–54
Networking:
    customized resumes and, 52–53
    effectiveness of, 16
    importance of, 10–11, 44
Newspapers, as resource, 40–41

O

Objective:
    in functional format, 114–115
    in hybrid format, 141–145
    omission of, 70
    professional qualifications brief and,
        70–72
    tailoring, 12, 66–70
Observational learning skills, inventory
    of, 32–33
O'Connor, Joyce, 177–179
Organizations, membership in, 78–79
Online, Olivia, 257–260
Oshman, Linda S., 132–136
Outplacement services, role of, 66

P

Paragraph format, bullets vs., 58–59

Part-time employment, 183–184
Penry, Bill, 165, 170–172
Performing skills, inventory of, 29
Personal data, 79, 185
Personal identity, 2
Personality traits, 12
Person-to-person contact, 4, 52–53
Persuading skills, inventory of, 28–29
Physical skills, inventory of, 35–36
Planning skills, inventory of, 30
Printers, types of, 20, 255
Prioritizing, 57–58
Professional associations, 220. *See also*
    Club membership; Organizations,
    membership in
Professional qualifications brief, 70–72
Professional writing service, 56, 84–85
Pronouns, 74
Proofreading, 57
Prospective employers:
    demographics and, 39
    recordkeeping, 278–279
    research on, 15
Prospect log, 278–279
Purposes of resumes, 3–5, 55, 161–162

Q

Quality, importance of, 20
Quintavell, Faith, 173, 175–176

R

Rapport, mutual, 5
Reason for leaving, 81–83
Recordkeeping. *See* Follow-up, tracking
    system
Reentry women:
    achievement, 203–204

functional vs. chronological format, 207
hobbies, 206–207
sample resumes, 209–215
transferable skills, 204–206
volunteer work, 205–206
References:
  choice of, 78–79, 83
  inclusion of, 83, 185–186
Rejection, dealing with, 61
Relationship:
  importance of, 16
Relocation, 38
Research:
  demographics and, 39
  on headhunters, 12
  importance of, 15, 236
  on prospective employers, 15
  sources of, 12, 39
Resumania, 52, 53, 55, 58, 59, 60, 62, 63, 69, 71, 80, 81, 82, 83
Resume-writing courses, 84
Return to the paid workforce. *See* Reentry women
Right-sizings, 15
Risk-taking skills, inventory of, 29–30
Rolodex, 20
Rugiero, John, 94–102
Rusk, Benetta L., 108–109, 272–273
Russu, Camille, 103–104

S

Salary history, 80–81
Sample resumes:
  career changers:
    generally, 221–225
    military resumes, 226, 231–233
  chronological format:
    before-and-after examples, 89–102

generally, 133–134, 137–140
good resumes, 107–111
success stories, 103–106
for first-time job seekers:
  generally, 186–187, 188–190
  good resumes, 197–200
  success story, 187, 193–195
functional format:
  good resumes, 123–129
  success stories, 118, 124–128
hybrid format, 135, 139–140, 152–159
reentry women:
  good resumes, 213–215
  success stories, 208, 209–212
resume from hell, 63
seasoned professionals, success stories, 237–247
Sampson, Bonnie, 118–121
Scannable resumes, 249–256
  bad news, 253
  databases, 253
  definition, 250
  examples, 257–260
  good news, 252–253
  samples, 265–275
  who uses:
    corporations and government, 250–251
    executive search firms, 251–252
    on-line employment service providers, 252
    resume banks, 252
  writing, dos and don'ts, 254
    content, 261–263
    formatting, 254–260
Scott, David, 89–93
Screening applicants, 3, 15, 17, 115
Seasoned professionals:
  background facts, 236
  chronological format and, 87
  dates and, 76–77

Seasoned professionals *(Continued)*
  disadvantages of, 236
  functional format and, 77
  job hunting tips, 240
  negative attitude and, 235–236
  sample resumes, 238–247
Self-confidence, maintaining, 15
Self-employment, 237
Serving skills, inventory of, 26–28
Skills inventory. *See* Functional and
    transferable skills inventory
Skills summary sheet, 23, 219
Slagle, Mark, 129
Smith, Alexandra N., 201
*Standard & Poor's Registry of
    Corporations, Directors, and
    Executives,* 39
Starrett, Elise, 141, 152–156
Stationery, types of, 20
Strengths, 52
Summary of qualifications. *See*
    Professional qualifications brief
Sutton, Marvin B., 237–239
Systematizing skills, inventory of, 33–34

T

Tailoring resumes:
  employer needs and, 51–54
  importance of, 3–4, 15, 17
  job descriptions, 54
  network contacts and, 52–53
Taylor, Joy, 173, 174
Taylorson, Rebekah A., 213–214
Telephone calls, follow-up, 282–284
Termination, 81
Terrara, Jacqueline, 136–140
*Thomas Register of American
    Manufacturers, The,* 40
Thomas Register Catalog File, 40

Thurston, William R., 126
Ti, Jiang, 196, 197–198
Tickler file, 207, 281
Time management, 20, 277
To-do list, 281
Trade journals, as resource, 12, 236
Training programs, listing of, 78
Transferable skills:
  career changers, 219
  first-time job seekers, 182–183
  inventory of (*see* Functional and
    transferable skills inventory)
  reentry women, 205–206
Travel:
  as accomplishment, 21
  as educational experience, 79
Truth, importance of, 60
Typefaces, 20, 59, 255

U

Unpaid work, 74–75. *See also* Volunteer
  work
Updating, 253

V

Verbal communication skills, inventory
    of, 25–26
Verb tense, 73–74
Vezina, Henri A., 165, 166–167
Voice mail, 66
Volunteer work:
  as accomplishment, 21
  in experience section, 75–76
  first-time job seekers, 181
  functional format and, 115
  reentry women, 205–206
  resumes for, 177

W

Wally, Liz, 124–125
Ward's Directory of Public and Private Companies, 40
Working with your hands and body, inventory of, 35–36
White space, 255
Wisdom, George, 127–128

Work-study programs, 180
Writing:
  guidelines for, 56
  preparation for, 5
  professional (*see* Professional writing service)
  reasons for (*see* Purposes of)
Written communication skills, inventory of, 25

4 WEEKS *FREE* OF

THE WALL STREET JOURNAL.

For your career and your future

Our first section gives you a quick, accurate read of your business day.

In Marketplace consumer and business interests are the issues.

Money & Investing: A wealth of financial information you can bank on

Keep your finger on the pulse of the day's major business, economic and financial news -- from the U.S. and around the world. Breaking stories. Current issues. Straight, unbiased reporting. Vital news that helps you stay focused, up to date and on top of your job.

Technology, Marketing, Law, Enterprise, And More. The Market place section expands your knowledge in many key areas that can help you make the right moves for your company and for you personally. From consumer trends and thinking to innovative corporate strategies, you'll get insight and ideas you can use to build your career and shape your future.

The Journal is the preeminent source for coverage of the day's financial markets, with personal and professional strategies for getting ahead. Helpful charts, easy-to-read stock quotes, plus our renowned investment columns provide timely information to help you make the most of every opportunity.

OUTGROWN YOUR CURRENT POSITION?

Subscribe to the publication that features **hundreds of jobs** at all salary levels including many high-end, high-salaried positions at top corporations. Each edition of the National Business Employment Weekly carries a week's worth of help-wanted ads from all regions of **The Wall Street Journal** plus ads you won't find anywhere else.

Special sections bring you Internet sites for job seekers, Sales and Marketing, Info Tech and Engineering Opportunities plus much more.

Every issue also brings **Career Advice** as well as special features on relocation, consulting and starting your own business.

To Subscribe call 1-800-JOB-HUNT (562-4868) Ext. 202